SHADES
OF BLUE

DAVID WHITE was born on 30 October 1967 in Manchester, England. A former professional footballer, he played as a forward from 1986 to 1997. He is best remembered for his eight-year spell at Manchester City. He also played for Leeds and Sheffield United, and was capped once by England.

JOANNE LAKE is the co-author of the *Sunday Times* bestseller *I'm Not Really Here*, the story of footballer Paul Lake's fight against injury and depression. She has since collaborated with World Cup referee Howard Webb on his autobiography, *The Man in the Middle*.

SHADES OF BLUE

The life of a Manchester City legend and the story that shook football

DAVID WHITE

WITH JOANNE LAKE

MICHAEL O'MARA BOOKS LIMITED

First published in Great Britain in 2017 by
Michael O'Mara Books Limited
9 Lion Yard
Tremadoc Road
London SW4 7NQ

Copyright © White Reclamation Limited 2017

All rights reserved. You may not copy, store, distribute, transmit, reproduce or otherwise make available this publication (or any part of it) in any form, or by any means (electronic, digital, optical, mechanical, photocopying, recording or otherwise), without the prior written permission of the publisher. Any person who does any unauthorized act in relation to this publication may be liable to criminal prosecution and civil claims for damages.

A CIP catalogue record for this book is available from the British Library.

Papers used by Michael O'Mara Books Limited are natural, recyclable products made from wood grown in sustainable forests. The manufacturing processes conform to the environmental regulations of the country of origin.

ISBN: 978-1-78243-770-3 in hardback print format
ISBN: 978-1-78243-782-6 in trade paperback print format
ISBN: 978-1-78243-772-7 in e-book format

1 2 3 4 5 6 7 8 9 10

www.mombooks.com

Follow us on Twitter @OMaraBooks

Every reasonable effort has been made to acknowledge all copyright holders. Any errors or omissions that may have occurred are inadvertent, and anyone with any copyright queries is invited to write to the publisher, so that full acknowledgement may be included in subsequent editions of the work.

Cover design by Claire Cater
Typeset by K.DESIGN, Winscombe, Somerset

Printed and bound by CPI Group (UK) Ltd, Croydon, CR0 4YY

To Tony 'Skip' Book,
who was a true inspiration to me, and who will forever remain my footballing hero.

To Glyn Pardoe,
whose ability shamed us all into becoming better players.

To Howard Kendall,
who deployed better footballers around me and simplified my game.

To Peter Reid and Sam Ellis,
who were hugely influential and made me feel irreplaceable.

To Dad,
who would have gone to any length to get me up that ladder.

Contents

Foreword by Peter Reid 9

PROLOGUE   Sheffield, 1998 11

CHAPTER 1   Bless 'Em All 13

CHAPTER 2   Project David 24

CHAPTER 3   Football Overload 35

CHAPTER 4   World of Opportunity 45

CHAPTER 5   Betrayal of Trust 54

CHAPTER 6   A Heavy Burden 63

CHAPTER 7   7: David White 75

CHAPTER 8   Skip and Glyn's Classroom 88

CHAPTER 9   Another Rung on the Ladder 100

CHAPTER 10   A Lifelong Dream 113

CHAPTER 11	Sid, Jack and Fred	127
CHAPTER 12	A False Dawn	142
CHAPTER 13	In a Good Place	159
CHAPTER 14	One-Cap Wonder	172
CHAPTER 15	Smashed Around the Edges	183
CHAPTER 16	The End of the Line	196
CHAPTER 17	A Bombshell	210
CHAPTER 18	Doing This For Dad	224
CHAPTER 19	A Flight to Mumbai	238
CHAPTER 20	Dusting Myself Down	253

Epilogue 268

Acknowledgements 277

Picture credits 280

Index 281

Foreword

BY PETER REID

David White and I go back a long, long way. I first became aware of him when I played for Everton in the mid-to-late 1980s, when I couldn't help but notice the presence of this powerful and pacey teenage winger, who posed a constant threat to his opponents. I really admired David's direct way of playing, epitomized by an extraordinary ability to gain half a yard on a defender before unleashing a perfectly weighted cross into the box. It was clear that this was a footballer with a great deal of raw, natural talent, and something told me that he'd go far in the game.

Whitie was still fairly young when I arrived at Manchester City as a thirty-four-year-old in 1990, but it was obvious that he had huge potential as a top-flight professional. He'd experienced a meteoric rise through the club's ranks, a product of City's fantastic youth team policy (spearheaded by Tony Book), which had reared similarly talented home-grown players like Andy Hinchcliffe, Steve Redmond and Ian Brightwell. David was undoubtedly one of Manchester City's shining lights – as a lifelong Blue himself, his love for the team and the shirt was plain to see – and I know that our manager at the time, the great Howard Kendall, thought the world of him.

I recall travelling down to Villa Park on 23 April 1991, and that night witnessing one of the most superb performances I'd ever seen from a forward. By then I'd replaced Howard in the hot seat, becoming City's player–manager, and occasionally I'd switch David from the right to the centre, to mix things up a bit. I'd opted to put Whitie up front in a striking position and he was simply unbelievable, verging on unstoppable. Our number 7's finish was truly brilliant, his four-goal tally helping us to a 5–1 victory and forcing a lot of people in the football world to sit up and take notice. They'd all been aware of Whitie's famous turn of speed, but his accuracy in front of the goal that night, against a very good Aston Villa side, was just beautiful to watch.

I found David a delightful person to work with. He had an extremely dry sense of humour – always useful at City – and was a charming, polite and well-rounded individual, the sort of lad you'd have been happy for your daughter to bring home. He came from a lovely family, too; I was lucky to meet his dad, Stewart, on a number of occasions and it was clear to see how much he adored his hugely talented son, as well as the club that had nurtured him over the years.

After he bid farewell to Manchester City, I continued to track Whitie's career, although it was sad to see his ankle injury blighting his progress at Leeds United and Sheffield United. This was, unfortunately, the main contributory factor towards his somewhat premature retirement from the game.

More recently, of course, David has attracted recognition for altogether different reasons. He, among other brave ex-professionals, has shown great courage in coming forward to publicly reveal his childhood trauma, and he has my utmost respect for doing so. It must have been hard enough to make the grade as a top professional footballer without shouldering the burden of such emotional heartache, and the fact that David somehow summoned the strength to continue playing top-level football – even gaining international honours – shows a remarkable depth of character. I applaud David for his honesty and candour – including the writing of this book – and hope that his openness will help to raise awareness of vitally important child protection and safeguarding issues.

Not only is David White a tremendous person, he is one of the finest footballers that I ever had the pleasure of playing alongside and managing. He brought so much joy to thousands of supporters during his career – particularly those of the sky-blue variety – and I'd like to wish him nothing but the best for the future.

PROLOGUE

Sheffield, 1998

Light rain was falling when I sauntered out of the Shirecliffe training ground. I stopped for a moment to switch over the strap of my kitbag to my left shoulder, reducing the burden on my troublesome right ankle which, this particular afternoon, was causing me to wince with every step.

As per usual, a couple of United fans were lingering outside the main entrance, sporting their red-and-white-striped scarves.

'All right, David?' they grinned, offering me their autograph books.

'Hiya, lads,' I replied, obliging with my usual loopy scrawl.

'Saw you jogging around the pitch before, mate. Reckon you'll be back in the squad soon?'

Ah, the big question.

'You never know,' I smiled, unconvincingly.

I didn't want to tell them that, the way things were going, I'd be lucky to get first-team football at Hereford United, let alone Sheffield United. Despite countless operations, my ankle wasn't getting any better, and my game was suffering as a result. The lightning pace and the pinpoint crosses that had been my hallmarks at Manchester City and, for a time, at Leeds United, had been blunted. My confidence on the pitch – I now dreaded kicking a football, such was my fear of the pain – had been dented. Sometimes it was hard to believe that, just five years earlier, I'd turned out for England. Times had indeed changed.

'D'you mind if we have a quick photograph, David?'

'Sure.'

I posed for the snap, shook the lads' hands and headed over to the players' car park. As I did so, my phone rang. I lowered my kitbag onto the gravel and reached for the Nokia vibrating inside my tracksuit pocket. *Unknown number.* My finger hovered over the red button for a second, but then I felt a sudden impulse to answer it.

'Hello?'

'Hi there,' said the voice at the end of the line. 'Is that David White?'

'Yes, it is … who's speaking?'

'Sorry to bother you, but I'm calling from Cheshire Police. We're investigating a former football coach of yours, Barry Bennell, and we're just wondering if we can ask you a few questions …'

The world, for a moment, stopped turning.

CHAPTER 1

Bless 'Em All

My earliest memory: I'm six years old, snuggled up in bed beneath a sheet, blanket and eiderdown; my dad is sitting at my bedside, singing me to sleep.

> Bless 'em all, bless 'em all
> Bert Trautmann, Dave Ewing and Paul
> Bless Roy Little who blocks out the wing
> Bless Jack Dyson the penalty king
> And with Leivers and Spurdle so tall
> And Johnstone, the prince of them all
> Come on the light blues
> It's always the right blue
> So cheer up me lads
> Bless 'em all

It was Dad's favourite Manchester City song, a rousing terrace tribute that prompted him to regale me with stories of bygone sky blue legends. Bobby Johnstone, the tricky inside forward who became the first player to score in consecutive Wembley FA Cup Finals. Jack Dyson, the maverick striker who went on to star for Lancashire Cricket Club. Bert Trautmann, the brilliant German goalkeeper forever remembered for his heroic display at Wembley in 1955 – broken neck notwithstanding.

When it was Mum's turn to be on night duty, however, she'd treat me to readings of traditional fairy tales and *Aesop's Fables*, bringing the stories to life by mimicking and gesticulating like an actress, and making me laugh in the process. If truth be told, I enjoyed Dad's Leivers and Spurdle battle cry as much as 'The Tortoise and the Hare', but I'd never have dreamt of telling Mum that.

I was born at Urmston Cottage Hospital, on the western fringes of Manchester, on Monday 30 October 1967, a son to Elaine and Stewart and a brother to two-year-old Steven. My parents had first met as teenagers at the Trinity Methodist youth club in nearby Patricroft, tying the knot at the adjoining church a few days shy of Mum's twentieth birthday.

The wedding had attracted a fair amount of interest, it seems, not only because it was the final ceremony to be held before the church's demolition (an omen, Mum has since said) but also due to the newlyweds' notable family ties. Mum was the daughter of Jack McCann, MP for Rochdale and erstwhile Mayor of Eccles. Dad was the grandson of Harry Wood, a successful rags-to-riches businessman and man about town. The hundreds of well-wishers gathered outside the church to welcome Mr and Mrs White bore testament to both men's popularity.

We lived in the Manchester suburb of Eccles, a working-class town located between the Ship Canal and the newly built M602 motorway, about ten minutes' drive away from Manchester city centre. As well as its world-famous currant-stuffed pastry cakes, Eccles was renowned for its rich industrial heritage, having spawned a cluster of silk and cotton mills in the mid-1880s. The Scottish engineer, James Nasmyth – inventor of the pioneering steam hammer – opened his ironworks in the Patricroft part of town, where a wide range of locomotives were produced.

Eccles' near neighbour, the old village of Barton, boasted the famous Aerodrome (used for military aircraft repair during World War II), the swing aqueduct and a gigantic coal-fired power station. The latter was demolished in 1979, and would eventually make way for a new B&Q; I remember standing with my mum, wide-eyed and open-mouthed, as the beige cooling towers disintegrated, the assembled crowd of thousands oohing and aahing as this familiar landmark was reduced to rubble.

Our family home was a large, modern, dark-brick bungalow set back from the B5211 Barton Road. The Bridgewater Canal – built in 1761 to link the Worsley coalmines to Manchester – ran adjacent to the road, just metres from our front door. At any given time of the day I could gaze out of the lounge window and watch gaudily painted barges chugging along the waterway, or bobble-hatted walkers striding down the towpath.

The old canal wasn't without its hazards, though, particularly at night-time; there were incidents of people toppling in, drunk or otherwise, and my brother Steve – during an alarming, late-1970s sleepwalking phase – was once found feeling his way along the towpath in his pyjamas, merely inches away from the canal's deep, dark waters.

My parents were very different characters, to put it mildly. Mum was a laid-back, free-spirited, creative type who loved art, literature and amateur dramatics. She was fiercely intelligent – she'd excelled at Eccles Grammar School – but had put her academic aspirations on hold in order to raise her two sons.

Dad, on the other hand, was a hard-nosed go-getter who'd happily quit Stretford Grammar School at the age of sixteen to join the family business. He was the archetypal alpha male who loved his pints in the pub, his Saturday afternoons at Maine Road and his Sunday roast lamb dinners.

They were poles apart politically, too. Mum had been a willing Labour Party activist from a young age – she'd helped her father's cause by delivering campaign leaflets and counting election-night ballot papers – and had carried her staunch socialist ideology into adulthood, supporting striking miners and sympathizing with CND protesters.

Over in the Blue corner, however, was Dad, a dyed-in-the-wool Tory who worshipped Margaret Thatcher and regularly championed her capitalist credo.

'I work hard for my bloody money, so I should keep my bloody money,' he'd grumble, slagging off the tax-grabbing loony lefties as Mum gave him daggers from across the kitchen table. That being said,

Dad's relationship with his father-in-law was deeply respectful and surprisingly amicable.

'Jack's the only man alive who could ever tempt me into voting for that shower,' he once said to Mum with a wink.

* * *

Compared with other households in the neighbourhood, the White family were relatively well off. This realization dawned on me as I started attending primary school, when I began to notice that our bungalow was more spacious than my mates' 1930s semis, that Dad's Volvo was flashier than those driven by other parents, and that we appeared to be the only family on our road that owned a static caravan in North Wales. Money was never an issue. If we wanted something – the latest Raleigh Chopper, or a new Sony Walkman – it was paid for, simple as that.

Steve and I genuinely appreciated these privileges – our mum wouldn't have tolerated any hint of ingratitude – yet we were under no illusions as to the source of our comfortable lifestyle. Dad's work ethic and business acumen was helping to build the family firm from a tiny working farm and scrap-metal yard into a large-scale recycling and reclamation plant, and our family unit was reaping the benefits.

The business, based on Worsley Road, had originally been owned and run by my great-grandfather, Harry Wood, a local rag-and-bone man who'd fancied trying his luck with a scrapyard. In the very early 1960s Dad began to work at H. Wood (Patricroft) Ltd, helping his grandad to reclaim and sell unwanted industrial scrap, ripping out iron girders, steel roofs and the like. Young Stewart must have made a good impression upon Harry, because when the old fella died he left the majority of his estate to his grandson, providing Dad with plenty of assets (but also a fair whack of inheritance tax liability). In any event, he'd been given a platform to expand and develop this fledgling business.

Harry's bequest, however, had effectively sidelined his only child, Lily – my nanna – for reasons known only to himself. Sadly, this decision was to have long-lasting repercussions. Lily, quite understandably, felt hurt and humiliated by this blatant snub – I don't think Dad's sister Judith was overly enamoured either – and, from that day on, the mother–son relationship was fraught with tension and resentment. At best, over the next five decades Dad and Nanna would tolerate each other. At worst, the underlying bitterness would badly affect the family dynamic, the feuds often turning into flashpoints which threatened to split the Whites apart.

The next few years saw Nanna and my paternal grandfather, Tom, continuing to live on the farm while my dad concentrated on developing the business. Also lodging with them was Bert Kidd, a hard-as-nails, street-fighting ragamuffin from Farnworth who'd come to work as a farmhand in 1949, when he was a teenager. Bert, it transpired, had suffered a horrendous upbringing. His troubled father had spent most of his adult life being shunted from prisons to asylums and, in his absence, young Bert had been elected the man of the house. He ended up doing everything from shovelling coal to delivering babies, and became all the more tough for it.

The story goes that one night, during the harvest, he'd been working very long hours in the fields, and my nan had made a suggestion.

'You've got to get up really early in the morning, Bert,' she'd said, 'so you might as well stop over.' He stayed the night and never left.

In the early-1960s, Tom, Nanna and Bert decided to leave the farm and relocate to Warrington to run a general store, although Bert also continued to work at the scrapyard. A few years later, however, the trio decided to return to Manchester, moving to a bungalow on the Worsley–Walkden border with a massive, manicured garden. My grandad died in 1971 (I have a hazy memory of him watching me pulling on my socks, and admonishing me because they were on the wrong feet) but Bert continued to live with Nanna, and they would become lifelong friends.

It was around this time that my dad suffered a horrific accident. He'd always been quite a fit young man – he enjoyed his running and his football – although he'd opted to retire from contact sports in his twenties, ever fearful that he'd injure himself and jeopardize the business.

Ironically enough, the accident itself happened in the workplace. Dad and Bert had been undertaking a gruelling job at an industrial launderette – dismantling some steelwork, apparently – but things had come to a dramatic halt when a heavy girder toppled over and crashed onto Dad's left leg. Incredibly, Bert managed to lift up the metal so my dad could crawl out, but the damage had already been done.

Dad was rushed to Accident and Emergency, whereupon he was told that his ankle had been smashed to pieces, and that amputation was more than likely. Thankfully the intervention of a brilliant orthopaedic surgeon saved his limb although, from then onwards, Dad would have to put up with constant and excruciating pain. For the rest of his days he would walk with a pronounced limp, the consequence of having a brittle ankle and one leg a couple of inches shorter than the other (Mum – and latterly my stepmother – would always have to alter his trousers accordingly). I don't remember a day that he didn't suffer and, deep down, I think it affected him more than his family and colleagues ever realized.

* * *

Steve and I would stay over at Nanna and Bert's every Friday, since this was Mum and Dad's Big Night Out. Among their favourite venues was the legendary Talk of the North, a cabaret club situated a stone's throw from our house, on the busy Liverpool Road. The place was renowned for attracting huge stars from the world of showbiz and music, and my parents would enthuse about the big-name acts rolling up to downtown Eccles, from Tom Jones and Shirley Bassey to Bob Monkhouse and Tommy Cooper.

So, as my parents partied the night away, my brother and I would loll on the settee and embark upon our weekly TV extravaganza. Nanna Tom – so named in affectionate memory of my late grandad – would sit contentedly on the other side of the lounge, knitting jumpers, darning socks or tackling the *Daily Express* crossword. Meanwhile Bert, sporting his regulation slacks, shirt and tie, would patrol his beloved back garden in order to shoot trespassing magpies and squirrels.

'How many have you popped so far, Bert?' I'd shout from the kitchen window. He'd probably be carted off in an RSPCA van for doing that now.

At 8.30 p.m., when it was time for *Gardeners' World*, Bert would return indoors – without his gun, thank Christ – switch to BBC 2 and turf us off the sofa. Undeterred, we'd respond by upping sticks and scampering down the road, knocking on a friendly neighbour's front door in order to continue our Friday-night telethon.

Wesley was a fifty-something fella who, like us, couldn't give a monkey's about Percy Thrower's petunias but who devoured sports broadcasts, particularly live athletics meetings. It was the era of the great British middle-distance runners – Sebastian Coe, Steve Cram and Steve Ovett – and we'd sit cross-legged on Wesley's living-room carpet, goggling at the screen as the gold, silver and bronze medals rained in from Oslo, Cologne and other chilly northern European cities.

This was also the heyday of Daley Thompson, the magnificent decathlete-cum-showman who was adored by crowds and cameras alike. Steve and I would watch, awestruck, as he powered over hurdles and catapulted himself over the pole vault. Sometimes he'd compete in individual disciplines as well as the decathlon, regularly trouncing event specialists in the long jump or 100m sprint.

Following our sport fix, we'd say a cheery bye to Wesley and skip back to Nanna's just in time for *Petrocelli*. A super-slick Arizona-based lawyer, Tony Petrocelli would win every court case in Tucson before returning home to his fit wife, a fresh pizza and a fridge full of Budweiser.

'Living the dream, that fella,' Steve would grin.

* * *

The FA Cup weekend was always the highlight of our couch-potato calendar. There existed very little live football back then, so that second Saturday in May was a rare treat for us, and was one of the few sporting events to be broadcast simultaneously on BBC and ITV. During the week-long build-up, regularly scheduled programmes like *A Question of Sport* or *Pro-Celebrity Golf* would adopt an FA Cup theme. On the day itself, after the end credits had rolled on *Noel Edmond's Multi-Coloured Swap Shop* – or *Tiswas*, its chaotic ITV counterpart – it was wall-to-wall cup fever.

First up would be the interviews with the players' wives, some shy and nervous, some bright and bubbly, but each of them justly proud of their menfolk as they approached the biggest day of their lives. Then it was back to the London studio for a wise slice of punditry from football icons like Brian Clough and Malcolm Allison, followed by – and this was the best bit – live footage from the respective team buses. As the vehicles wound their way towards Wembley, the likes of Liam Brady and Pat Jennings would be interviewed by Gerald Sinstadt, with the frequent breaks in sound and signal just adding to the immediacy of it all. It was brilliant, brilliant television.

Dad, probably shaking off the remnants of a beery hangover, would collect us from Nanna and Bert's at around midday, by which time the pre-FA Cup tension would be ramped up good and proper. As three o'clock approached, the streets of Eccles quietened and the traffic receded. In those days the country almost came to a standstill, no matter which teams were playing. It was like a state occasion.

The giddy White males would camp out in the lounge for the afternoon, eating and drinking the contents of the fridge, all three of us glued to the action from the first pass to the final whistle.

'Fabulous this, isn't it lads?' Dad would say, savouring this rare opportunity to watch real-time football on the box.

Most mid-to-late 1970s finals are now etched upon my memory, so deep was my fervour and so clear is my recall of all the players, results and goals. How could I ever forget Liverpool's stroll against Newcastle in 1974, Alan Taylor's 1975 brace for West Ham or Bobby Stokes' disputed late goal in 1976? And then there was Manchester United's 1977 victory over their arch-rivals Liverpool, followed by Roger Osbourne's shock winner for Ipswich Town in 1978.

Sadly, FA Cup Final day on 12 May 1979 would remain lodged in my memory for very different, and much darker reasons.

* * *

Despite their lingering animosity, neither Dad nor his mother let anything come between the grandparent–grandchildren bond during our childhood, and Steve and I enjoyed a close relationship with Nanna Tom. Similarly, the rapport with our maternal grandmother, Alice, was wonderful. Like Lily, she was a widow – Jack had sadly died in 1972 – and she too was given a grandad-related name by the family, who dubbed her 'Nana Jack', with one 'n'.

Following Jack's passing, Alice's elder sister Betty came to live at her neat, red-brick semi on School Lane in Eccles. Their home was ideally located for me, as it faced my school – Godfrey Ermen Memorial Primary – and backed onto Patricroft recreation ground. It was commonplace for wayward footballs to soar over Nana's fence and thud into her flower beds, and she and Betty became notorious for refusing to return them.

'Aw, Dave, can you grab us our ball from your nan's back garden?' my mates would plead. 'It's a brand-new Mitre and she won't flamin' give it us back …'

Despite their fearsome reputation among local kids, you really couldn't have met two nicer, kinder ladies than Alice and Betty. Both grey-haired and slightly built, Betty was much the smaller at just 4 foot 6 inches tall, a serious childhood illness having stunted her growth. However, while Betty may have been tiny in stature, she more than made up for it in character. I recall her driving a cumbersome white Austin Allegro which, as she was so dainty, had to have ten-inch wooden blocks screwed into the pedals to enable her little legs to reach them.

As she became older and more frail, Betty developed a pathological fear of making right turns in her Allegro, so would take great pains to find a route that comprised entirely left turns. This amused Steve and I no end, and we'd often find ourselves sitting on the *faux*-leather back seat of Betty's Allegro, furiously pointing at the football pitch on the right that she'd agreed to take us to.

'It's that park just over there, Aunty Betty!' we'd yell, prodding the window and pissing ourselves laughing as she completely ignored us and drove off in the opposite direction. She'd then proceed to make left turn after left turn, conducting a tortuous detour of backstreet Eccles until we finally reached our destination. Steve and I soon learnt that any journey with Turn-Left-Betty would take twice the normal time.

As schoolkids, Steve and I would visit Nana and Betty's every Tuesday straight after school. Mum would turn up shortly afterwards, her arrival prompting the teatime ritual to begin in earnest. First, the mahogany drop-leaf table would be wheeled into the centre of the small lounge-cum-dining room before being theatrically opened up and given the Mr Sheen treatment. The Rediffusion telly would then be switched on, taking a few moments to warm up before Meg Mortimer and her Crossroads Motel beamed in from Birmingham.

Then Nana and Betty would meticulously set the table, positioning the lace placemats and arranging an array of vintage diningware. This included their treasured cruet, a delicate sterling-silver condiment holder with a round handle that had to be politely passed round the table when anyone requested salt or pepper. Steve – horror of horrors – once clumsily shoved over the salt cellar to Aunty Betty without the cruet; it was the first and last time he'd commit this heinous social faux pas.

Betty's shriek of 'STEVEN! The cruet!' has since become a White family in-joke, any social event having become incomplete without a daft, drunken game of 'Cruet' (basically an opportunity to loudly shoehorn any rhyming phrases – *blew it*; *knew it*; *threw it* – into our conversation).

Teatime at Nana Jack's operated on a strict three-week cycle. Week One comprised individual home-made minced-beef pies, lovingly topped with pastry 'D' and 'S' initials for us boys and served with home-made gravy and a choice of peas or baked beans. Mum, Nana and Betty would share a big plate-sized meat pie, and the pet dog Tina – a pampered white poodle with a human food fetish – would gnaw on the leftover beef and gristle.

The following week our dinner plates would groan with sausage and mash, and week three would herald a speciality shepherd's pie. Occasionally Nana and Betty would throw in a roast pork dinner curveball – my aunty made the best roasties ever – which was gratefully received and devoured by the ravenous White brothers. And Tina.

Nana's signature dessert was a traditional trifle. She'd carefully arrange layers of sponge, fruit, jelly and custard in a gigantic cut-glass bowl before smothering it with whipped cream and a sprinkling of hundreds and thousands. Then she'd wield this huge silver serving spoon, plunging it into the trifle and spooning it out like Billie Jean King serving for match point, Steve and I stifling our laughter as red and yellow clots dripped onto the tablecloth. From then on, any food-related heavy-handedness in the White household would be referred to as 'doing an Alice'.

But that wasn't the end of our weekly Eccles banquet. As the trifle slithered towards the pit of our stomachs, Nana would present us with Day-Glo pots of Birds Eye Supermousses and wedges of freshly baked chocolate cake. However, as soon as we'd finished this conveyor belt of desserts – and when Nana felt that she'd done her job in filling up her strapping grandsons – Steve and I would be told in no uncertain terms to go and play outside so she could have some quality, uninterrupted time with her daughter. It was almost a case of, *I've fed you lads, now shove off.*

'Come on then, boys,' she'd say as she bundled us out of the door, zipping up our anoraks, slotting Toffee Crisps into our pockets and handing us Colin Bury's mud-encrusted football that she'd confiscated earlier that week.

We never had a problem with this abrupt turfing-out; we appreciated how much Nana valued her weeknight catch-ups with her daughter. And, with half a pound of Tate & Lyle coursing through our veins, my brother and I would spend the next couple of hours careering around the playing field under the orange glow of the street lights, chasing and dribbling our borrowed football until home time.

CHAPTER 2

Project David

My brother and I always looked forward to our legendary family trips to North Wales. Three or four times a year the White clan would head off to our static caravan at St Asaph, perhaps best known for being Great Britain's second-smallest city. Other relatives would often tag along, too, and Steve and I would keenly anticipate their arrival. Without mobile phones to track journey progression, we'd sit at the window for hours, whooping with joy when we suddenly caught sight of Aunty Betty's white Allegro trundling along on the horizon, no doubt having avoided every right turn from Eccles to Rhyl.

Located eight miles from the coast, the Eryl Hall site was split into four huge fields in order to accommodate hundreds of caravans of all shapes and sizes. Therein lay a friendly, close-knit community of holidaymakers, a home-from-home for hordes of Mancs and Scousers in need of some sea air and – if they were very lucky – some sunshine.

A proper kids' paradise, each field had a perimeter road that was perfect for biking and skateboarding, and the various playgrounds and open spaces invited all manner of boisterous ball games. But no other attraction quite eclipsed the legendary Eryl Hall Chip Machine. Forget your Sinclair Spectrum or your Pioneer music centre; as far as Steve and I were concerned, this was the finest technological breakthrough of the twentieth century. Each night we'd grab a Tupperware bowl from the caravan, eagerly shove it under the machine's hatch and slot in our 10p pieces. Following a couple of minutes of spits, sizzles and internal rumbles, a portion of steamy, salty chips would be dumped into your bowl. It was a truly special moment.

'Aunty Betty's inside that machine, frying them chips,' Steve would say, a vision that always made me chuckle.

We'd sometimes venture further afield to the Criccieth area, which boasted a stunning stretch of coastline. The craggy bays of Borth-y-Gest were brilliant for hide-and-seek, and Black Rock Sands was so wide and flat that Dad was able to drive his car onto the beach, occasionally allowing Steve and I a turn at the steering wheel.

'Go on, Niki Lauda, put your foot down,' he'd grin, as I squealed in the front seat.

We'd also pay visits to the touristy beaches of Prestatyn, Llandudno and Colwyn Bay for games of cricket, rounders and – inevitably – football. Unsurprisingly, come rain or shine, Dad insisted upon playing hour after hour of beach soccer, which I absolutely adored. He'd mark out all the familiar lines, spots, arcs and circles in the damp sand before shamelessly removing the poles from the family windbreaker to use as goalposts. My mum would glower at us as she sat shivering on the tartan rug, her coat wrapped tightly around her to combat the squally Welsh winds.

* * *

Despite some happy family times – particularly in North Wales – it came as no major shock when my parents announced their separation. Raised voices and slammed doors had become commonplace in our family home, and it became quite clear to Steve and I that this was no marriage made in heaven.

One winter's night, Mum had tentatively primed me for the bad news, perching on the end of my bed to gently explain that she and Dad weren't getting along, and that things might soon be changing.

'I wonder how you'd feel if I went to live down the road?' she'd asked, her eyes glistening. 'You and Steve could come and see me whenever you liked, y'know ...'

I was seven years old when my parents confirmed the inevitable. I remember sitting in the lounge, prior to my weekly Cubs meeting, togged up in my grey shorts, green jumper, neckerchief, woggle and sporting my newly sewn-on Home Help badge.

'Your mum's going to move down the road,' Dad said, matter-of-factly, before explaining that Steve and I would be able to stay at her house most weekends, but would continue to live with him in the bungalow during the week.

Leaving the family home had been an awful decision for Mum to make – I later learnt that she'd received lots of flak from judgemental gossipmongers – but Steve and I realized that she'd acted with our best intentions at heart. And while my brother and I were naturally upset about the split, it came as something of a relief that the fierce arguments and moody silences would now be consigned to history.

'Everything will be okay, boys,' grinned my Dad, his cheeriness at odds with the gravity of the situation. 'Now don't you be late for Cubs, eh ...' he said, marshalling us out of the front door.

A bigger bombshell was about to be dropped, however. Steve and I had an inkling that something was afoot when Dad, just days after Mum had moved out, announced that he was treating us both to lunch. The pressures of work and his lack of spare time meant that we rarely ate out together.

Maybe he's just trying to cheer us up, I remember thinking to myself. It hadn't been the easiest couple of days, after all.

As we settled ourselves around a table at our local pub, Dad happened to mention, almost in passing, that a friend of his called Margaret and her two daughters would be coming to live with us at the bungalow.

'You know Janet and Carol from school?' he said airily, as Steve and I exchanged confused glances. 'Well, the girls and their mum are going to be moving in.'

Breaking our long, shell-shocked silence, Dad then picked up the laminated menu and peered at its contents.

'Are you ready to order or what, lads?' he asked us.

By the time we returned home the trio were already in situ, having plonked themselves on our brown leather sofa after they'd unpacked their belongings. While we vaguely knew the girls – bizarrely, Janet and Steve had been born in adjoining hospital beds within a day of each other – we certainly didn't count them as friends. The fact that Carol was sporting *my* boxing gloves taken from *my* bedroom made that prospect even less likely.

Her opening gambit of 'D'you wanna fight?' probably wasn't the best thing to say in the circumstances, either, but there you go.

Suffice to say that the boys and the girls never really got on; they did their own thing, we did ours, and that was that. It was extremely weird and intensely awkward. We seldom came into contact with Janet or Carol at school, we rarely walked home with them and we spent little time with them during holidays. We just didn't have that connection. They had an older brother, too – Phil – although he'd chosen to stay with his father.

As regards Margaret, there was no traditional stepmother dynamic – even after she and Dad had tied the knot – and our relationship at that time was distant, shall we say. I don't think the new Mrs White took too kindly to me or my growing football fixation, no doubt seeing me as a drain on Dad's attention. Looking back, she probably had a point. Dad loved having kick abouts in the garden, and spent a ridiculous amount of time with me as opposed to his new wife and the other three kids.

Happily, my relationship with Mum went from strength to strength. Her house was located just a couple of miles down the Bridgewater Canal, yet its relaxed, chilled-out vibe felt aeons away from the stresses and strains of Dad's place. Since their split, Mum had enrolled on a degree course at Manchester Polytechnic Theatre School, and I loved chatting about her new incarnation as a Film and TV student, and learning about all the actors, writers and directors with whom she was now rubbing shoulders.

I eagerly volunteered for cameo roles in her amateur dramatics productions at St Catherine's Church, too. Everyone said I excelled in my role as Bird 2 in *The Owl and the Pussycat*.

* * *

I probably spent my happiest times as a child at Patricroft recreation ground. I'd never been remotely interested in hanging around street corners, instead preferring to mess about with my brother and assorted mates at Patty rec, as it was affectionately known.

A third of the rec was taken up with an old-style concrete playground (before the advent of any spongy, fracture-preventing flooring) that housed the usual cluster of slides, see-saws and roundabouts. This was the site of some mildly mischievous antics: stamping on lads' knuckles as they idly dangled from the climbing frame; jamming swing chains around the top bar so the seats became stuck; clambering atop the roof and balancing on the ledge of the little electricity substation. This hardstanding area was also the site of wall-y, bars-y and various other repetitive footy challenges ending in 'y'.

Dividing the playground from the grass was a green metal fence, two bars of which we'd prised apart to provide a lazy short cut to our Football Central. This consisted of one carefully marked pitch with proper nets for serious 11 v. 11 matches, surrounded by a swath of green space for ad-hoc, jumpers-for-goalposts kick abouts. And it was while hurtling around on that lush expanse of grass that I swiftly realized that I had a real flair for football. Most of the lads I knocked about with were older than me and, like my brother, were tough, sturdy and athletic. Yet, despite the age gap and the size difference, I found that I could more than match them for skill and technique. Not only that, I was fast. Very fast.

Steve's pals would often force me to go in goal (perhaps to take this pesky eight-year-old down a peg or two) but I really didn't care. As long I was on a football pitch, with my mates, in the fresh air, I'd play anywhere. I was smitten.

My first taste of competitive match action came courtesy of my Cub Scouts and school football teams. While I had my eye on the right-wing position – this was 1976, at a time when the heroic Dennis Tueart and Peter Barnes were lighting up the flanks at Maine Road – I also realized that, as a new recruit, I couldn't just waltz into my preferred role. So I spent a season in goal, biding my time and coveting the winger's shirt from afar as I patrolled the muddy hollow between the sticks.

Like many primary schools in the 1970s, a shortage of male teachers meant that our training sessions and matches at Godfrey Ermen Primary were organized and overseen by females. Nothing wrong with that, of course, but by their own admission Miss Irwin and Miss Robinson weren't master tacticians. Their passion, commitment and enthusiasm, however, was second to none. Even on the darkest, chilliest midwinter evening you'd find them both out on the pitch, clad in cagoules and wellies, loudly encouraging us to do our best and try our hardest.

Then, in the summer of 1977, things began to fall into place for me. A talented goalkeeper called Andrew Gorton joined our school in the fourth year (or year six, as it is these days), releasing me to play on my favoured right wing. The 'Goddies' unit somehow clicked and a plucky, spirited side was born (not a bad outcome considering there were only about thirty lads to choose from). Three of us would even go on to play professional football: other than myself, Andy the keeper turned out for Oldham, Stockport and Lincoln, and centre back James Collins secured contracts with Oldham and Bury. Miss Irwin and Miss Robinson were obviously doing something right.

Around that time, when I was nine years old, Andy, James and I were selected to play for Eccles Town FC's Under-11s. My dad was thrilled, of course, although there were no hugs, backslaps or congratulatory words. As far as he was concerned, my football progress was to be expected, not exalted.

It was at our team's home ground, Alder Park School in Winton, that I met my new team captain, an impressive midfielder called Simon. One evening, following our weekly training session, Simon explained how he'd been recruited by Whitehill FC, a highly regarded junior team with close links to Manchester City. It was a side renowned for its hotshot coach and its ability to nurture and develop talented young players, many of whom ended up signing associated schoolboy forms at Maine Road.

'It's brilliant, lads,' he said excitedly. 'I'm at City's training ground every week, and I'm with Whitehill on a Sunday. Play your cards right, boys, and you might get the chance yourselves.'

Simon's words ricocheted around my head as I lay in bed that night. In my eyes, Manchester City was the Promised Land, and I was going to do all I humanly could to get there.

* * *

Eccles Town FC was one of the more successful teams in the Salford area and I soon made the right-wing berth my own, playing alongside boys a year older than me. Our Saturday-morning fixtures became a honeypot for talent scouts working on behalf of professional clubs across the north-west. You could spot these blokes a mile off: they'd always arrive late, parking up their Cortinas and their Rovers before sauntering over to the sidelines in their regulation sheepskin coats or padded Adidas jackets. Some liked to underline their importance by conspicuously upping and leaving ten minutes before the final whistle; others would loiter around afterwards to have a quiet word with the mums and dads of any lads who'd caught their eye.

Among the parents, rumours and speculation were rife as to which scouts were in attendance (easy to suss) and which boys were the focus of their attention (not so easy to suss). It could be an incredibly competitive, cut-throat environment in which envy, jealousy and one-upmanship abounded, each parent holding the highest hopes for their offspring.

'That United scout rang me twice last week, Geoff,' you'd hear one dad saying to another. 'Reckons our Jamie is the best central defender he's seen in a long time. Sorting a trial out for him. Says he's a star in the making.'

'That's great news, that,' would be a typical response, the other dad smiling on the outside, but probably seething from within.

As a rule, Eccles Town competed against neighbouring teams in the Manchester area like Urmston Town or Irlam Town. After training one night, sometime in spring 1978, our manager announced to a hushed dressing room that we'd be lining up against the esteemed Whitehill FC that weekend. I greeted this news with a mixture of excitement and trepidation. While I was buoyed at the prospect of sharing the pitch with one of City's renowned satellite teams, I was equally worried that I'd have an off day and not do myself justice. Both Dad and I realized the importance of this friendly fixture, and the opportunity it presented.

I remember the game so clearly. It took place at the old Shell Sports Club in Carrington, a vast area of moorland bordering onto the former M63 motorway that, twenty years later, would become home to City and United's state-of-the-art training complexes. Even back then it was a marvellous facility, and was a hundred times better than our divot-ridden pitch at Alder Park.

Our team wasn't accustomed to losing, but that day we did so in some style, suffering a 4–0 mauling by a superior Whitehill side. The gulf in class was plain to see, but so it should have been. However, while our slick opponents certainly bore the hallmarks of some elite coaching, a few of us Eccles lads felt we'd held our own and given a decent account of ourselves.

More than anything, the match underlined the level of graft and ingenuity required if I was to have any chance of achieving my dreams, and making it as a professional. Lost in thought and deep in contemplation, Dad and I didn't exchange a word during that evening's journey back home to Eccles.

* * *

From that day onwards, Project David went into overdrive. I continued to impress at Eccles Town – a conveyor belt of talent scouts were regularly checking me out – and Dad became increasingly convinced that his youngest son had what it took to make the grade. As far as he was concerned, success could only be achieved if we matched each other's dedication and commitment, both working in partnership to come up with the goods and reach our common goal. Sometimes it felt like he was applying his business principles to my budding career, designing the blueprint and masterminding the strategy to propel me towards Manchester City.

Dad went to extreme lengths to support this mission. While he called it his passion, others called it an obsession. He spent a huge proportion of his time criss-crossing the north-west to ferry me to a variety of fixtures, where he'd chat animatedly to assorted scouts, coaches and parents on the touchline, gleaning as much advice and information as possible.

Our home life became totally monopolized by football, too; in fact, I'd go so far as to say that it eclipsed everything. We'd spend entire mornings together in the front garden, Dad battling through the pain barrier as he launched balls towards me to control, set up cones for me to dribble around, and marked targets on the wall for me to aim at. He'd always strategically park his car so that I could take full advantage of the wide, in-and-out drive to practise my ball skills, and so that I could shoot against the side of the garage. In the throes of winter he'd get up early to clear the drive of snow, enabling me to continue my quest towards football perfection. Nothing, but nothing, was allowed to get in the way.

'No excuses, David,' he'd grin as he wielded his shovel, his cheeks chapped red with the cold. 'We'll not let the weather stop us, eh, son? Let's work on that left foot of yours. We might get a couple of goals out of that this weekend.'

One day, Dad proudly presented me with a Peter Barnes Football Trainer that he'd bought from Hurley's, our local sports shop. This contraption comprised a ball attached to an elastic cord that was in turn linked to a belt, the idea being that the football would ping straight back when you kicked it away, allowing you to hone your reflexes. No disrespect, Peter, but it was absolutely shite. More often than not it would smack you square in the bollocks, and to me it was an implement of torture rather than a training aid.

Dad refused to be browbeaten by this godforsaken gadget, however, and – as resourceful as ever – promptly transformed it into the Dave

Watson Heading Trainer. He rigged it up in an alleyway at the side of the house, positioning the dangling ball high enough for me to connect powerfully with it, in an attempt to emulate the City captain's aerial supremacy. Unbeknown to me, each week Dad would raise the football slightly in order to – quite literally – keep me on my toes.

He even went to the lengths of building a large, cage-like construction at the rear of the garden, housing a mini-pitch with goals at either end. The chicken wire prevented the ball from being booted over next-door's fence or onto the adjoining bowling green, an outcome that would infuriate my dad since it meant wasting valuable playing time.

You'd have been forgiven for thinking that my big brother was peeved with Dad's preoccupation with me. To Steve's eternal credit, that simply wasn't the case, and I can honestly say that I never once detected any envy, rivalry or resentment on his part. Our closeness as siblings no doubt helped matters. While Steve and I were different in many ways – he was a go-getting, gregarious type while I was more reserved and strait-laced – we loved each other's company and were best mates as well as brothers. He could be quite protective over me, too; I hung around with his school friends quite a lot – probably more than my own – and he'd be the first to wade in if they ever gave me any stick.

Our quarrels were few and far between, although I do recall Steve chucking a red snooker ball at my head following a rare falling-out, and him once forcing me to kiss some poor girl who'd been watching our Patty rec kick about one evening.

'You're not going home until you snog her,' he demanded with an impish glint in his eye, knowing full well that I was obsessed with getting home on time, and only had seconds to spare before my self-imposed nine o'clock curfew. So I closed my eyes, puckered up and legged it, wiping my mouth with my cuff as I hotfooted it back home.

Over the years, Steve became well accustomed to Dad's football obsession. He also quite genuinely wanted me to succeed. He would regularly act as my practice partner and my pacemaker, gladly accepting his role as Best Supporting Sibling while I took centre stage.

* * *

It was in the aftermath of the Whitehill defeat, and while sharing a lift to training with our captain, Simon, that I received the news that would immeasurably change my life. It's a moment in time that remains etched upon my mind, probably more so than any other in my football career.

'So will you be coming to training with us, then?' asked Simon that particular evening.

'What d'you mean, Si?'

'Whitehill, Dave. Will you be coming along? Have you said yes or what?'

My confused expression told Simon that I had no idea what he was talking about, and that this news had obviously reached him before me. The Whitehill coach, it transpired, had been massively impressed with my performance against them, and was keen for me to start training with his select squad as soon as possible.

His name was Barry Bennell.

CHAPTER 3

Football Overload

That night's training at Eccles came and went in a blur, my legs wobbling and my head swimming as I tried to digest Simon's glad tidings. When Dad arrived to collect me it was confirmed by our manager, John Chapple, that Whitehill FC had indeed made overtures and were keen for me to hook up with them as soon as possible.

'Barry's asked that you give him a ring when you get home tonight, Stewart,' said John. 'He reckons Whitehill will do wonders for David's game, and he can't wait for him to meet the other lads. Exciting times ahead, eh?'

John's emotions were mixed, however. He was very protective of his young protégés – and he was averse to the idea of lads playing too much football – but even he realized that this was too good an opportunity for me to miss.

Dad was overwhelmed, but maintained an air of calm as he accepted all the handshakes and high-fives from the other fathers. Everyone in local football circles knew precisely how much energy and effort Stewart White had devoted to his talented son's cause, and watching him receiving praise and plaudits made me feel so proud. I was able to breathe a huge sigh of relief, too. All Dad's toil and trouble hadn't been in vain, and Project David appeared to be well on schedule.

* * *

Being a mad-keen City fan made the Whitehill news all the more thrilling. At that stage I'd become a regular visitor at Maine Road, having attended my first proper match in August 1975, a 3–0 defeat of Norwich City.

Prior to that game, Dad had proudly presented Steve and me with a bulky brown envelope. Within it we'd found a trio of tiny powder-blue Manchester City season-ticket books, each one imprinted with MAIN STAND, BLOCK E, ROW F. My heart leapt when I realized that one of these beauties was mine, all mine. It would turn out that the three of us would keep those same seats for the next twenty years.

My Maine Road initiation came at a time when the club was regrouping following one of the most successful periods in its history. Dad had been lucky enough to witness the Blues' late 1960s and early 1970s winning streak, which had seen manager Joe Mercer, coach Malcolm Allison and captain Tony Book masterminding a trophy haul that included the 1968 First Division Championship, the 1969 FA Cup, the 1970 League Cup and the 1970 European Cup Winners' Cup.

Like many of his fellow City fans, Dad idolized the supremely talented triumvirate of Colin Bell, Francis Lee and Mike Summerbee. He'd also wax lyrical to Steve and me about his other big favourite, star striker Neil Young. He delighted in telling us how, in May 1968, he'd seen 'Nelly' scoring two vital goals in the 4–3 victory at St James' Park, enabling City dramatically to snatch the championship away from Manchester United.

'Tell me again, tell me again,' I'd beg Dad at bedtime, imploring him to guide me though every kick of this classic match of yesteryear.

Fast-forward to 1975, however, and many of those sky blue stalwarts had been transferred or retired, the baton having been grabbed by a new breed of heroes. Their names became indelibly stamped upon my mind, so much so that, while walking to and from school, I'd often find myself reciting this legendary line-up.

Macrae, Hammond, Donachie, Doyle, Booth … I'd say to myself, in time with my footsteps' rhythm as I paced down Barton Road. *Oakes, Summerbee, Bell, Marsh, Hartford, Tueart* …

Match days became magical occasions for me. Saturday afternoon games at 3 p.m. were the norm, but it was the evening midweek fixtures that really used to get my adrenalin pumping. I would sit in my classroom at Godfrey Ermen Primary, willing the clock on the wall to go faster, my spine tingling every time my thoughts switched to a floodlit Maine Road. Sometimes I'd also have a school match on the same day, resulting in a severe case of football overload that was almost too much to take in. *Can life get any better?* I'd think to myself as I pulled on my maroon-and-gold school kit.

I came to love the routine and rituals associated with match days, none more so than the journey to the ground. Dad would always drive us there, his pal Mike Lewis usually occupying the passenger seat and Steve and I sitting in the back, often with my good friend Colin Bury shoehorned between us. All three of us would lean forward to either join in the footy banter being traded between Dad and Mike or listen to the pre-match chatter on Piccadilly Radio.

The route was never straightforward, however. Dad hated being stuck in standing traffic – he'd rather be mobile for an hour than marooned in a mind-numbing jam for twenty minutes – and he devised a backstreet, congestion-free detour that took us through Stretford and Trafford Park. We'd always pass by the Kellogg's factory on Barton Dock Road, a red-brick building that used to bear a huge red 'K'. As we approached this Mancunian landmark, a distinctive toasty, cornflakey smell would waft into the car, a comforting sign that we weren't too far from our destination.

We'd then head past Old Trafford's football and cricket grounds, continuing through Chorlton and crossing over Princess Parkway, one of the major arterial routes into Manchester city centre. It was here that we'd start to see blue-scarved City fans pounding the pavements, many of them spilling out of The Parkside pub, a legendary pre-match drinking den.

After zigzagging our way through Moss Side's narrow streets we'd park up in St Crispin's church car park on Hart Road, where we'd go through the rigmarole of the same hi-vis-jacketed jobsworth trying to guide us into a space.

'Bit more … bit more … bit more … *STOPPPPPP* …' he'd yell, beckoning theatrically before slapping his palm on the boot of Dad's car.

After a ten-minute stroll, with the glare of the bright white floodlights looming ever closer, we'd finally reach the stadium forecourt. It would be teeming with City fans, some buying the early edition of the *Pink Final*, others queuing outside the tiny souvenir shop. Sporadically, the BBC's outside broadcast lorry – with its mass of cables and aerials – would be parked near the main entrance, guaranteeing us a showing on that night's *Match of the Day*.

Dad would always buy me a match programme and a bottle of Coke (never Bovril; I couldn't bear the stuff) and, after filing through the clanking turnstiles, Steve and I would dart to our seats. Dad had played a blinder with the season tickets, securing us a brilliant vantage point that positioned us adjacent to the players' tunnel and behind the City dugout. This meant that my brother and I could lean over the whitewashed wall of the tunnel as the players jogged past for their warm-up, both of us within touching distance of Doyle, Donachie and their teammates. Half an hour later, when both teams ran out for kick-off, Steve and I would almost come to blows as we jockeyed for position in order to catch a glimpse of our sky blue heroes.

Being so close to the pitch, we could also hear the yells and curses coming from manager Tony Book, coach Ian McFarlane and physio Freddie Griffiths in the dugout, together with their interactions with the opposing bench and the match officials. Back then it was quite literally a dugout, too, as the coaches' eyelines remained at ground level; it can't have been easy to track a game from that perspective.

If we turned around and craned our necks, Steve and I would be able to see City's much-maligned chairman, Peter Swales, as well as a variety of celebrities and ex-players occupying the surrounding VIP seats. The club's head honcho would sit right at the front of the Directors' Box, and I remember being struck by how worried and pensive he often looked.

Throughout the match a blanket of swirling smoke would shroud the Main Stand, since most fans near us puffed on fags, cigars and pipes.

It really didn't bother me, though; in fact, the smell of tobacco, beer and pies almost became part and parcel of the match-day atmosphere. During half-time I'd often find myself gazing over to the Kippax Stand opposite where, at any given second, I could spot a cigarette lighter being sparked up. Then it was time to check out the half-time scores by squinting at a sandwich board paraded around the ground by some poor volunteer. A few years later, chairman Swales would install a single-line digital scoreboard atop the North Stand, but it wasn't exactly the appliance of science.

Saturday games would usually be done and dusted by 4.45 p.m., back in the day when half-time comprised a strictly observed ten minutes, and when there were no add-ons for goals and substitutions. Once Dad, Mike and us kids had fought our way through the sea of supporters flowing towards the exits – huge, clammy crushes were commonplace – we'd up our pace to ensure we got back to St Crispin's before BBC Radio Two's *Sports Report*. With its iconic theme tune, followed by James Alexander Gordon's crisply read results, it became a match-day institution.

In those days, that programme was the quickest way to find out all the full-time scores. It's hard to believe now, but in the early 1970s we'd often leave the ground totally unaware of the other results, unless we were pacing behind some statto with a transistor radio attached to his ear. No one in Dad's car would utter a word as the First Division match reports filtered through, delivered beautifully by the likes of Peter Jones and Bryon Butler. And, as was his wont, Dad would often take a meandering, congestion-dodging route back home to Eccles, using his in-built Manchester A-to-Z to pinpoint a clear run home.

* * *

City's manager at the time was Tony Book, the club's former captain. He'd taken on the full-time role in 1974, having previously acted as caretaker in the wake of Malcolm Allison and Johnny Hart's ill-fated stint. Despite his impeccable coaching credentials, Big Mal had been unable to sustain the remarkable success he'd previously enjoyed with Joe Mercer as manager.

Luckily for Book, City stars like Mike Doyle, Alan Oakes, Colin Bell and Tommy Booth were still going strong in the mid-1970s. Bolstering this array of legends, however, were new signings such as striker Joe Royle, midfielder Asa Hartford and left-winger Dennis Tueart, all of whom helped City to maintain a consistently respectable position in the First Division's top half.

For a football-mad kid like me, it was a pleasure to watch these brilliant players at close quarters. One of my favourites, Dave Watson, was a giant of a centre half. I remember once watching in awe as he connected with an opposing goalkeeper's kick, before heading it all the way back to him without a single bounce. The guy was immense. Willie Donachie, who like Watson was an experienced international, emerged as a superb full back, able to operate equally well on the right side or the left.

Much hope had been invested in Rodney Marsh – he of the mercurial talent and flamboyant persona – when he'd arrived at Maine Road in 1972. However, it was well documented that, despite his flashes of brilliance, some players felt that Marsh disrupted and hindered the team, and would regularly confront Tony Book to tell him so.

Joe Corrigan, after a shaky start, eventually developed into a fantastic goalkeeper. He'd suffered ridicule early in his career following a couple of high-profile errors but, while many players wouldn't have recovered from such criticism, City's number one was made of sterner stuff. He knuckled down and grafted until he proved his critics wrong, to such an extent that he'd eventually invite comparisons with greats like Frank Swift and Bert Trautmann.

By the end of my first full season as a spectator, however, the City careers of Marsh and Bell had effectively ended. Marsh swapped Moss Side for Tampa Bay, having never quite gelled with his teammates on the pitch. Colin Bell, our supremely talented midfielder, suffered a horrendous injury at Maine Road following a clash with Manchester United captain Martin Buchan. The incident, which occurred during a League Cup tie in November 1975, saw both players going for a fifty-fifty challenge; the ball was at knee height as Buchan connected, however, and Bell sustained torn ligaments in the resulting collision. City's 4–0 victory was scant consolation as news spread of Bell's fate.

'Don't worry, boys, we'll soon see him back in action,' said Dad, convinced that his absence would be short-term.

Having worked tirelessly on his rehab, Bell attempted a comeback a couple of years later which, tragically, never materialized. I remember my heart sinking as I sat in the stands, watching him limping badly on the field of play. How he even made it out of the tunnel, let alone finish a game, was beyond me. At the age of twenty-nine, and having chalked up nearly 500 appearances for the Blues, Colin the King reluctantly had to hang up his boots.

Apart from the crushing disappointment of losing Colin, I absolutely loved my inaugural season as a fully fledged City fan. My very first away game – at Sheffield United's Bramall Lane, just two days after my eighth birthday – was a truly brilliant experience and prompted a lifelong obsession with football stadia. I developed a real fascination for English grounds, captivated by their unique construction and their individual little quirks.

The match itself finished 2–2. Keith Macrae had worn the number 1 shirt that night, despite not being named in the initial squad; in those days, teams didn't often take a second keeper. It transpired that Joe Corrigan had fallen ill a few hours earlier and, having received a frantic phone call, Keith sped over the Snake Pass towards Sheffield, arriving just in time for kick-off.

Tommy Booth played up front and scored our first goal – I guess he'd been deployed there following Rodney Marsh's departure – with eighteen-year-old starlet Peter Barnes slotting in the other. Barnes, a prodigious young winger (and son of ex-City player Ken) had progressed through the youth-team ranks at the club and, due to his formidable speed and direct approach, was fast becoming my main role model.

City managed to lose their two-goal lead at Bramall Lane – leading to a glum return journey over the 'tops' – but I remember our mood lifting as we heard an entertaining radio report from the Baseball Ground describing the fisticuffs between Derby County's Francis Lee and Leeds United's Norman Hunter. On-pitch scraps were commonplace in the mid-1970s, but this one sounded like a humdinger.

'Can't wait to see footage of that in the highlights,' laughed my dad.

The Blues managed to finish the 1975–6 season in eighth place, despite the fact that their consistently brilliant form on their own turf was more akin to a top-three team (they won as many home games – fourteen – as First Division champions Liverpool).

Our silverware that year came courtesy of the League Cup. The tournament itself had commenced with a wobble – it had taken three second-round games for us finally to overcome Norwich City – but, from then on, it was all plain sailing. Our Wembley date against Newcastle United was booked following a semi-final victory over Middlesbrough, the Blues having triumphed 4–1 on aggregate. Dennis Tueart was suspended for the second leg, having been dramatically sent off in an FA Cup tie against Hartlepool United. Our star winger, who'd already scored twice, had been gratuitously kicked by 'Pool's George Potter as he lay on the floor, attempting to retain possession. City's number 11 saw red, headbutted his opponent – who just happened to be an old pal of his from Teesside – and was immediately dismissed. Dennis wasn't someone to be messed with, mate or no mate.

Potter, meanwhile, was poleaxed – he eventually had to be stretchered off – yet, as he lay there unconscious, the referee decided to brandish a red card in his face. It was all very surreal.

'There's only one Dennis Tueart,' chuckled Dad as he read the *Manchester Evening News* match report. 'Fracturing your mate's cheekbone in a game that you've virtually won, when you're on the verge of a hat-trick. Now that's what you call a competitor, son.'

* * *

The Whites' trip to Wembley, on Saturday 28 February 1976, was a day to remember. Dad, Mike, Steve and I set off from Eccles at 7 a.m., my brother and I wrapped up in anoraks, our treasured City scarves draped around our necks. The anticipation mounted with each motorway service station that we stopped at, Steve and I calming our nerves by playing Space Invaders while Dad and Mike enjoyed a quick cup of coffee.

I can still recall the scenes when the rival fans merged on the Yorkshire stretch of the M1. Leaning out of their car windows, supporters bedecked in sky blue or black and white exchanged jeers and banter, most of it – but not all – good-natured. My brother and I would meet any cries of 'You Manc bastards!' with a selection of hand gestures, confident in the knowledge that Dad's new shit-off-a-shovel Daimler wouldn't be caught by the mouthy Geordies in their Vauxhall Victors.

My eyes were on stalks when I first caught sight of Wembley stadium; for a football nut like me, glimpsing those iconic twin towers for the first time was a truly amazing experience. As we followed the crowds along the famous Wembley Way, joining in all the City chants with gusto, we spotted an old guy selling sky blue scarves emblazoned with WEMBLEY 1976. This prompted a passing Magpies fan, swigging from a bottle of Newcastle Brown, to give him some verbals.

'You'll not be selling too many of those this afternoon, pal,' he laughed, nudging his mates.

'Maybe I won't sell any this afternoon,' the bloke retorted in a heavy Mancunian accent, 'but I'll sell fuckin' thousands tonight …'

Our Cup Final seats were located at the royal box side of the ground, almost level with the penalty area at the tunnel end. The feverish atmosphere was like nothing I'd ever encountered before, and I remember eagerly counting down the minutes until kick-off.

My heroes didn't let me down. Early in the game, Mike Doyle headed an Asa Hartford free kick back into the area. Newcastle could only partially clear the ball into the path of Peter Barnes who, approaching from the right, waited for the ball to sit up nicely before hitting it crisply into the ground, past keeper Mike Mahoney and into the Newcastle goal. The ecstasy on young Peter's face was a sight to behold. I found it utterly intoxicating that a born-and-bred Manchester lad had just scored a Cup Final goal for his favourite team.

'There you go, son,' yelled Dad, hoisting me into the air. '*That's* what it's all about.'

My joy turned to jitters, however, when Newcastle equalized on 35 minutes, Alan Gowling finishing accurately with his left foot, having latched onto a Malcolm Macdonald cross.

'Things are going to plan, don't you worry,' Dad's pal Mike reassured us at half-time. 'It'll be our ribbons on that cup, lads, mark my words …'

His sentiments were spot on, thankfully, because shortly after the interval we'd witness one of the finest match-winners in football history. Willie Donachie had taken a pass from Alan Oakes, and had hit a left-footed cross over to the far post. Tommy Booth had risen to head the ball back into the penalty area, where there looked to be no immediate threat from a City player.

The lurking Dennis Tueart knew differently, however. Seemingly from nowhere, he unleashed an astounding bicycle kick, expertly steering the ball past the diving Mahoney and in at the far post, sending the blue half of the stadium crazy. What an athlete. What a goal. What a memory.

I felt overwhelmed and was close to tears when Mike Doyle, Manchester City captain and proud Mancunian, held aloft the League Cup trophy, adorned with those blue and white ribbons. His valiant teammates – including a battle-scarred, blood-spattered Dave Watson – mounted the steps behind him to collect their much-deserved winners' medals.

As the City songs were belted out, and the assorted scarves were held in the air, I had a private moment to myself. I closed my eyes, clasped my hands and said a little prayer.

Please, please let me play in a Wembley final one day. I'll work so hard, I promise …

Little did I know that, twenty-one years later, my dream would come true.

CHAPTER 4

World of Opportunity

By 1978, at the age of ten, I was playing more football than ever before, turning out for my school team during the week, Eccles Boys on a Saturday and Whitehill under-12s on a Sunday (not forgetting all the training sessions in between). Being part of the Whitehill set-up was as fantastic as I'd expected. I felt honoured and I felt special; sometimes it was like playing for Manchester City themselves, so strong were the ties.

The side's crème de la crème recruitment policy guaranteed our constant top-of-the-league status. My teammates were ridiculously talented; embarrassingly good, in fact. We once played Unsworth 'A' and Unsworth 'B' back-to-back, beating them by a combined score of 20–0, and shortly afterwards thrashed another hapless team 36–0. Teams from all across Manchester would dread facing the shit-hot Whitehill boys.

My dad, with his win-at-all-costs mentality, lapped it up. He never missed a training session and attended every single match. For the next six years we probably spent more time on a football pitch than at home; the bungalow became a pit stop, almost; a place where we'd refuel, wash kits and scrub boots.

Whitehill opened up a whole new world of opportunity for me. We had the best of everything: access to brilliant facilities, top-quality kits and equipment and, crucially, one of the best young football coaches in the business.

Barry Bennell was known as 'Benny' to most people, but he insisted on his name being spelled 'Bené' with an accent over the second 'e', as in Pelé. Lean, athletic and aged in his early twenties, he sported a mop of dark brown curly hair and wore the trendiest designer football gear. He'd always bound around with a huge smile on his face – he was incredibly eager and enthusiastic – and his friendly charm and approachability ensured his popularity among dads and lads alike.

By all accounts, Bené had been a budding professional footballer – at Chelsea, apparently – whose chances of hitting the big time had been scuppered by injury. Ever since then he'd built up a new career as a youth coach and a talent-spotter, going on to forge close ties with big clubs including Manchester City, Stoke City and Crewe Alexandra, and working with a network of junior sides in the region.

While Bené may have failed to make the grade as a professional, he'd managed to retain an impressive repertoire of football skills and tricks. No one could juggle a ball or maintain their keepy-uppies quite like Bené. After training sessions he'd happily show off his astounding agility, drawing in clusters of cooing admirers as he balanced the ball on his head, and deftly trapped it on the nape of his neck. He was like a latter-day freestyler.

'Bloody hell, Bené, we could do with you at Old Trafford,' you'd hear some parent saying. 'You've got skills to die for, mate.'

Dad and I agreed that we'd never met such a diligent and dedicated coach. The guy radiated professionalism and set notoriously high standards for every lad in his squad. None of us could be a minute late, for example. Everybody's attitude and application had to be spot on. We had to show respect to officials, opponents and spectators. Anyone having the nerve to defy him would be shown the door, as simple as that. He was keen that we all looked the part, too; our shirts, shorts and training kits – all supplied by Bené – were the flashiest in the league, and had to be absolutely pristine.

The star-struck parents on the sidelines could only gaze in wonderment.

'Wow, these boys are only ten and eleven,' they'd exclaim, 'but just how professional do they look?'

Bené was the football guru with the nous and the know-how, the expert coach with the contacts and the connections. Desperate to impress him both on and off the pitch, the Whitehill boys would hang onto his every word and would do exactly as he said.

Bené was a godlike figure to Dad and me. We both thought the world of him, and worshipped the ground he walked on.

* * *

The annual Isle of Wight tournament was an eagerly anticipated football festival that was staged at the Warner's holiday camp over a July weekend. It was attended by many of the UK's top junior teams, most of whom were affiliated with professional clubs like Arsenal, Leeds United and Glasgow Rangers. On the couple of occasions I was invited to take part, Dad booked a beachside property for a few days so the family could stay nearby and enjoy a welcome break; no one complained, since the Isle of Wight was a superb holiday destination. I'd spend the weekend at Warner's with Bené and my teammates before hooking up with Dad, Steve and the girls the following Monday.

Bené was in his element on the Isle of Wight. His days were spent encouraging his Whitehill lads from the sidelines – I seem to remember our side doing pretty well – and his evenings were devoted to keeping us all amused and occupied, like some kind of children's entertainer.

'Come on, boys, you've worked really hard all day. Let's relax and have some fun tonight, eh?' he'd grin.

Bené would do his utmost to ensure that he was the centre of attention, whether it was performing elaborate card tricks, telling us daft jokes and riddles or demonstrating his amazing football trickery. It was like he had his own theatrical spotlight following him around.

His favourite party piece was a nunchaku demonstration. Made famous by Kung Fu legend Bruce Lee, this fearsome-looking weapon comprised two thick rods of wood connected by a weighty chain, which Bené would swing around at great speed, often within inches of our faces. My teammates and I would sit rooted to the spot, mesmerized by this multi-talented performer.

Every night, once darkness had set in, our coach would take us for long walks to remote locations – clifftops, woods, beaches – and we'd all trail obediently behind him, following in his footsteps as though he was some kind of Pied Piper. He'd then sit the lads down in a circle and, in a low voice, regale us with a series of scary, spooky stories. He'd tell tales of unsolved murders, ancient mysteries and ghostly episodes, simultaneously captivating us and terrifying us.

'Don't worry, boys, it's only make-believe …' he'd then say, perhaps sensing that some of us were feeling a bit freaked out as we sat shivering in a freezing-cold, pitch-black forest, listening to 'The Story of the Screaming Skull'.

'… and you know you're always safe with Bené', he'd add, flashing us a toothy grin before leading us all back to Warner's.

The tournament also gave Bené the opportunity to speak frankly about our football prospects, and I remember being hugely affected by one particular pep talk he gave us towards the end of our stay. 'You've all done me proud this weekend, but I'll count myself lucky if just one of you lads goes on to make it as a professional,' he'd said, scanning the front room of the Warner's chalet that we'd squeezed into.

'And that person will be the one who works hardest for me, who listens to me and who doesn't give up.'

His stark sentiments almost brought me to tears, as I felt 90 per cent sure that this extra-special footballer wouldn't be me. I was a year younger than the rest, for starters, and had convinced myself that our Whitehill side comprised players who were far more skilful and assertive than me. The centre forward, for example – a strapping lad called Mike – was streets ahead of any of us. My pal Simon was another shining light who'd rightly earned a reputation as a complete midfielder with a golden future. I was utterly disconsolate.

Bené's remarks remained etched into my psyche. Whenever I saw a decent player falling by the wayside (Mike being a case in point, ironically enough) I'd recall my coach's blunt words, persuading myself that, if I kept on toiling, and did as he said, the odds of David White becoming The Chosen One would surely shorten.

* * *

It was around this time, with my stock rising at Whitehill, that Dad's 'Project David' went up a gear. Now that I was playing for a renowned feeder team, and was advancing up the football ladder, it was time to pinpoint my next big objective. Signing schoolboy forms for Manchester City was soon identified as the target to aim for, the big be-all-and-end-all.

Dad's philosophy in life, as he frequently expounded, deemed that happiness was driven by success, which was in turn driven by hard work. From his go-getting perspective, grafters were winners and slackers were losers. The only way that I'd flourish, according to Dad, was through practice, commitment and dedication. Everything else – including any foolish concepts of downtime, relaxation or chilling out – was regarded as wasteful. Luckily for me, I was doing really well at school so had no classwork or homework problems to thwart my sporting progression.

In order to maximize my chances, warned Dad, every spare minute of every day had to be justified from a footballing perspective.

'You can't let up on your training, David. You've got to be ready to perform for the King at the weekend,' he'd grin as we played head tennis on the driveway ('The King' being the reverential nickname that the Whitehill parents had coined for Bené).

Any outdoor activities, he informed me, had to benefit my game directly. If they didn't have purpose or relevance, they'd be off limits.

At weekends, for example, my school pals and I would go 'trekking', an outdoor challenge that merged hide-and-seek with a treasure hunt. This pursuit met with Dad's approval, since it involved sprinting and jogging, which ultimately aided my fitness. Weekly swimming sessions at Irlam Pool were justified in his eyes too, as were trips to the local tennis court or a game of pitch and putt with Steve.

When the annual Silcock's funfair rolled into town, however, I decided to keep away, despite the fact that I desperately wanted to go. It was the highlight of the summer for many thrill-seeking Eccles kids but as far as Dad was concerned, hooking ducks, chucking darts and bumping dodgems held no sporting merit whatsoever. With his words ringing in my ears, I reluctantly stayed at home, glumly booting a ball against the garage wall as the sounds and smells of the fairground drifted across the garden.

Soon enough, Dad's master plan began to take its toll. Football was still my pastime of choice – there was nothing else I'd rather do – but the constant pressure to excel started to have a detrimental, almost attritional effect. Even at the tender age of ten, the joy and passion I had for the game was already being eroded by feelings of dread. I worried myself daft about not putting in enough effort in a training session, for example, or not using every waking hour wisely. I fretted about losing a split second of pace, overhitting a cross or not heading that bloody ball-on-a-string hard enough. I forever analysed Dad's comments and criticisms, my stomach churning as I contemplated the heavy fixture schedule that lay ahead, and the necessity to play out of my skin and do myself justice.

Along with this angst came chronic sleep problems. Realizing the importance of a decent night's kip, I always ensured that I was back home from my training sessions or my Patty rec runabouts by 9 p.m., and would set myself target times to drop off by. Lying in bed, though, I often found myself staring at the ceiling, unable to switch off as my mind whirred with football-related anxieties.

The spectre of failure – and the fear of disappointing Bené or my dad – could sometimes keep me awake until the early hours. This sleep deprivation, together with my unrelenting training regime, left me exhausted in the mornings and drained by the weekend. I was trapped in a vicious cycle of pressure, fear and insomnia, but was far too young to realize it.

Things got so bad that I started to dread getting into Dad's car after matches, because if I ever had a crappy game he'd go absolutely ballistic.

He never accused me of a lack of effort – I always gave 100 per cent, no matter what, and my winning mentality in those days was unquestionable – but if I made some careless mistake or didn't heed his or 'The King's' advice in some way he'd let rip, big-style. He'd slaughter me all the way home, banging the dashboard and revving the engine in anger.

'What the bloody hell happened there, David?'

As he ranted and raved I'd nod meekly and shrug my shoulders before waiting for the shit-storm to blow over.

On the other hand, if I put in a show-stopping Man-of-the-Match-winning performance he'd spend the entire journey grinning like a Cheshire Cat while re-enacting all my best moves. I'd recline in the passenger seat, waves of relief washing over me as we sped back down the M63.

I came to realize that Dad's Monday-to-Friday state of mind depended entirely on my performance on a football pitch. If he was curt and tetchy all week, I'd blame myself because I hadn't converted a couple of chances the previous weekend. If he was cheery and upbeat, I'd breathe a sigh of relief that I'd managed to bag that second-half hat-trick.

I was as desperate to play well as I was to please Dad, but the pressure of the first dictating the second was almost too much to bear. For a ten-year-old lad to have to wrestle with that dilemma was totally counter-productive.

At least I had some respite at my mum's, who had a totally laissez-faire attitude to sport and to life in general. She knew I had the potential to make it in the game, but also realized that I possessed the intelligence to succeed in life even if my football went down the pan. The low-pressure environment at Mum's contrasted starkly with the highly strung life at the bungalow.

'If you want to train outside on the fields, that's fine,' she'd smile as she put my fish 'n' chips supper on the kitchen table. 'But if you want to lounge on the sofa and watch telly with Steve, well that's okay, too.'

I rarely chose the latter, if I'm honest, but it was nice to have the choice all the same.

* * *

Despite all the external pressures and intensities, my football progression was on an upward trajectory. I was impressing all and sundry (including a variety of City scouts) and Dad was always thrilled when Bené took him aside after games to sing my praises.

'He's doing great, Stewart ...' he'd say, 'but we just need to work on his heading, and maybe get him to think more about his defensive responsibilities.'

'You're dead right, Bené,' Dad would reply. 'We'll work on it over the weekend.'

In 1978 my Manchester City dream seemed to be edging ever closer, and I think I quite literally jumped for joy when my father told me that I'd been invited to some school-holiday training sessions run by the club.

Each morning for the next three weeks Dad drove me from Eccles to Maine Road, my heart pounding like crazy when those familiar stands and lofty floodlights came into view. He dropped me off on the forecourt car park, where a bus would be waiting to ferry a twenty-strong group of hopefuls to the club's training facility in Cheadle, near Stockport. Whitehill were clearly not the only Sunday-league feeder team, I soon realized.

The intensity of those sessions was ridiculous, but I loved it. Every touch of the ball felt like life or death to me, but the joy of scoring or making a goal was just so sweet. For a City-mad young 'un like me, the Cheadle ground was a thrilling place. There were two pitches, a standard-sized one on the far side that we'd use most of the time, and another massive, full-sized pitch with its own little stand. When City coaches like Bill Taylor – and sometimes even manager Tony Book – came down to watch, we'd be asked to upgrade to the bigger pitch, presumably so we could best showcase ourselves to the Maine Road powers-that-be. If we picked up a knock we'd even be treated by the first-team physios, too. This was the real deal, and I wanted more of it.

Furthermore, not only were we able to rub shoulders with some of the older schoolboy players, we even bumped into some of the professionals, like Dave Watson and Peter Barnes, which totally blew my mind.

At the end of each week, City's chief scout – an affable guy called Ted Davies – would hand us a fiver for our 'expenses'.

'Buy yer mums some flowers,' he'd wink at us all. 'Just don't tell yer dads I said that …'

* * *

It was in the spring of 1979 that Dad burst into my bedroom to tell me about the latest development in my football journey.

'Fancy a trip to Spain next month, David?' he asked excitedly. 'Bené's asked me if he can take you and another lad to Majorca during the Whit holidays.'

'Majorca?' I said, incredulously. 'Really?'

'Yep. Really. He knows how hard you've worked over the past few months, and he thinks a nice break in the sun will do you the world of good,' he grinned, explaining that Bené had also agreed to lay on some special warm-weather training sessions, too, designed to make me an even better player.

'So what d'you think, son?'

'Why not?' I said, flashing him a smile. I'd never been abroad with my family before – let alone my football coach – and it all sounded like great fun. And, as Dad had suggested, anything that was going to improve my football – and my chances of success – was bound to be a good thing.

'You need to make the most of this opportunity, David,' he added. 'How does it feel to be in Bené's good books, eh, you little superstar?'

'Feels great,' I laughed, genuinely thrilled to see my Dad looking so happy.

CHAPTER 5

Betrayal of Trust

On Saturday 5 May 1979, with my holdall stuffed with summer clothes and suncream, Dad and I set off for Manchester Airport. I felt really excited as we crossed the Cheshire boundary; aeroplanes, runways, flights and hotels were all new to me and I couldn't wait for my first foreign adventure.

Waiting in Departures to greet us was a tracksuited Bené, standing beside my Whitehill teammate and holiday buddy, who I'll call Mark.

'Enjoy yourself, son,' winked Dad as he handed me my shiny new passport and pressed a wad of notes into my coach's palm.

'You sure, Stewart?' he asked.

'Treat yourselves,' came Dad's reply. 'I'm looking forward to seeing two new, improved players when you come back.'

He then firmly shook Bené's hand, thanked him for giving me this fantastic opportunity, and headed back to the car park.

'Right, lads,' grinned our coach, as Dad disappeared out of the terminal. 'Let's get this show on the road.'

The flight to Majorca was smooth enough, and I remember feeling thrilled when I caught my first glimpse of Cala D'Or, the picturesque resort on the island's east coast that was to be our base for the next seven days. The azure sky, the golden sun, the sparkling sea, the sandy beach; it was like a miniature paradise, a far cry from my wet weekends in Wales.

Within minutes of the coach dropping us off at the Hotel Cala D'Or, Mark and I were flinging our suitcases onto our own little beds – Bené had reserved us a triple room for the week – before unpacking all our bits and bobs.

This is just amazing, I remember thinking as I skipped out onto the balcony and surveyed the beautiful, tropical-style complex.

Bené then told us to put on our swimming trunks, grab our footballs and head to the pool. He couldn't wait to get our holiday started; he was like a hyperactive little kid.

'Chop chop, boys,' he said. 'We don't want to waste a minute, do we?'

The small pool area was jam-packed with tourists – British families, predominantly – lazing on sunloungers and sheltering under parasols. Bené found some space to lay down our towels, before producing a bottle of coconut oil from his sports bag.

'Don't use that, David,' he said, as he watched me flip open my tube of Factor 20 Uvistat. 'You want to go back home to Manchester with a tan, don't you?'

I nodded. I'd never really had a proper suntan before.

'Well this is the stuff you need,' he smiled, throwing over the brown plastic bottle. 'Trust me.'

As with all Bené's advice, I did as I was told. He knew best, naturally. I slathered on the coconut oil – as did Mark – and, by the end of the stay, our pale Mancunian skins had deepened into a mahogany brown.

Then, with a nod and wink, he handed us both a football and led us to the poolside where, in front of all the holidaymakers – and to our mild embarrassment – he encouraged us to demonstrate our array of soccer skills. Bené, as per usual, was the centre of attention as he expertly juggled, controlled and flicked the ball, attracting ripples of applause from appreciative onlookers.

After finishing our impromptu routine, Bené beckoned Mark and me to join him in the pool. We all larked about in the water for a while, splashing and dunking each other, before our coach loudly set us a challenge to see who could swim the most lengths underwater (he won, naturally).

From what I can remember, nobody at the hotel seemed to bat an eyelid that a twenty-something bloke was fooling around with a couple of eleven-year-olds. If they didn't already know that he was our football guru – Bené would brag about his sporting connections to all and sundry – they'd have probably assumed that we were two nephews having a laugh with their charismatic uncle, or perhaps three close-knit cousins having some fun in the sun.

When we weren't sunbathing by the pool or playing football on the beach, Bené would take us for trips out in the resort, most of them of the daredevil variety. One afternoon we hired a hulking great motorbike, Mark and I riding pillion as our coach sped down tree-lined avenues. We soon screeched to a halt, in the middle of a dense forest.

'Go on, David, you have a go,' he'd grinned, wheeling this beast of a machine towards me. I'd never ridden a motorbike in my life, of course, and after straddling the seat, starting it up and revving the engine I promptly crashed it straight into a huge concrete block that had been left lying around from an old construction site. Luckily I was more shaken than hurt.

'Are you all right?' laughed Bené, brushing the gravel off my back. 'Might be a good idea not to tell your mum and dad about that, okay?'

He also thought it would be fun to take Mark and I night fishing. Cala D'Or was studded with jagged little coves, and we spent hours traipsing through the darkness to find the best spot. I remember Mark and I perching precariously on some massive rocks in the early hours, gripping our fishing rods with just an expanse of blue-black sea before us. I felt absolutely petrified.

'Who fancies some stories, then?' Bené had asked at one point, before proceeding to chill us to the bone with ghoulish tales of bloodthirsty piranhas and man-eating sharks. As with our trip to the Isle of Wight, Bené seemed to revel in propagating a feeling of peril and danger, before taking great pains to emphasize that he was our chief protector, our guardian angel, our responsible adult.

'Don't worry, you'll always be fine with me, lads,' he reiterated, as he gathered up our fishing rods and, with a hand on each of our shoulders, steered us away from the cliff edge.

* * *

The following day we enjoyed yet another action-packed afternoon by the pool and, after a few glasses of Coke and a couple of card games on the balcony, the three of us went to bed. I remember lying there, chit-chatting to Bené and Mark about football for a while, before feeling myself drifting off. The non-stop poolside games had worn me out, and I'd have probably been fast asleep by ten o'clock.

It must have been in the early hours when I awoke to find someone else in my bed. I knew instinctively that it was Bené. His body was pressed against mine and he was stroking me, touching me.

It took me a few groggy seconds to realize exactly what was going on. I just froze in shock. I could hardly breathe. I felt paralysed with fear. By then he must have known I was awake, but he didn't stop what he was doing. He merely carried on regardless, for what seemed like an eternity.

This can't be happening to me, I remember thinking to myself. *Surely Bené – my coach, my guide, my hero – isn't doing these horrible things to me.*

Mark, meanwhile, was sleeping soundly on the other side of the room, seemingly unaware of what was taking place just a matter of metres away.

And then, when it was over, and without saying a word, Bennell just slid out of my bed, quietly crept back to his own, and quickly fell back to sleep.

For hours I just lay staring at the ceiling, stunned and horrified, hoping to God I was in the middle of some appalling nightmare that I'd soon jolt myself out of. *Why, why, why?* I asked myself, over and over again, my mind beset with confusion and bewilderment. And, while there had been no violence, force or pain, I was old enough to realize that there was something very, very wrong with what had just occurred.

As the Majorcan sun began to rise, and as the reality of the situation began to hit home, I climbed out of my bed and walked out onto the balcony. I'm not exactly sure why. Maybe I felt safer there because I could hear some early risers chattering beside the pool below. Perhaps

I was contemplating yelling a desperate *HELP ME* to a passing family, or a member of staff. Maybe I just needed to breathe in some fresh air to try to clear my thumping head. I really don't know. I just remember feeling so scared and helpless. Here I was, on an island in the middle of the Mediterranean, hundreds of miles from my home and my family, trapped in a hotel with a man who within a matter of minutes had gone from mentor to monster.

Bennell must have heard me stirring, and within minutes he had followed me out onto the balcony. My heart pounded as I sensed him standing right behind me, but I didn't dare turn around. I couldn't bear to face the man. A few moments passed before he punctured the silence with a question.

'Has anybody done that to you before?' he whispered into my ear, without any trace of apology, regret or contrition.

A chill ran down my spine. *What sort of sick question was that?* I didn't afford him a reply. I ignored him and continued staring straight ahead, blinking back the tears that were now beginning to well up.

After an interminably long pause – I could feel his breath against my neck – Bennell padded back into the hotel room. I, however, remained rooted to the balcony until breakfast.

* * *

There was to be no repeat act in Cala D'Or. However, I was left feeling emotionally drained for the remainder of the week. I was simply unable to fathom why this figure of trust, this friend to all parents, this pillar of the community, could have done something so hideous and humiliating to a young lad like me. I also felt angry and ashamed with myself for not having the presence of mind to shove him away or to shout for help.

The following day Bennell acted as though nothing had happened – I think brazen is the word – cheerfully chatting to me and Mark over lunch and taking us to the nearby beach for yet another football skills showcase. I felt I had no other option but to play along with the whole charade. First, I didn't want any frosty silences or knowing looks to arouse any suspicions from Mark, who didn't need to be privy to what had gone on. At one point I did wonder whether my friend had suffered the same fate, but nothing about his behaviour or demeanour suggested that this had been the case.

Second, despite feeling totally heartbroken that Bennell had betrayed my trust, I didn't want to rock the boat. So I gritted my teeth, painted on a smile, and carried on as normal.

Events took a particularly strange turn that evening, though. Bennell had taken Mark and I to a nearby bar for a game of ten-pin bowling and, after a few rounds, I'd found myself topping our leader board, well above Bennell in second place. This was a rare occurrence. He was notoriously brilliant at every sport he played; like most coaches he was ultra-competitive and a terrible loser.

The last thing I wanted to do was annoy or aggravate him, so I deliberately chucked it in. I ignored that ingrained winning instinct of mine and knowingly bowled wayward balls, totally bypassing the pins so that he could leapfrog me into first place. Bennell wasn't daft, though, and sussed out my logic good and proper. When Mark was out of earshot he turned to me.

'You're throwing in the towel because of what happened last night, aren't you?' he asked, almost dismissively.

'No, I'm not,' came my defensive reply. He was spot on, though.

This Cala D'Or capitulation represented a huge psychological turning point for me. Like Bennell, I also had a win-at-all-costs outlook, and simply couldn't bear the thought of being beaten. My family would rib me about my deadly serious approach to caravan-based card games, for instance, when I'd make up my own rules as I went along to ensure certain victory.

'If I pick up a heart next, I win,' I'd say to Steve, sternly. 'And if you pick one up, you lose.'

There's no way I'd ever tolerate any kind of defeat – it simply wasn't in my DNA – and never in a million years would I have purposely let somebody beat me. But that night, for the first time ever in a competitive environment, I found myself backing down, giving up and caving in.

***

We flew back to the UK on the morning of Saturday 12 May 1979. It happened to be FA Cup Final day, with Terry Neill's Arsenal due to line up against Dave Sexton's Manchester United at Wembley Stadium.

The two-hour flight gave me a lot of thinking time. In fact, I don't think I uttered a word to anybody from Majorca to Manchester, apart from a polite thank you to the air stewardesses as they handed out drinks and peanuts. As we soared over mainland Spain – Bennell chose to sit between me and Mark – I gazed out of the little round window and calmly assessed the situation. I came to the conclusion that, for mine and my family's sake, I just had to put the horror of Cala D'Or behind me and consign it to the dark recesses of my mind.

I decided not to tell a soul about what had happened. My dad, in particular, could never, ever find out about what Barry Bennell had done to me. By revealing my ordeal and unmasking our celebrated football coach, I'd not only be breaking my father's heart, but would also be shattering our dreams and destroying all our hard work. As Dad never tired of telling me, 'The King' held the key to a possible career in professional football, and I didn't want to do anything that would jeopardize my progress or hamper my chances.

The joy I felt at seeing Dad waiting for me in Arrivals almost matched the relief I felt seeing Bennell head off to the taxi rank. I was elated to be home, safe and sound, and couldn't wait to get back to Eccles for a glass of pop, a bag of chips and a slice of top-quality FA Cup football. As it happened, we arrived at the bungalow just in time to see all those late-in-the-day goals raining in at Wembley, most notably Alan Sunderland's dramatic winner for Arsenal.

'Looks like I've missed one of the best Cup Finals in years,' frowned Dad. 'I hope that trip was bloody worth it, son.'

''Course it was, Dad,' came my reply.

If only you knew, I thought to myself. *If only you knew.*

***

It was with a huge sense of dread that I had to face Bennell again the next day. Somehow I can't imagine being too talkative during the short drive over to Oldham, where Whitehill FC were due to play a league match on some pitches near Boundary Park.

When we arrived, I noticed that our coach was enthusiastically doling out a brand-new, all-white kit to my teammates. *That's a bit odd*, I remember thinking to myself, bearing in mind that we were approaching the tail end of the football season.

'Wow, these shirts are sound, Bené,' I heard the lads saying as they pulled them over their heads, their parents nodding in approval at the latest top-notch gear provided by the ever-professional Barry Bennell.

Just prior to kick-off, he beckoned me and Mark over to the pitch. Bedecked in our new kits, he insisted that we both stand either side of him and pose for a photograph.

'C'mon, boys, look happy!' he grinned, his arm draped casually around my shoulder as I forced out a smile. None of the onlookers, including my father, thought anything was amiss, of course. If anything, the other lads and dads might have felt slightly envious that Mark and I – having just returned from a week in Majorca – were yet again being singled out by our coach for special treatment.

Looking back, I'm convinced that there was an ulterior motive behind these whiter-than-white kits. I reckon Bennell knew perfectly well that they'd enhance our brown-as-berry suntans and, more likely than not, had bought them specifically for this purpose.

I think he was showing us off, like a pair of gleaming trophies.

* * *

Some weeks later, following a Wednesday night training session, I overheard Bennell talking to my dad in the car park.

'Stewart, you can bring Dave to my place after the City game on Saturday if you want,' he said nonchalantly. 'He can stay overnight, no probs. We can even take in a match in the morning, if that's all right with you,' he added, giving Dad some spiel about a cracking right-winger he was coaching who I could watch and observe.

'Are you sure, Bené? That's really decent of you, mate,' replied my father, glancing across at me as I leaned against his car. 'David will be chuffed to bits.'

I'm not sure that I will, Dad... I thought to myself, hoping to God that my Cala D'Or ordeal was just a one-off.

Three days later, I found myself sitting in the passenger seat of Dad's car, with a football perched on my knee, being driven to the home of my abuser.

'You'll have a great time, David,' trilled Dad as we made the eighteen-mile journey from Manchester to Chapel-en-le-Frith, the small town in the Derbyshire peaks where Bennell lived.

'Take every piece of his advice on board,' he added, nodding his head sagely. 'What Bené doesn't know about football isn't worth knowing, remember …'

I'm sure that my father thought he was doing this for my own good. I'm sure that he visualized my coach and I having a great time poring over back issues of *Shoot!* magazine, discussing tactics and dissecting *Match of the Day*. I'm also sure that he had absolutely no idea that his nervous, anxious son was aching to yell, '*Turn round NOW, Dad, I want to go home.*'

My heart sank as we slowly drew up outside Bennell's stone-built terrace.

'Enjoy yourself, David,' said my father, giving me a cheery thumbs-up as I closed the car door behind me.

CHAPTER 6

A Heavy Burden

Barry Bennell's place, which I found myself reluctantly visiting on a number of occasions, was noisy, messy and chaotic. The TV was constantly on transmit, and the music centre was always blaring out at full blast. You could hardly move for all the clutter, whether it was kids' comics and football magazines piled up on tables, the latest sports gear hung up on coat hangers, or LPs and video cassettes strewn across the floor.

All the latest films would be there at our disposal, especially scary movies like *Jaws*, *Halloween* and *Alien*; I think Bennell ran some kind of video shop or stall, hence the boxes and boxes of hot new releases.

He owned the full gamut of computer and console games, too – *Asteroids*, *PacMan*, *Manic Miner*, *Daley Thompson's Decathlon* – but if you didn't fancy anything screen-based, there was also the pool table, the jukebox, an assortment of fruit machines and, I seem to recall, an array of animals for us to pet and play with. You'd never go hungry at Bennell's, either; takeaway fish 'n' chips dinners were commonplace, and the kitchen was like a sweet shop, stocked to the brim with cans, crisps and chocolate.

'Take what you want,' he'd say. 'Make yourself at home.'

He had created a kids' paradise, a treasure trove, an Aladdin's Cave; it was more like a teenagers' youth club than a twenty-something's bachelor pad. Every time I visited there'd be at least four or five other young lads milling around, taking full advantage of his hospitality.

When the night drew in, we'd all crash out. Some boys would kip on his bedroom floor or in his spare room, but I'd be asked to sleep in the lounge, alone. Bennell would hand me my holdall, tell me to get changed into my pyjamas and gesture towards my makeshift bed, an ottoman-style piece of furniture that he'd pushed against a wall. Then the curtains would be drawn, the lights would be dimmed, and he'd head off to his bedroom.

Fearful and nervous, I'd lie completely still on the ottoman, staring into the darkness, unable to sleep. I'd clutch a blanket up to my chin, desperately wishing I was cocooned in my comfy bed at Mum's instead of being cooped up in this cramped little house. And then, once everyone had fallen silent, I would hear the lounge door slowly creaking open, and I would sense Bennell's footsteps getting closer.

And closer.

And closer.

* * *

Sometime in spring 1980, after I'd had a number of overnight stays at Bennell's, I learnt that I was to accompany my coach and some other young footballers to Butlin's in the Welsh town of Pwllheli. It was a very popular holiday camp in its heyday, largely down to its budget family accommodation, its *Hi-de-Hi!*-style entertainment and its 'Funland' theme park. As conniving as ever, my coach knew that Dad was keen for me to gain match practice with older age groups ('I don't think our David's being challenged enough, Bené,' he'd told him), so he'd suggested I join his under-13s team at a weekend football camp at the Welsh resort.

Please, not again, I said to myself, when Dad packed me off with my holdall and my football. Once more I was being lured away from my home by Bennell, yet there was nothing I could do and nothing I could say to prevent it. I just had to bite my lip and do as I was told, as per usual.

While I wasn't totally confident that I could compete with City wannabes two years my senior, I was 100 per cent convinced of Bennell's motives. Within hours of my arrival in Pwllheli my worst fears were met. The embarrassment of being nutmegged on a football pitch by lads twice my size was nothing compared to the shame of being cornered by my once-hallowed coach in a locked Butlin's chalet.

Pwllheli and Chapel-en-le-Frith weren't the only stay-overs that I experienced with Bennell; there were other occasions, probably spanning a couple of years or so, when I was left alone and vulnerable with this vile individual. All too often I'd find myself praying for my dad to pick me up, counting down the hours until I was back in Eccles and out of harm's way.

Why me? I'd ask myself as the abuse took place. *Why is this happening to me?*

How I wished I'd been able to come up with some plausible excuses to get me out of those godforsaken trips. But I couldn't. I was trapped, I was compromised, and Bennell knew it. He'd handpicked me as an ideal victim, of course, well aware that I was an obedient, compliant sort of kid who'd meekly go where I was told with no questions asked. To him, no doubt, I was an available, easily accessible child who'd never do anything daft like feigning illness or inventing an injury in order to evade him.

Bennell was a master manipulator who knew that, with me, he didn't even have to resort to threats or intimidation. It was never a case of 'Tell anyone and I'll drop you', or 'Blab to your dad and you'll regret it', because he'd sussed out the reasons why I'd never disclose the abuse and blow his cover. First, because I was petrified of endangering my chances of making it at Manchester City and, second, because he knew I'd be shit-scared that my father would find out. Bennell's abuse was psychological as well as sexual. He knew that, with all his promises of stardom, he had a hold over me. He was an adult who was prepared to play mind games with a kid.

Aware that his victim was too scared to expose the truth, my coach was also safe in the knowledge that my family never suspected a thing. As far as I was aware, Mum and Dad never detected any risk whatsoever and, in all honesty, why would they have done? Bennell was a sly, scheming master of disguise who'd become an expert in hiding his true nature behind a cloak of respectability and responsibility. People like my dad were so blinded by the lure of professional football, and were so in awe of 'The King' and his promises, that Bennell could dupe and deceive them with ease. By ingratiating himself with unwitting adults, he was also able to make them part of the whole grooming process.

In fact, I don't think any of the Whitehill parents were aware of the monster in their midst and, without any warning signs or alarm bells to alert them, had no inkling that their beloved boys were being coached by a predatory paedophile. Moreover, during the 1970s and '80s the stereotype of a child abuser tended to be a scruffy old bloke in a grimy raincoat, not a handsome young chap in an Adidas tracksuit. Police Identikit photos of child molesters would often depict narrow-eyed, lank-haired fifty-somethings, not fresh-faced, curly-locked twenty-somethings. Barry Bennell just didn't fit the mould, and he knew it.

It remains hard to comprehend, however, how Bennell's actions didn't appear to arouse any suspicions among those mums and dads. Times have clearly changed. I can only imagine the reaction nowadays if a twenty-five-year-old football coach took a father to one side, seeking consent to whisk his school-age son off to Majorca for a week. First, in all probability, the dad would tell him he was crazy even to suggest it. Second, he'd doubtless advise him to fuck right off. Third, he'd most likely pick up the phone and call the police.

But I concede that society was very different in those days. Public awareness of paedophilia and child sexual abuse was limited – inside and outside the sporting arena – which meant that, when I was a kid, parents were perhaps more trusting and less sceptical.

And as for the youngsters themselves, a culture of shame and silence prevailed which made disclosure to friends or family both improbable and unlikely. Moreover, alternative channels for flagging up abuse were virtually non-existent. I was never aware of any organizations that empowered and encouraged children to blow the whistle, and I shudder to think how many other kids like me were left alone and afraid, persecuted by their abusers and petrified to spill the beans.

It was this climate of fear, secrecy and ignorance that enabled sex offenders like Bennell to thrive within the world of youth football. Not only that, clubs didn't have in place any child protection policies, criminal record checks or welfare officers that could have rooted out these individuals. This dearth of safeguarding measures meant that paedophile scouts and coaches were able to foster close links with junior teams at will, thus providing them with all the access and the opportunity they needed.

Barry Bennell was able to dangle the Beautiful Game as bait, of course. Under the auspices of 'improving David's skills', he lured me to holidays, to tournaments, to camps and to sleepovers, all with the full approval of my football-obsessed father. My coach had the temerity to persuade Dad that the primary purpose of our Majorcan 'holiday' was rest and relaxation – with a dash of training – when, in reality, it was all just a smokescreen. All that man ever wanted to do was to separate me from my loved ones and have me for himself.

Looking back, I must have transmitted some negative vibes to my father during this miserable chapter in my life. Whether conscious or subconscious, I'm sure there were occasions when I'd seemed strangely quiet during the journey to Chapel-en-le-Frith or, conversely, times when I'd been overly excited to burst through the front door on my return from Butlin's. But, in all honesty, I don't think Mum or Dad ever sussed that anything was remotely awry. These shrewd and intelligent people had no idea what kind of hell their son was going through. Not a clue.

That said, my insistence on remaining silent was unwavering. I felt that the abuse I'd suffered, while hideous, wasn't severe enough to be worth upsetting my parents about. In my eyes, Bennell hadn't gone so far as to physically attack me or try to kill me, and I didn't believe that any dramatic confessional on my part would be worth all the potential tumult and heartache.

Lying in my bed at night, all those worst-case scenarios would play on my mind. I'd flinch with fear as I imagined Dad discovering the truth about Bennell, driving to his house, beating him to a pulp, getting arrested by the cops for GBH and ending up in a Strangeways prison cell. Alternatively, I'd picture Dad being so racked with guilt and remorse that he'd do something daft like jump off Barton Bridge at rush hour.

As these grisly, irrational thoughts constantly whirred around my little head, I concluded that it was my responsibility to ensure that none of this ever materialized. It was my duty to pull down the shutters and lock away the secrets so Dad would never find out. I knew that Bennell's behaviour was wrong – so very, very wrong – but I didn't think it bad enough to destroy the dream and devastate my family.

It was an appallingly heavy burden for an eleven-year-old child to shoulder.

* * *

While Bennell undoubtedly blighted my childhood, I count myself lucky that I had some good times to offset the grim. My second trip to the football Mecca of Wembley, with Dad and Steve in tow, was a case in point.

The FA Cup Final between Manchester City and Tottenham Hotspur in May 1981 was a cracker of a match, and our fantastic vantage point – more or less opposite the royal box – couldn't have given us a better view of the game's two major incidents. John Bond's blue boys opened the scoring on the half-hour mark, courtesy of the oldest player on the pitch, thirty-three-year-old midfielder Tommy Hutchison. Our Scottish number 10 had thrown himself at a first-time cross whipped in by Ray Ranson, his flying header soaring into the top corner and whizzing past Spurs' keeper Milija Aleksic.

'*GET IN, HUTCH!*' yelled Dad, as Steve and I leapt out of our seats, waving our City scarves around our heads like helicopter rotor blades.

Our happiness turned to heartbreak, however, when Hutchison scored an infamous own goal. In the 79th minute Spurs had been awarded a free kick, and we watched on nervously as Osvaldo Ardiles lined up to take it while the City wall assembled itself. Hutchison positioned himself on the inside, perhaps expecting it to be a left-footed shot.

However, as Ardiles shifted the ball to Steve Perryman on his right, Hutchison suddenly darted to the other side of the wall to act as an additional shield. Glenn Hoddle promptly hit a curling shot around the wall which, to us, looked like it was heading wide of the goal. However, as the ball flew past Tommy he flicked his head, connected with the ball and unintentionally diverted it into the net, past a stunned Corrigan. Hutchison was inconsolable, as was I.

'These things can happen in a Cup Final, David,' said Dad as I sat there dejectedly, my head in my hands.

After 90 minutes the score remained 1–1, which meant a replay the following Thursday. This wasn't good news for the White boys. Steve's O-level Geography exam, scheduled for the Friday morning, meant that we couldn't make the return trip down south. We were both gutted.

Instead, we had to watch one of the most gripping Cup Finals in modern times from our lounge in Eccles, looking on in envy as the TV cameras panned across stands festooned with sky blue scarves, flags and rosettes. My brother and I sat nervously on the edge of the sofa as referee Keith Hackett blew his whistle to get things started. We were punching the cushions when Spurs' Ricky Villa struck to open the scoring after eight minutes, but were punching the air when City drew level shortly afterwards thanks to Steve MacKenzie's first-time, right-foot piledriver, arguably among the finest goals in FA Cup history.

Honours remained even as the second half kicked off, but within five minutes City striker Kevin Reeves calmly converted a penalty to make it 2–1. From then on City flagged; Spurs took the ascendancy and Garth Crooks scored from close range to level the tie.

And then came Wembley's Goal of the Century, which saw Argentinian midfield maestro Ricky Villa waltzing into the City area and leading our defenders a merry dance as he took a deft touch to the left, then a jink to the right before slotting the ball home under an advancing Joe Corrigan.

'Can't believe I've just seen that,' said an ashen-faced Steve as the net bulged, and the Argentinian wheeled away to celebrate. 'Ricky bloody Villa ...'

This Wembley defeat may have been soul destroying, but even Steve and I had to admit, albeit grudgingly, that Villa's wonder goal was worthy of winning any game. It remains one of the most replayed football moments on television, much to the dismay of every Blues' fan who had their FA Cup Final dreams shattered that night. Ricky bloody Villa.

* * *

A few weeks later, the family – me, Steve, Dad, Margaret and the girls, that is – went on holiday to Malta. It was the first time we'd ever been abroad en masse. There was some kind of mix-up when we arrived – I remember having to spend our first night in a crummy, cockroach-infested hotel – but the next morning Dad kicked some serious ass and secured us an upgrade to a swanky apartment complex.

Steve and I spent most of our time swimming and splashing in the pool, although we did haul ourselves out to watch Prince Charles and Lady Diana's wedding on the bar-room TV. In the evening the family usually went out for a bite to eat in one of the St Paul's Bay tavernas, often hooking up with other British holidaymakers to share a few Cokes and cocktails.

One night proved to be more memorable than most. We'd been enjoying a meal in a nearby restaurant when Dad happened to strike up a conversation with a twenty-something bloke from Birmingham. As was often the case, he proceeded to tell him about my football achievements and aspirations, including my burning desire to play for Manchester City.

'Our David's hoping to sign schoolboy forms when he's fourteen,' said Dad as I sat there sandwiched between him and Steve, tucking into my chicken and chips. 'He's just got to make sure he keeps those standards up, hasn't he?' he added, giving me a playful nudge.

The Brummie fella's response stopped me in my tracks.

'I once dreamt of becoming a footballer,' he said dolefully, shrugging his shoulders. 'Sad thing was, though, I had loads of talent but I just didn't work hard enough.'

He rested his cutlery on his plate and looked me straight in the eye.

'My advice to you, lad, is to practise for at least two hours a day. That's the only way you're going to make it, believe me. Whatever you do, don't get lazy and mess things up like I did.'

This random guy's words hit me like a thunderbolt. There was no science behind his pronouncement – he was neither a footballer nor an athlete, and had no coaching background to speak of – but, for whatever reason, this layman's advice in a Maltese bar deeply resonated with me. For the next few years, this 'two-hours-a-day' mantra wormed its way into my psyche and would become something of an obsession. It was all a bit bizarre, really.

As a direct consequence, during my time as a schoolboy and apprentice footballer, I made a personal pledge to devote at least two hours to training, every single day. More often than not I'd put in nine or ten – especially during school holidays – but whatever the day, whatever the weather, whatever my mood, I became fixated on that two-hour benchmark. In my mind, I couldn't cut any corners and become a failure like the fella in Malta. I simply had to make the grade.

* * *

I left Whitehill FC when I was about thirteen, making the natural progression to another feeder team associated with City, Blue Star FC, that was managed by another coach, thankfully. After two years'-worth of violation and humiliation I was finally able to escape Barry Bennell's clutches, and the relief I felt was indescribable. No longer under his charge, and no longer within his sphere of influence, he'd now run out of valid reasons to lure me away. As far as I was concerned, the horrible abuse had ended and this hideous man was history. I resolved to banish this awful experience to a dark corner of my mind, hoping and praying that Bennell would never taint my life again.

I continued to play for a variety of Manchester City satellite teams every Sunday morning – for some reason they had weird names like

Pegasus, Xerxes and Midas – and, mercifully, was able to feel totally relaxed around my coaches. Between the ages of twelve and fourteen, however, there was a real dearth of competitive, Saturday-morning football in the west Manchester area. The age range for Eccles Boys was capped at eleven, and the next rung on the regional football ladder – Salford Boys – only ran an under-15s side, which I was too young to play for. This football vacuum really frustrated me – I'd become accustomed to wall-to-wall matches at weekends – so I decided to fill the gap with some high-school football.

Eccles C of E's school team was, let's be frank, a bit shit. In fact, it was so shit that one of the PE teachers, Ken Swales, informed me one day that, if I fancied it, I could manage, train and pick the team myself. Having clearly lost all hope and motivation, he seemed more than happy to entrust a thirteen-year-old with that responsibility, particularly one who'd benefited from years of elite coaching and advice.

'I'd love that, Mr Swales,' I said, naturally leaping at this unexpected player-coach opportunity.

Each Monday I'd carefully consider my best squad formation, before neatly writing out the team sheet and pinning it up on the PE noticeboard. I'd also deliver the team talks before our Wednesday afternoon matches, telling Colin Bury to lead the back four and ordering Stuart Hamnett to get crosses in from the right.

Being in charge of scouting and recruitment (yep, I was Director of Football too) meant that I would scrutinize and talent-spot fellow pupils during playground kick abouts or games lessons.

During one PE session I remember my attention being caught by a tall, rangy pupil called Chris Spalding and his smaller mate, another lad named Stuart. Neither of them looked like natural sportsmen – in fact, they seemed utterly disinterested with any type of ball game – but I detected some hidden talent.

'D'you fancy doing me a favour, lads, and turning out for the school team?' I asked, approaching them both one lunchtime.

'Are you fuckin' mad or what, Dave? We hate football,' came their reply.

My powers of persuasion won the day, though, and Chris and Stuart ended up doing a sterling job for Eccles C of E, surprising themselves in the process. We hardly won any games – we were still pretty shit – but I found myself relishing the laid-back, chilled-out attitude of school football. Playing alongside my carefree, couldn't-give-a-toss classmates came as a welcome change to lining up with all the cut-throat, elite-level contenders on a Sunday morning. Our calamitous displays against the likes of Walkden High and St Patrick's RC may have been error-strewn, but they were always laughter-filled.

My dad's absence from the school-field touchline definitely helped me to relax and loosen up. He never came to watch me play for Eccles C of E – we were far too tinpot for him to be bothered, I think – and, in any case, his work commitments often clashed with our afternoon fixtures.

'How did you get on today, Dave?' he'd ask – perhaps a little half-heartedly – when I returned home from school.

'Twelve-three, Dad.'

'Were you the twelve or the three?'

'The three, Dad.'

He'd tut and shake his head, but I'd just chuckle.

* * *

My PE teacher was very kind to me in many respects. Mr Swales realized the seriousness of my football ambitions – I think he was really proud that one of 'his own' was doing so well – and often allowed me to duck out of the obligatory rugby, cricket and cross-country. As the other kids wrestled in scrums and learnt how to bowl, Mr Swales would let me spend entire games lessons kicking a football against the gym wall or dribbling around plastic cones. If I wanted to sharpen my heading or practise my volleying skills, he'd even go to the lengths of pairing me up with a couple of friends, one to put crosses in and one to go in goal. Unsurprisingly, this preferential treatment wasn't very popular among other pupils.

'How is it that David can faff around playing head tennis, when I have to run through muddy puddles on the school field?' a classmate would complain following a cross-country session.

My PE teacher would just shrug and grin. Top fella, Mr Swales.

* * *

In late 1981, around the time of my fourteenth birthday, a sponsored Saab drove up the gravel driveway leading up to my dad's scrapyard in Eccles. Working outdoors that afternoon – alongside fifty-one-year-old Bert – was a teenage yard-hand. Dad and I were sat in the office, the open window enabling us to hear the pair's conversation.

'Hey, it's that fella from Man City,' exclaimed the young lad as the car pulled up, and the Blues' youth-team coach and erstwhile manager got out. 'It's Tony Book!'

Bert sighed and shook his head.

'You'd better tell Booky that I'm not interested,' he said.

'What d'yer mean, Bert?' replied his wide-eyed workmate.

'He wants me to sign for the first team, doesn't he, but I can't be arsed. Tell him thanks, but no thanks. I'm quite happy here at the yard.'

Bert's helper promptly burst into the office where Dad and I were sitting behind a desk, poised to sign my long-awaited schoolboy forms that would commit me to the club for the next two years.

'Guess what, Mr White!' the lad panted. 'Tony Book's here to sign Bert for Manchester City.'

Once we'd stopped laughing we gently put the lad straight, asking him to hold the door open for Tony as he strode in, armed with the all-important paperwork. Just a few weeks earlier he'd informed my parents that I'd greatly impressed the hierarchy during my various training sessions with the club, and that they'd wanted to sign me up.

As our esteemed visitor took a seat in the office, Dad and I looked at each other, both bursting with excitement. Tony took a pen out of his pocket and flashed a smile.

'Let's get this done and dusted then, eh?' he said.

CHAPTER 7

7: David White

Girls, unlike football, had never been at the top of my teenage agenda. Once I'd started to make a name for myself locally, however, I'd noticed random lasses hanging around to chat with me after training, or sitting on the wall outside my mum's house, whispering and giggling as I walked past.

'Hi David,' they'd say, beaming at me and swinging their legs. 'We're going to watch you play at Irlam next week. Score a goal for us, eh?'

Other lads would have probably loved the attention but it made me feel uneasy. I'd get all red-faced and tongue-tied whenever any of them smiled sweetly at me or tried to strike up a conversation, lowering my head and scuttling past as quickly as possible. I wouldn't have blamed them for mistaking my shyness for aloofness.

That said, at high school I struck up close friendships with a couple of great girls, Tracy and Joanne, who I'd hang around and chat with during lunch and break times. It was a weird state of affairs, really, as I found myself alternating between the two of them, gravitating to Tracy when I became bored with Joanne (and she with me), and vice versa. Neither were conventional boyfriend–girlfriend relationships, though; I wasn't your hearts-and-flowers type of lad, I wasn't into public displays of affection and I hardly ever met them socially outside of school. They were both acutely aware that football remained my priority, and that I didn't have much spare time for cinema visits or Wimpy burgers. To be honest, I'd often find myself wondering why they bothered with me in the first place.

I was always conscious of what my dad would think, too; he frowned upon the idea of serious relationships because, as far he was concerned, girls were both a hindrance and a distraction.

'Football comes first, David,' he'd warn as he spied some lass giving me the glad eye on the touchline.

I made sure nothing got in the way of my selection for the renowned Salford Boys side in 1982, though, and I was chuffed to bits to get through their gruelling trial process. Comprising fourteen-year-old lads handpicked from local schools, the team staged its home Saturday-morning fixtures on the pitches at Broughton Lane, with midweek sessions taking place at The Cliff, Manchester United's training ground. At Salford Boys, discipline was tight and expectations were high. If you missed training for whatever reason, or were just a few minutes late, you'd find your name wiped off Saturday's team sheet. This was serious stuff. There was no messing about.

This elite environment saw me crossing paths with other Manchester City associated schoolboys who, like me, had been selected for their school boroughs. There were plenty of these lads around, too, due in no small part to City's celebrated scouting network which, at that time, was the best in the north-west. Among those making an immediate impression upon me were Andy Thackeray, a brilliant centre forward who played for Huddersfield Boys; Steve Crompton, a superbly agile goalkeeper from Warrington, and Steve Redmond, a tough and tenacious Liverpudlian who made defenders' lives a misery. At that time, however, the one player who was head and shoulders above the rest was Bolton Boys' Paul Moulden. The finest fifteen-year-old striker that I'd ever seen, he was built like a fully grown adult. Virtually unplayable and ridiculously prolific, his claim to fame was an official entry in *The Guinness Book of Records* for scoring 289 goals in one season for Bolton Lads' Club.

Vying with the region's cream of the crop was a double-edged sword, though. While the improved standard definitely helped me to up my game and hone my skills, by the same token I felt threatened by these astoundingly good footballers. They too had ambitions to turn professional, and represented serious competition for big-club apprenticeships.

As someone who was prone to self-doubt, playing for Salford Boys certainly made me question whether I had enough talent and ability to break through. I'd watch Mouldy and Reddo in action – like them, I'd been deployed as my side's centre forward – and would think to myself, *Jeez, they're both miles better than me.* These lads were oozing with desire and dedication, and I knew that they wouldn't be falling by the wayside any time soon.

My season at Salford started promisingly, but later that year I suffered a major setback. I began to experience grinding pains in my hips and groin, severe enough for Dad to arrange a consultation with ex-City physiotherapist Freddie Griffiths at his central Manchester clinic. Mr Griffiths came up with a diagnosis of osteochondritis, an inflammation of the bone and cartilage.

'You'll need rest and rehabilitation for eight to ten weeks,' he advised, and my heart sank. It was a devastating blow for me amid such an important season.

Dad approached this stumbling block with his usual pragmatism. He did everything he possibly could to ensure my swift and speedy recovery, including driving me to and from the school gates between Monday and Friday and enforcing my strict rehabilitation regime. We had a small snooker table in our games room, and every single day I'd have to lie atop it for half an hour while Dad patiently helped with my stretches, as instructed by the physio. It was my job to try to flex my muscles and resist these actions, and it hurt like fuck.

'Bloody hell, David, I'm sweating cobs here …' Dad would say afterwards – we were both exhausted by the end of it – but it was all worthwhile. Doing things by the book meant that, following two tedious months on the sidelines, I found myself fixed up and back on the pitch. Sadly, I was nowhere near fit enough to attend the England Schoolboys trials; although, if I'm being brutally honest, I don't think I'd have been selected in any case. At that stage I was good, but not that good.

Closer to home, I began to worry that my chances of securing an apprenticeship at Maine Road were diminishing. Along with my injury woes, I was conscious that there was a talented glut of fellow forwards waiting in the wings. The very capable Darren Beckford, who'd played for England Schoolboys, was a year my senior but was already involved with City's much-vaunted youth side, also known as the 'A' team. Paul Moulden was the kingpin of our age group, although Steve Redmond and Andy Thackeray, both superb attackers themselves, weren't far behind.

'I reckon I'm way down the pecking order,' I'd say to my dad, who'd reassure me that this wasn't the case.

Deep down, though, I think he probably shared my reservations, and at one point he encouraged me to accept trials with two other clubs, Leeds United and Nottingham Forest. The Leeds situation was a bit of a farce, really, comprising one of the coaches from Salford Boys' bundling some of us into his car one night and driving over to Elland Road for an ad-hoc trial game. It was a waste of time, frankly, and ended up amounting to nothing.

The trip to Nottingham, which spanned three days, was far more professional. I was paired up with Andy Hinchcliffe, a fellow Manchester City schoolboy, and we had a blast. Staying in digs near the stadium gave us an insight into life as an apprentice, and our daily training sessions alongside the River Trent were top-notch.

'If I don't get offered terms at Maine Road, I'm coming here instead,' I grinned as we jogged towards the City Ground.

* * *

While I crossed my fingers for a call-up to City's youth team, the club's seniors were coming to terms with life in the Second Division, having been relegated in May 1983. They were also getting acclimatized to yet another new manager. Billy McNeill – nicknamed 'Caesar' – was a dapper and articulate Glaswegian who'd lifted the European Cup with Celtic as a player before progressing into management. Having had stints at Clyde, Aberdeen and Celtic, he'd finally decided to try his luck south of the border.

His penchant for Scottish players soon became apparent. Derek Parlane, Gordon Dalziel, Jim Tolmie and Neil McNab were among his first signings for City, and legend had it that club secretary Bernard Halford had to rush through the transfer of Mick McCarthy before McNeill discovered he was a Yorkshireman from Irish stock, not Scottish.

'Get him signed, for God's sake, before Billy finds out he's from Barnsley ...' was the gist of it, apparently.

In October 1983, just a couple of days before my sixteenth birthday, I took an important phone call from the club.

'Hi there, David,' said a City receptionist. 'Could you report to Platt Lane at nine o'clock on Saturday morning? You've been picked for the 'A' team fixture against Manchester University.'

I doubt she realized that the lad at the end of the line was bouncing up and down like a yoyo, almost too thrilled for words. Finally, I'd been selected for a bona fide City youth game. Here was my big chance to impress the coaching staff and secure that coveted apprenticeship. I could hardly wait to tell Mum, Dad and Steve.

That Saturday morning, however, my mood dipped when I opened the lounge curtains to see a thick, wintry frost coating the front garden.

'Match abandoned, I reckon,' sighed Dad half an hour later, as he backed his car out of the drive and flicked on the heated windscreen. 'But let's go and check it out for ourselves, eh?'

Our spirits sagged when we eventually arrived in Moss Side and caught sight of the Platt Lane pitch. We got out to have a closer look and discovered a frozen-solid surface that was nowhere near playable. My big youth-team debut clearly wasn't happening any time soon.

Within moments, however, we noticed Tony Book's Saab swinging into the car park.

'*MR WHITE, DAVID!*' he yelled, gesturing for us to get back into our car. 'Change of plan. We're playing over at Maine Road. There's undersoil heating over there, and the pitch is fine.'

I couldn't believe my ears. My first ever game for a Manchester City side was taking place at my beloved stadium, the venue of so many memorable Saturday afternoons.

'Don't get too excited, David,' warned Dad as we made the five-minute trip to the ground. 'You're only in the squad. You might not even get a game.'

However, when we reached the dressing room and scanned the team sheet, my name was among the starting line-up, in big bold typewritten letters. 7: DAVID WHITE.

Running out onto the pitch, alongside other young players like Earl Barrett and Jamie Hoyland, was a truly magical moment. There must have only been a couple of hundred spectators rattling around the Main Stand, but I didn't care. The fact that Dad was in their midst meant the world to me, and he too must have felt incredibly proud that bitterly cold December morning.

I had a decent game, fortunately, holding my own in an open-age affair against a team of physically strong opponents. Dad's long-standing insistence that I practised with older sides probably paid dividends that day, as did all those 1970s kick abouts with my elder brother Steve and his pals.

The width of the Maine Road pitch suited me down to the ground, too, allowing me the space to use my trademark power and pace. I managed to score one of our four goals, racing beyond the University team's defence to slot the ball into the far corner of the net.

This is heaven, I thought to myself as I pumped my fist in front of the empty Platt Lane stand and almost floated back towards the centre circle.

* * *

In the wake of my first Maine Road appearance I received a couple more call-ups to the 'A' team, and also featured in the side's Lancashire Youth Cup campaign (we hammered Manchester United 4–0 in the semi-final and beat Bolton by the same scoreline in the trophy decider).

7: DAVID WHITE

The following March I happened to be playing in an inter-house game at school when, midway through the second half, I spotted my dad standing on the sidelines, gesturing frantically in my direction. I was taken aback; he rarely watched my school football team, let alone a run-of-the-mill house game.

I shot him a quizzical 'What are you doing here?' look, until a break in play enabled me to amble over.

'You've got to come off, David,' he wheezed. 'They want you at Maine Road for the reserve game tonight, son. Kick-off's in a couple of hours.'

I had to exit the pitch there and then – the PE teachers fully understood, bless 'em – before bombing back to the bungalow, where I quickly threw on my City tracksuit while Dad furiously scrubbed my muddy football boots.

I made a 70th-minute appearance that evening, playing my part in a match that saw City overcome Chesterfield 2–0 with goals from Clive Wilson and Paul Simpson. This run-out with the reserves marked another major step forward in my career, as I'd demonstrated that I felt very comfortable among the senior professionals. My stock had risen, it seemed, as had my confidence.

A few months later, in June 1984, my yearned-for apprenticeship offer arrived in the post. An official letter, embossed with the familiar, circular MCFC crest, informed me that I'd be joining Manchester City's brand-new Youth Training Scheme, the YTS being the government's rebranding of the traditional apprenticeship, with some education thrown in. My pay packet would amount to £27 per week, and my family would be entitled to a lodgings allowance of £25.

The good news didn't end there, for I managed to leave school that summer with eleven O levels under my belt. While my heart had always been set on a career as a City player, it was still reassuring to know that I had some formal qualifications as a backup should things not go to plan. Not that I intended to leave the world of academia for good, though. I'd enrolled on an A-level course ('Don't turn your back on your education,' Mum had advised) which, if all went well, I hoped to combine with my football.

* * *

My life as a full-time YTS trainee began in July 1984, and I soon found myself spending much of my week at Maine Road. On my very first day I woke up at dawn in order to get showered, dressed and out of the house by 7 a.m.; the journey from Eccles to Moss Side was a long haul – it involved two bus rides and two short walks – and I couldn't risk being late on such a momentous day. I remember tentatively waiting at the bus stop near my house, toting a little toilet bag containing deodorant, toothpaste and some Kouros aftershave that I'd been bought the previous Christmas.

The YTS lads reported to our new coaches, Tony Book and Glyn Pardoe, in the away-team changing room, effectively our base for the next two years. As we filed in we were greeted with some good-natured stick from older players such as Gary Jackson and Paul Simpson who, having graduated from the youth team, were now exempt from the menial jobs tasked to first- and second-year trainees.

'No more scrubbing bogs for us any more,' they laughed. 'Hope you've brought your Marigolds …'

Among that year's cohort were Steve Redmond, Paul Moulden and Ian Brightwell. Add into the mix great lads like Ian Scott, Steve Crompton and John Bookbinder, and I soon found myself part of a close-knit band of brothers. But it was Andy Thackeray who I'd become closest to. Huddersfield born and bred, and perhaps not as loud and lairy as the others, Thacks was a lovely lad and we got on famously.

Upon arrival at Maine Road I was given a squad number – 21 – along with a dark blue, heavy cotton training kit. Next we were assigned duties; I was handed the 'general cleaning' gig, which included sweeping the first-team changing room, disinfecting the toilets, hosing down the entire washroom area, before wiping the dirty tidemark off the side of the bath.

This suited me fine, particularly as it meant avoiding any boot-room tasks. I'd always hated cleaning boots – at home I just used to shove them under the tap at home and cram in some newspaper – and I really didn't fancy spending half a day with my hands full of mud, shite and dubbin.

The boot room itself fascinated me, though, with its wall-mounted racks of wire brushes, spanners and files, as well as box upon box of studs of varying lengths and materials. Some 'extra grip' studs even had nails running through them, which would be filed down so that they were just protruding (how these evil-looking things ever got past referees I'll never know). I discovered there was a whole new vocabulary for me to get to grips with, too. Studded boots were 'leathers', moulded boots were 'rubbers', and trainers were 'flats'.

Other morning chores included helping out Joyce in the laundry room. A warm, bubbly and friendly woman, she loved a laugh and a gossip and treated us lads like her own.

'C'mon boys,' she'd say. 'Let's work at double speed today. Many hands make light work ...'

We'd gladly help her organize all the kits for the senior professionals, sorting out shirts, shorts, socks, slips (football-speak for underpants), jockstraps, sweatshirts and wet tops. They'd all be wrapped in a numbered towel and rolled up like swimming kits before being packed into an enormous wicker basket, which would then be wheeled to the home changing room.

Tony (or Skip, as everyone called him) liked us to help out City's groundsman, too, whenever jobs needed doing. Stan Gibson was a Maine Road institution whose semi-detached house adjoined the souvenir shop. He also happened to be a die-hard Blue who wouldn't hold back if he was unhappy with a result or a performance.

'You fuckin' should have scored that on Saturday, young David,' he'd say, handing me a rake and pointing me in the direction of the centre circle.

My fellow apprentices and I did our utmost to complete our daily jobs before the first-teamers returned from training, simply because we were prime targets for some serious piss-taking. Many YTS lads – particularly the more vocal among us – would be despatched to ask Maine Road's office staff for 'long stands', 'tartan paint' or 'a flask of steam' as the senior pros peeped through the doorway, sniggering.

You learnt to keep your gob shut if it was your birthday, too, because chances were you'd end up being shoved into a laundry skip with your bollocks smeared in dubbin, before being unceremoniously hosed down with water and dumped on the stadium forecourt. Somehow, thank God, I kept my nose clean and managed to avoid any harsh treatment.

The trainees were able to wreak their revenge at Christmas, though, as we were allowed to don fancy dress and perform daft songs with the sole intention of ripping shreds out of the senior pros. The deal was that we could be as controversial or as personal as we wanted – we'd taunt them about their crappy first touch, their balding head or their latest conquest – and they'd just have to sit there and take it. It was great craic.

* * *

Taking place every July at Manchester University's sports ground at Wythenshawe Park, the club's pre-season training was seriously strenuous. The first fortnight would see the apprentices and professionals mingling together as one big, fifty-strong group. We'd begin our day with a warm-up run supervised by the physio, Roy Bailey, who knew the park like the back of his hand and would lead us through fields and woodland, and past canals and lakes. Eventually we'd stop, stretch and do some 'bodies', which were basically sit-ups performed every which way possible, and which made us sweat like pigs.

Roy would then give the nod for Tony Book or Billy McNeill – both taskmasters extraordinaire – to take over. We soon discovered that our physical and emotional state at the end of the session would be determined by which word Skip or Caesar would utter next. 'Rubbers!' meant ball-work (usually bearable), and 'Flats!' meant running (generally unbearable).

Not that ball-work was always the easy option; in mid-July the weather could be boiling hot, the playing surface could be rock hard, and the blisters on the soles of your feet – usually exacerbated by new boots – were often horrendous.

'This is just disguised running anyway,' you'd hear players moaning as they staggered around the pitch, their worn-out bodies bent double.

Every single player was scrutinized by the management and coaching staff during these runs, drills and kick abouts. Any shirkers or slackers would be singled out for special attention, and would be told in no uncertain terms that they had to get in shape in time for the new season. There were no hiding places.

We'd return to the clubhouse at lunchtime feeling utterly exhausted, and would grab a light meal of chicken or ham salad followed by a piece of fruit. We were clearly being fed to stave off our hunger pangs rather than to refuel, since fats and carbs were strictly off the menu. We would, however, be encouraged to neck a whole pint of full-fat milk, glugging it straight from the bottle (there were no isotonic drinks for us during pre-season).

Then, prior to our backbreaking afternoon training session, we'd be given half an hour to recharge our batteries. We'd often spend this precious respite spreadeagled on the grass, basking in the summer sunshine. Sometimes pre-season training would coincide with the British Open Golf Championships, so we'd rig up a portable telly in the clubhouse, gathering round the screen as Greg Norman and Sandy Lyle drove off from Turnberry.

Training days were often rounded off with my favourite discipline, namely the 'Snake Run'. This was a race-type pursuit, perfect for a sprinter like me, whereby you'd leg it towards one of the coaches – often Glyn Pardoe – who stood 500 yards ahead. The first player to reach him would have to lie down on their back, then the second player would step over him and do the same, until there was a long line of prostrate players along the field, like a human train track. The stragglers in our midst, often slower players like goalkeeper Andy Dibble and defender Nigel Johnson, would find themselves having to heave themselves over fifty bodies. And then, with our bones aching, we'd be told to do it all over again.

'Where the hell are we?' a weary player would moan, having tramped across yet another player-strewn hillside. 'Have we reached the Yorkshire fuckin' border yet?'

While our session usually finished at four o'clock, the apprentices' chores continued until much later. Despite feeling absolutely knackered, we were still expected to collect all the dirty, sweaty training kit before lumping the laundry skips onto the minibus and transporting them back to the ground. And that wasn't all. Invariably we'd be ordered to sit in the big communal bath at Maine Road, with the tap constantly running, so that we could scrub every crust of mud and every blade of grass from thirty white Mitre footballs. We'd then have to towel dry them all until they gleamed, in preparation for the next day's training.

I remember one day having to shift two tons of rubble from one part of the ground to another. It was only about ten yards and it would have probably cost about twenty quid to hire a machine to do it, but Skip was insistent that we complete the task. He was big on fostering team spirit and togetherness, was Skip. He didn't give a shit if we all hated him; it was just part of his 'band of brothers' mentality.

In those early days, we didn't always realize the method behind Skip's madness. For instance, after we'd finished our daily jobs, our coach would regularly leave us waiting in the changing room for what seemed like an age.

'We're all done, Skip,' Reddo would say as he rang up to his office.

'Hope everything's clean and fuckin' shipshape,' he'd reply. 'I'll come and inspect in a minute. Stay put until I come down.'

An hour later we'd still be awaiting his appearance, desperate to pack up and go home, wondering why we were being punished in this way. What we never appreciated at the time, though, was that it was all premeditated. Skip knew full well that, during this time, we wouldn't just be sitting there in silence. Jokes would be shared, play-fights would abound, and banter would be traded. Out of that would come a climate of friendship, camaraderie and team bonding that couldn't be taught, no matter how good a coach you were.

When he finally surfaced to send us home I'd think, *Bloody hell, Skip, why the long wait?* but as I grew older I realized exactly what he was up to. His methods were so simple, so clever, and so effective.

My usual walk–bus–walk–bus trek home meant that I'd often end up staggering through the front door at six o'clock, feeling absolutely bushwhacked. Once I'd wolfed down my tea I'd drag my tired body up to bed, feeling far too fatigued to watch any TV or make coherent conversation with Dad or Steve. While I genuinely loved my life as a Manchester City apprentice – it's what I'd always dreamt of – I hadn't realized quite how draining it would be. Not only did we have the usual Monday-to-Friday grind; we also had games to play on Saturday mornings and, in the afternoon, would be expected to stick around to watch the first team or the reserve team in action. Occasionally we'd be asked to assist Stan or Skip with a few post-match tasks on the pitch or in the dressing room.

My day-to-day routine became much easier when, in the spring of 1985, I passed my driving test. I inherited my first car from my brother – an Escort Mark II, registration VOA 358S – although I immediately set about customizing it, organizing a respray to change the paintwork from red to blue, for obvious reasons. Having a set of wheels was a godsend. As well as cutting my daily journey time, it allowed me to conduct a more grown-up relationship with Tracy, who by that time had permanently replaced Joanne in my affections. Instead of walks out to local cafés and burger joints, we were now able to venture further afield to city-centre bars and pizza parlours.

I was always back at home before the clock struck nine, though, ever mindful of the need to rest my body and recharge my batteries.

CHAPTER 8

Skip and Glyn's Classroom

I'd always been well aware of Tony Book and Glyn Pardoe's City pedigree. When I was a kid, Dad used to give me the low-down on Book's brilliant captaincy – he'd lifted every domestic trophy during the club's purple patch, and had been voted the league's Player of the Year in 1969 – and would wax lyrical about Pardoe's prowess as a silky skilled left back.

Across two decades, Skip's role at the club had undergone many different incarnations. Prior to chairman Swales appointing him as youth-team coach in the mid-1980s, he'd assumed the mantle of first-team captain, of general manager and of first-team trainer. Some may have viewed this job with 'the kids' as a sideways move – a demotion, even – but Skip appeared to relish his new position as chief custodian of Manchester City's young talent.

At that time, Skip's job was pivotal at Maine Road. With his stretched resources, Peter Swales was unable and unwilling to pursue big-money signings – he'd had his fingers burnt during Malcolm Allison's infamous 1979 spending spree – so the need to find home-grown players was particularly pressing. In order to stabilize the finances, Skip was tasked with seeking and nurturing a steady stream of young, local footballers with enough promise and ability to propel them into City's senior squad and save Swales some dough. It must have been quite a pressured role for the man from Bath.

'You've got two years with this crop of lads,' Tony, I imagined the chairman saying to him in his broad Manc accent. 'I want as many of 'em as possible knocking on the door of that first team …'

Skip became one of the busiest blokes at the club, a plate spinner extraordinaire. Not only was he overseeing the youth team from a coaching and administration perspective – he'd don a kit one minute, a suit the next – he'd also been asked by the hierarchy to keep his hand in with the first-team training. You wouldn't have blamed Skip for storming over to the chairman's office and kicking up a fuss about his increased workload, but I doubt he ever did. He never seemed to have any qualms or complaints; he just got on with it, for the sake of the club he loved.

Neither Tony nor Glyn possessed an ounce of ego. The club's ridiculously meagre staffing levels on the playing side – essentially a manager, an assistant manager, two coaches and a physio – meant that everybody had to muck in, and it was commonplace to walk into the dressing room to find one ex-City legend folding and packing the kit while another loaded up a laundry skip. They did these menial tasks without hesitation and with minimal fuss. Nothing was beneath them. I couldn't help but admire their humility and self-effacement.

But, while I liked Skip very much – and respected him immensely – there's no denying that there were times when the guy petrified me. In his two-year quest to mould us into bona fide first-teamers, he subjected us to an unfailingly harsh training regime.

'My goal is to help you become professional footballers, to transform you boys into men,' he barked during one of our early get-togethers. 'Now that may be at Maine Road, or that may well be elsewhere, but one thing's for sure. If you're not prepared to give me one hundred per cent, and if you're not willing to listen and learn, you'll be out on your arse.'

He stressed that there was an awful lot of growing up to be done in a short space of time, and explained that there wouldn't be any room for niceties and pleasantries.

'With your talent you should walk this league,' Skip would say to us, 'but that counts for nothing if you don't end up as a first-team player. Prepare yourself for a rough ride.'

The training pitches at Platt Lane were effectively Skip and Glyn's classrooms. There, they'd school us in how to 'control and play, control and play', which was by far their favourite phrase. Another favourite maxim of theirs was 'straight balls will get you killed', which Skip would yell while encouraging us to play forward passes on an angle, to avoid our opponents cutting them out and breaking on us.

Our coaches' demands were never unrealistic, though, and they rarely asked us to do something that they couldn't do themselves. In one instance, the lads and I were practising inswinging free kicks on the Platt Lane Astroturf but were consistently botching the delivery.

'C'mon, Glyn, show them how it's done, for fuck's sake,' Skip would say, whereupon the forty-year-old would despatch a set piece with inch-perfect precision. This would happen time and time again.

'I've still got it, lads ...' he'd grin as the ball hit the back of the net, glancing off the head of one of our on-running forwards.

Every single move we made on the training pitch would be scrutinized, enabling Skip to pinpoint any weaknesses, which our coach would immediately – and ruthlessly – set about rectifying. His sights were frequently set on me, with the positive elements of my game – my pace, my crossing of the ball – being conveniently ignored as he honed in on my faults and frailties.

'C'mon you, David, you twot,' he'd say ('twot' was a pet insult of his, halfway between 'twit' and 'twat', I suppose). 'You're six foot one, son, but you look like you're five foot one when you jump for a header.'

On other occasions he'd bemoan my defensive abilities or my lack of aggression in challenges, intrinsic weaknesses that would always be frowned upon. This cruel-to-be-kind approach was all for my benefit, of course. Any deep-seated flaws had to be purged if I was going to improve, to progress and to make the grade. Skip's job, as far as he was concerned, was to dish out home truths, not pats on the back. Any lads who didn't grasp this, or who couldn't stomach his methods, often ended up quitting City's YTS programme.

It could be pretty brutal at times, I admit. I vividly remember playing Manchester University again one Saturday morning and really struggling to get my act together on the pitch (I'd been feeling laboured for the previous couple of weeks, to be fair). This hadn't gone unnoticed by Skip, who set about fixing the problem.

For the entire ninety minutes he stalked the sidelines, tracking me up and down the wing, bollocking me when I erred and encouraging me when I excelled. His running commentary was relentless.

'Get your fuckin' heels on the line, you twot,' he'd growl. 'Fuckin' go and check. Create yourself some space.'

If I found myself drifting inside the pitch and getting caught on the ball, he'd go apeshit.

'What the fuck did I just tell you, David? What the fuck did you expect?'

It was purgatory, possibly the hardest ninety minutes of my football life.

'Well done, son,' Skip said to me after the game, acknowledging my perseverance rather than my performance, I think.

* * *

Do I want to report for training today? Do I want to keep putting myself through this? I remember asking myself the next morning when I woke up feeling physically and emotionally battered. The answer, of course, was a resounding yes. Hard though it sometimes was, I knew that I was benefiting from first-rate training from a top-notch coach, something that Dad would constantly remind me of.

'Dig deep, David, stay focused,' he'd say. 'Count yourself lucky that you're learning from a past master. It'll all be worth it in the end, I promise.'

Luckily, Glyn was always around to help counteract Skip's sternness. While he had his own ruthless streak – he certainly didn't suffer fools – he possessed a sense of calm that his ex-teammate lacked. If he ever noticed my head dropping during training, for example, he'd make a point of collaring me afterwards to offer me some comforting words or to dole out a little pep talk. While I don't think Skip and Glyn consciously engineered some kind of Good Cop/Bad Cop act, their slightly different approaches were very complementary.

In the early days of my apprenticeship I remember him sitting me down to explain why, during a session at Platt Lane, Skip had lambasted me for my naïve approach.

'David, gone are the days of being able to knock the ball outside a full back and run around the inside to retrieve it,' he said.

'I know he can be a bit harsh, but Skip just wants you to realize that you won't get away with that at a professional level. You need to stop doing it. You need to find another way.'

Sometimes, however, I suspected I got a rough deal from our head coach, and that he reserved some of his most abrasive treatment for me. Maybe all the apprentices felt that way, I don't know. I think Skip sometimes looked at me and saw a molly-coddled lad who'd enjoyed a pampered, privileged upbringing, and who'd never wanted for anything. I was a kid born with a silver spoon in his mouth who'd been cajoled and cosseted throughout his easy life. I was someone who no doubt had a job waiting for him at Daddy's company if his football career went tits up. Skip would regularly accuse me of not 'wanting it' badly enough because – in his opinion – I didn't *need* it badly enough.

'And you … you can fuck off back home,' he once snarled at me after one mediocre display.

'Play like that again, son, and you *will* need another job,' he continued. 'But you won't need to go to fuckin' Aytoun Street Jobcentre like the rest of us, will you, David? Your old man will fuckin' sort you out. He'll fuckin' look after you, won't he, son?'

I never dared answered back – I just let him rant on – but deep down, I knew that no malice was intended. If anything, his caustic comments were part of a plan to toughen me up. Even so, his words would often linger when I lay in bed at night, feeling a bit wounded and sorry for myself. Skip wasn't to know of the trauma that I'd gone through as kid – I was still adhering to my vow of silence, of course – but I used to wonder whether he'd have acted as harshly had he known that my life wasn't quite as charmed as he'd thought.

Any accusations that I lacked desire were a load of old bollocks, to be fair. I'd worked relentlessly hard to become a footballer and, in my mind, none of my fellow apprentices had grafted more than me. They simply couldn't have done. It was physically impossible. I'll hazard a guess that no other young player in the country could have put in more hours, more time or more effort than me. From the age of seven I devoted every fibre of my body to the beautiful game, 24/7. In time, I'm sure Skip came to realize this.

Without that degree of dedication – and without Dad's encouragement – I wouldn't have found myself at Manchester City Football Club, that's for sure. While I possessed a fair amount of natural talent, I couldn't claim to have the finest skill and technique in the world. I always reckoned my success was down to 75 per cent graft and 25 per cent style, and without that in-built work ethic there's not a chance I'd have secured an apprenticeship.

I think Skip was also a bit bemused by my academic aspirations, too. He wasn't the only 1980s youth-team coach to view formal education as an unnecessary distraction for his players, and my decision to study A levels during my apprenticeship – Economics, History and General Studies – wasn't exactly the norm. Most of the other YTS lads enrolled on a basic day-release football-coaching course every Monday, but me and our goalie, Steve Crompton, chose to go down the more traditional education route. I studied Economics via a correspondence course, and my former History teacher, Brian Carroll, home-schooled me on a weekly basis. I'd soon discover, however, that juggling an intensive exam course with a football YTS scheme wasn't going to be as straightforward as I'd thought.

* * *

Skip and Glyn had been tasked with building a team that would make some serious headway in the Lancashire League and the FA Youth Cup. As the 1984–5 season commenced, and with their targets in mind, they decided to reshuffle the pack. Our side of sixteen- and seventeen-year-olds was lacking a right back, so Andy Thackeray – strong, adaptable and the embodiment of Skip's no-nonsense spirit – was moved from attack to defence, with Colin Finlinson partnering him on the left side.

Steve Redmond had spent the majority of his junior career as a centre forward, but it was decided he'd be best deployed deeper down the pitch, as either a central midfielder or a centre half. Much to my relief, our coaches chose not to tinker with my position and I was allowed to remain in my favourite role, bombing up and down the right flank.

The Lancashire League was a tough old division. It pitched youth teams – or 'A' teams – from the likes of Liverpool, Everton and Manchester United against senior reserve sides from lower-league clubs like Stockport County and Tranmere Rovers. Joining the fray were second-string teams from non-league outfits such as Morecambe, Marine and South Liverpool. This diverse mix meant that our team either found itself up against similarly aged apprentices who, like us, were keen to gain knowledge and expertise, or up against hardbitten older players who were more bothered about teaching us a lesson and kicking us off the park.

'You've got to grow up quickly in the Lancashire League,' I remember Glyn saying, 'but there's no better place to learn.'

As the season developed we gradually found our feet, benefiting hugely from the experience of competing against uncompromising, rough-and-ready teams across the north-west. As was the plan, we also progressed nicely in the FA Youth Cup. I scored a brace as we demolished Preston North End 6–0, and we followed this up with an eventful match at Billingham Town, near Middlesbrough. This Northern League team were desperate to make their mark as Youth Cup giant-killers – there were a few choice words hurled at us when we assembled for kick-off – and the partisan crowd was as hostile as hell. They soon shut up, though, when we thrashed them 10–1 thanks in part to hat-tricks from myself and Darren Beckford.

'Well done, lads, that told 'em,' said Skip. 'Now let's get the fuck out of this place …'

Nottingham Forest were our next victims, who, despite rolling up at Maine Road with the well-regarded Franz Carr in their side, received an

8–0 hammering. Carr was a lightning-quick right-winger who'd already made waves in the senior squad, but who – thanks to Andy Hinchcliffe's superior marking – hardly got a kick all match. I managed to bang in another couple of goals, too, which put a smile on my dad's face.

I'm sure Skip must have been delighted with our tally of twenty-four strikes in three games – what manager wouldn't have been – but, if so, he certainly didn't let it show. Without fail, and regardless of the margin of victory, Skip would give us a ferocious tongue-lashing. We'd regularly win 4–0 or 5–0 and still get a bollocking. As far as Skip was concerned, massaging our egos and blowing smoke up our arses had no merit whatsoever.

Some YTS trainees would also be handpicked for City's Central League reserve team which, with its high headcount of senior players, certainly had its plus points for a young apprentice. I got a real buzz from sharing the pitch with seasoned professionals, and would spend the ninety minutes watching, listening and learning.

Once, on the coach to a reserve game at Hillsborough, Skip casually informed us that Sheffield Wednesday were planning to field their first team as they'd been thrashed the previous Saturday.

'There might be a few familiar faces there tonight, boys …' he said. That evening we lined up against Lee Chapman, Brian Marwood and Nigel Worthington, pitting our wits against big-name, top-dog professionals. You couldn't buy that kind of experience.

Later on in my career I'd find myself playing against Sunderland reserves and coming up against the legendary Alan Kennedy, the former Liverpool defender who'd just happened to score the winning goal in two European Cup Finals. I was so in awe of him I could hardly run straight. But, with my adrenalin pumping, I went on to have a blinder.

'Well done, lad,' said Alan after the game, and my evening was complete.

Being picked for the reserves allowed you to visit some of the League's most famous venues – Anfield, Elland Road, Villa Park – which was great for an obsessive stadium-spotter like myself. One of my very first reserve fixtures took place at the iconic Goodison Park, where the long-serving full back, John Bailey, spent the whole game shadowing me closely and upending me at every opportunity.

Featuring in the club's second-string team also upped your profile among the City faithful. Hundreds of Blues' fans would attend reserve games, wielding their season-ticket books to guarantee free entry through the turnstiles. Many of these hard-core supporters liked to track the up-and-coming players, enjoying the kudos of talent-spotting the latest starlet to hit the first team ('That Redmond lad, I knew he was special when I saw him in the Central League …')

Occasionally, though, the reserve-team hotchpotch of junior and senior players could sometimes present problems, and could end up bringing you down. You'd find yourself playing alongside jaded, out-of-favour thirty-somethings, many of whom had a beef with the manager and the club and who, as a result, would put in lacklustre performances to a soundtrack of continuous moaning.

'You've got to be careful,' Dad would say to me. 'Ignore those negative vibes, David, and don't be picking up any bad habits.'

'I'll try not to,' I'd reply.

* * *

Manchester City's first-team manager, Billy McNeill, cared deeply about youth-team affairs. He'd often come to watch our games in the youth cups and Central League, occupying a prime position in the Director's Box. If matters on the pitch were going well, he'd just leave Skip and Glyn to it, sometimes paying us a post-match visit to offer his congratulations. If our performance wasn't up to much, however, he'd invariably disappear down the tunnel, enter the dressing room and hijack the half-time team-talk. I don't think he intended to undermine Skip; it was more a case of him trying to impart the managerial wisdom that he'd accrued over the years.

The manager would waltz in, wearing a smart trench coat over one of his immaculate navy suits. He'd then hang up his coat and jacket, before neatly tucking in his shirt and waiting for Skip to give him the floor. He was brilliant at analysing and evaluating a game, was McNeill, and

(**Right**) Left to right: Dad, Mum, Nana and Grandad Jack at the annual Rochdale Observer Ball, 1962.

(**Left**) Grandad Jack presenting Manager of the Year 1967/8 to Matt Busby at Old Trafford.

(**Right**) Left to right: Nanna Tom, Aunty Betty and Nana Jack in the mid 1970s.

(Above) Black Rock Sands, North Wales, c. 1971. Left to right: Mum, Steve, Dad, Nana Jack, Grandad Jack, Me, Nanna Tom, Grandad Tom. Bert is behind the camera!

(Above) Me and Dad on holiday c. 1973.

(Left) Me and Steve in our school photo c. 1975.

(Left) Whatever the weather. Proper bowl haircut and my favourite Stylo moulded, studded boots. This was taken in the back garden of Dad's bungalow.

(Below) Early days at Whitehill c. 1979. Barry Bennell is standing on the far left.

(Left) Me sporting a Manchester City youth team kit handed down to our junior team c. 1982.

(Below) Anticlockwise from left: Paul Moulden, Steve Crompton, me and Ian Scott at my house.

(**Above**) Left to right: Jimmy Frizzell, Billy McNeill and Tony Book in 1986.

(**Below**) After winning the FA Youth Cup in 1986 we paraded it at Maine Road before the next home game. Back row, left to right: Ian Brightwell, David Boyd, Paul Lake, John Clarke, John Bookbinder, Andy Thackeray. Front row: Steve Crompton, Ian Scott, me, Steve Mills. We went through the entire competition with the same starting line up. Missing from this picture are Steve Redmond, Paul Moulden, Andy Hinchcliffe and Steve Macauley.

(**Above**) Left to right: Glyn Pardoe, Steve Redmond, me, Paul Lake, Andy Hinchcliffe and Tony Book in 1989.

(**Below**) It took me far too many games but my first senior goal against West Ham on 13 December 1986 was sweet.

(**Top**) Howard Kendall and Niall Quinn in 1990.

(**Above**) Peter Swales, Manchester City's Chairman.

(**Left**) Jimmy Frizzell and Mel Machin in 1987.

(**Above**) Lining up with England Under-21s in Toulon in 1987 alongside the likes of Vinny Samways, Michael Thomas, Gazza, David Platt, David Hirst, Julian Dicks, David Rocastle, Steve Redmond and Nigel Clough. I'm on the bottom row, second from the right.

(**Below**) Peter Reid and Howard Kendall.

would recall everything with forensic detail, without any notes. While he was never a ranter-and-raver in the Tony Book mould, he could mete out a good old-fashioned roasting when necessary.

'You need to understand, young David, that not everyone is as quick as you,' he'd say in his broad Glaswegian twang.

'In the thirty-fourth minute, Scotty played you in with a beautiful pass, and your pace allowed you to get there and knock a great cross in,' he'd say. 'But it was to no one, son. They were all ten yards behind you. You have to think, engage your brain. We can all hit a good cross to nobody, David ...'

There's no doubting that McNeill was an impressive individual, a person who commanded respect throughout the football world. You were certainly under no illusions as to who was The Boss.

That being said, though, I did find myself questioning the quality of some of the manager's new signings during the 1984–5 season. Many simply weren't up to scratch, struggling even to make a mark in the reserves, let alone the first team. A handful had been made offers they couldn't refuse to come south of the border, but plainly didn't give a shit about Manchester City. In fairness to the manager, he saw the error of his ways, offloaded the players in question and subsequently exercised a little more caution in the transfer market.

We finished the season disappointingly, with Newcastle United dumping us out of the FA Youth Cup at the quarter-final stage. A couple of issues had really irked us beforehand, though. First, the tie had been refereed by a local, George Courtney from Spennymoor, who was allegedly a Magpies' fan. Second, the icy conditions at St James's Park had rendered the pitch almost unplayable and, by rights, the match should have been postponed.

It had been one apiece when Andy Thackeray, our right back, had eased the ball out for a goal kick. Newcastle's winger proceeded to shove Thacks roughly onto the rock-hard pitch, but Courtney opted to award a free kick against us, citing obstruction.

As a winger, there was nothing more frustrating than a full back shielding the ball over the line instead of playing it. There must have been hundreds of occasions when I'd pushed or kicked out in frustration but, without fail, I'd always conceded the free kick. I was fuming when Courtney's decision went the other way, as were Skip and Glyn, who prowled along the touchline, berating the ref and his linesman.

The eighteen-year-old Paul Gascoigne took the resulting free kick, Joe Allon latched onto it, scored with a header, and bundled us out of the Cup.

'We've been done by their three big hitters,' I moaned on the coach back to Manchester. 'Gascoigne, Allon and Courtney ...'

We picked ourselves up, however, triumphing in the Lancashire Youth Cup after beating Manchester United in the semis and trouncing Wigan Athletic 5–1 in the final. I finished my first YTS season with a grand total of 20 goals from 36 games.

'You can't really argue with that tally, son,' said Dad as he drove me away from Maine Road, my cup winners' medal jangling in my pocket.

* * *

The first team had enjoyed a decent season, too, in spite of its relatively feeble strike force. Tony Cunningham, a Jamaican target-man bought from Sheffield Wednesday at the beginning of the season, had proved to be yet another City misfit. Most of the goals had instead been generated from midfield, mainly through Gordon Smith and David Phillips. The latter represented a great piece of business, McNeill having drafted him in from Plymouth Argyle for a paltry £90,000. A hard-working Welsh international with fantastic vision, Dave had a habit of scoring spectacular, long-range goals – he won two Match of the Day Goal of the Month's that season – and went on to make 620 senior club appearances throughout his career. Only 81 of those were in our shirt, unfortunately; for some hare-brained reason he was sold to Coventry City after just two years.

As the final game of the 1984–5 campaign approached, Manchester City needed to beat Charlton Athletic to secure promotion back to

Division One. They did so courtesy of a stylish 5–1 victory, with the goal-getting Phillips bagging the first and the last. The star of the end-of-the-season show was nineteen-year-old Paul Simpson, however, who'd successfully broken into the first team a few weeks earlier, and whose subsequent six goals had reignited the promotion push.

Simmo was a very direct, old-fashioned winger who always looked like he had a goal brewing within. We shared lots of similarities as players, although he was a lot smaller than me, and was probably blessed with more technical ability. While I could have been jealous, witnessing a former apprentice being blooded in the first team just served to further inspire and motivate me.

I want a piece of that, I remember thinking as I watched the goals rain in from my seat in Block E, my smile as wide as Simmo's when his vital strike – City's fourth goal of the day – hit the back of the net.

CHAPTER 9

Another Rung on the Ladder

My first season as an apprentice had been exciting, but exhausting. By the time summer arrived I was ready for a break, and jetted over to the Majorcan tourist trap of Alcudia with Steve Redmond, Andy Thackeray, Ian Scott and Colin Finlinson. It marked my first visit to the island since the 'holiday' with Bennell, but I refused to allow that ordeal to get in the way of some quality time with my teammates. Cala D'Or, I convinced myself, was some distance away, both geographically, historically and emotionally.

We had a fabulous time – albeit low-key – our focus being on chilling by the pool rather than partying in the clubs. Despite being nearly eighteen, I didn't touch alcohol that holiday, opting instead for fizzy drinks and frothy milkshakes. Being a pretty sensible, risk-averse kid, I wanted to avoid any booze-induced recklessness that might jeopardize my football career. That particular summer there'd been press reports of a well-oiled Manchester lad who'd caused himself serious damage by diving into an empty hotel swimming pool, and it had lodged in my mind.

Football, unsurprisingly, monopolized much of our time. In fact, the first thing we did after we'd landed in Palma was to buy a new Mitre ball to take to the beach every day. There, we'd stage five-a-side routs against unwitting tourists ('Fuckin' 'ell lads, you're good … you should get yourselves signed up!') or hour-long games of head tennis.

And, since there was no World Cup or European Championships to entertain us on the beach-bar TVs in the evening, our conversations would invariably turn to football back home, whether it was Norman Whiteside's FA Cup Final winner that May, or Gary Lineker's close-season transfer to Everton.

Within a week or so of our return to the UK, the usual pre-season training regime at Wythenshawe started in earnest. A couple of weeks later, the first-teamers left to go on tour, thus giving us second-year apprentices the opportunity to get to know the fresh intake of young City hopefuls. Some of the new apprentices I'd already come across: the talented pair of Andy Hinchcliffe and Paul Lake, for example, were fellow Mancunians who I'd encountered on many occasions in our schoolboy days, and who'd already made appearances for the youth team.

The 1985–6 season swung into action in August. I was surprised that McNeill hadn't bought in any big names over the summer, though, instead recruiting a handful of cut-price signings. Centre half Nigel Johnson and veteran midfielder Sammy McIlroy arrived at the club – from Rotherham United and Stoke City respectively – but perhaps the most interesting purchase was midfielder-cum-striker, from Huddersfield Town.

The twenty-five-year-old signed on the dotted line for the random fee of £132,000 which was, apparently, a figure set by a Football League tribunal, no doubt as a result of the cost-conscious Peter Swales bartering for the lowest possible fee. It ended up being an inspired signing on McNeill's part, since Lillis – contrary to many expectations – went on to become a big fans' favourite at Maine Road. I'm sure Mark himself would have conceded that he wasn't the most technically gifted player in the world, but what he lacked in skill he more than made up for with passion. He ran himself into the ground every game – his dedication to the cause was paramount – and the die-hards in the Kippax Stand loved him for it.

Bhuna – that was his nickname; don't ask me why – also happened to be an absolute diamond of a fella, a really cheerful, kind-hearted soul who loved a good laugh and enjoyed the odd wind-up. He was a role model to me – I'd track his every move as he led the attack in my coveted number 7 shirt – and he also became something of a mentor, often sitting me down to impart his advice and guidance.

Mark was among the many players who shared in my joy when, on the day I turned eighteen, I signed my first professional contract. For the next two seasons I'd be earning the princely sum of £85 per week, and it was truly the best birthday present I could have wished for.

My family were delighted with this development of course, particularly my dad and my brother. Steve continued to be my best pal and cheerleader – I couldn't have had a more supportive sibling – and he was ever so pleased for me.

'That's another rung on the ladder climbed, Dave,' he smiled. 'No one deserves it more than you, mate.'

The youth team had an electrifying start to the season. I scored a hat-trick as we trounced a hapless Oldham Athletic 12–0 in the Lancashire Youth Cup, breaking our own record previously set at Billingham. The following week we began our FA Youth Cup campaign at Prenton Park, hammering Tranmere Rovers 7–1. I bagged two goals, earning me a Man of the Match award and prompting a beaming Billy McNeill to collar me after the game.

'If the net hadn't been there for your first goal, David, that ball would still be flying,' he grinned.

His comments meant everything to me. Not only had I been praised by a legend of the game, I'd been made to feel like a world-beater.

After thrashing Blackburn Rovers by the same 7–1 scoreline, we earned a third-round tie away to Blackpool. A few days beforehand, the other lads were off doing an exam for their day-release course, so Skip had spent a whole afternoon session with me and our keeper, Steve Crompton, working on crosses and finishing.

'Right, let's do some spot kicks, boys,' said Skip. I proceeded to score twenty-five out of twenty-five with power and precision, placing every single one to Cromps' left.

'It's official then, David,' smiled Skip. 'You're our new penalty taker.'

This wasn't the best decision that my coach had ever made. The spot kick I took during our game at Blackpool was comfortably saved (my blushes were spared, fortunately, thanks to Scotty's match winner) and a few days later I missed another during an 'A' team game. My penalty-taking career was over almost before it had started. Believe it or not, I never took one again in a competitive setting. My confidence had been shot to smithereens, and I simply couldn't risk the possibility of missing the target and letting my team down.

'Don't ever ask me to do that again, Skip,' I said sadly, and my coach duly obliged.

Next up in the FA Youth Cup were Leicester City, who we stuffed 4–1. It was a bloody freezing night, though, and following the final whistle we were eager to return to the warmth of the changing room. As we swaggered in, full of the joys of yet another win, Skip swiftly brought us back down to earth.

'Good result, lads, but I've seen you pass the fuckin' ball much better than that. Now get your flats and your sweatshirts on and go and help Stan divot the pitch …'

Five minutes later we were back in the cold night air, our hands turning blue with cold as we helped our groundsman replace clods of Maine Road turf. For a whole sodding hour.

* * *

Our victory over Fulham in March 1986 secured our place in the Youth Cup semi-final, which would see us pitted against the much-fancied Arsenal. Just ten days earlier, however, I'd received an unexpected boost, having being named in the senior City squad to play in a testimonial game for the Dundee FC defender, Bobby Glennie. The mood on the Scotland-bound coach had been somewhat downbeat – the first-teamers had suffered a 1–0 defeat at the hands of Arsenal the day before – but I couldn't hide my excitement at the thought of making my first-team debut (neither could Steve Redmond, Paul Moulden and Ian Brightwell, who'd also been given the nod).

Sitting in the driver's seat of our Finglands coach, as always, was the inimitable Derek Sutton. Small, squat and ox-strong, legend had it that, back in the day, he'd been a professional wrestler alongside the likes of Big Daddy and Giant Haystacks. His fighting name had been The Hooded Lunatic, apparently, which always used to make me chortle.

Derek didn't suffer fools and didn't give a toss. If we ever hit motorway traffic en route to a game, for example, he'd take matters into his own hands and brazenly drive on the hard shoulder for fifty miles, knowing that he'd be able to talk round any aggrieved traffic coppers. During our hotel stays he'd be our Mr Fixit, playing hell with the reception staff if anything wasn't up to scratch.

He became very much part of the club set-up, did Derek, so much so that on a match day he'd often wangle himself a seat in the dugout, sitting in between the manager and the physio. He did the same at Manchester United, apparently – Finglands laid on buses for them, too – until Alex Ferguson arrived at Old Trafford and turfed him out.

Derek even had the brass neck to dole out half-time advice to the players.

'Whitie, you need to get more crosses in, mate,' he'd pipe up, sometimes interrupting the manager as he gave his team-talk. While these interventions used to get my hackles rising, I'd have never dared tell the much-feared Hooded Lunatic to shut the fuck up, scared that I'd end up in a headlock.

The Dundee game was a major stepping stone for me, and the fact that I held my own among the seniors made it even sweeter. I was also thrilled to earn myself a namecheck in Billy McNeill's programme notes the following week.

'David White did enough to indicate the extent of his potential,' he wrote. 'His pace on the flank set up the first goal and there were other flashes of his speed which got him away from the opposition, and allowed him to deliver some good balls into the attacking area.'

The club also enjoyed a trip to Wembley that season. I had no idea what the Full Members' Cup was – or why a First Division side were playing in this superfluous, newfangled cup competition – but victories over Leeds United, Sheffield United, Sunderland and Hull City in the northern section had ensured our place in the final. Chelsea were to be the opponents on Sunday 23 March despite, for some unknown reason, both sides having been required to play their league fixtures the previous day (City had ventured over to Old Trafford for the Manchester derby). It was all a bit of a dog's breakfast, to be honest; the competition had failed to capture much attention, the crowds had been meagre, and the authorities' sanctioning of footballers to play twice in twenty-four hours was both reckless and ridiculous.

It turned out to be a memorable couple of days for my pal Steve Redmond, though. He'd played at Old Trafford in the wake of Mick McCarthy's suspension and then, due to an injury to Kenny Clements, had found himself being picked for the Cup Final. Paul Moulden had been involved in both matches, too. While it was wonderful to see my mates playing their part in two big matches, I can't deny that I felt some envy. Games at Wembley were few and far between and I was frustrated that this one had arrived a little too early in my career. My dad was sitting in the crowd that day – Chelsea narrowly beat City 5–4 – and he'd have definitely shared in my disappointment.

Playing in a youth-team five-a-side on the Wembley turf prior to kick-off came as some consolation to me, though. Only a fool wouldn't have enjoyed the experience of performing in front of thousands of fans in the most famous football stadium in the world.

* * *

Both Youth Cup semi-final games proved to the toughest of my career at that stage, largely due to the fact that I was marked by Michael Thomas. Arsenal's star protégé, Thomas had already established himself as a regular first-teamer and was a fantastic player and formidable opponent. He was considerably stronger than me and, unlike many left backs that I'd come up against, easily matched my pace and often edged me off the ball. His ability to negate my game left me feeling incredibly frustrated.

How have I copped for this? I remember thinking as Thomas body-checked me for the twentieth time. *They've got one player who's head and shoulders above everyone else, and he just has to playing against me, doesn't he?* Rarely had I felt so sorry for myself on a football pitch.

We lost the first leg at Highbury 1–0, setting up a crucial return tie at Maine Road the following Thursday. Thomas dominated that match, too, as did his equally impressive teammate, Paul Merson. Luckily for us, another Paul – Moulden – was wearing his goalscoring boots that night, banging in two to counteract Arsenal's earlier strike. We went on to win a nerve-shredding penalty shoot-out, with Ian Scott driving in the decisive winner. While I was as relieved as Skip, Glyn and the rest of the lads (Arsenal, in fairness, were the superior team), I left Maine Road in contemplative mood. The cream had risen to the top over those two legs – Thomas, Merson and Moulden were way ahead of any of us – and I realized that I had a lot of ground to make up.

When I returned home, though, I remember flaking out on the lounge sofa, feeling completely exhausted and fraught with worry. The Cup Final first leg – against Manchester United, at Old Trafford – was due to be played just two days later, and I felt miles away from peak fitness. My fears were justified. By the time our Saturday kick-off had arrived, I was mentally and physically drained and I ended up having a nightmare of a game. I simply couldn't put a foot right. We did well to come away with a 1–1 draw, though, Paul Lake having followed up his own penalty to score via a rebound.

My mate Thacks was dismissed as a result of a bust-up with Aiden Murphy; thankfully he wasn't banned for the second leg so, for the ninth tie running, Skip was able to name an unchanged eleven. While I'd played well enough during the campaign to secure my place in the team, I knew I needed to liven up and get my act together.

Incredibly, over 18,000 fans rocked up to Maine Road on Tuesday 29 April 1986, prompting club officials to hastily open up other areas of the ground in order to accommodate the overspill. Right from the first whistle we never looked like losing the tie. We took an early lead through a David Boyd header and sealed a sweet, sweet victory in the second half, Mouldy having converted my saved shot (my performance that day was okay, albeit unspectacular). While our captain Steve Redmond was being presented with the trophy, I noticed that Andy Thackeray was nowhere to be seen. An FA jobsworth, it seemed, had stopped him from collecting his winners' tankard due to his first-leg dismissal. Thacks was distraught. It would take twenty-seven years for the stuffed suits at the FA to relent and rightfully hand over his memento.

The champagne corks were popping in the post-match dressing room, when Manchester City club captain Paul Power joined in the celebrations.

'Brilliant lads, you should be proud of yourselves,' he smiled. I think we earned a little more respect from the senior pros that day. Our Youth Cup win had been a huge accomplishment – the culmination of two years' worth of seriously hard graft – and I think they all appreciated that.

Once we'd got showered and changed, Skip let us visit a nearby Moss Side pub for a few extra bevvies, but only under the terms of his strict curfew.

'Let's not overdo it, lads; no more than an hour, please,' he said. 'Back to the grindstone on Monday morning.'

He wasn't wrong. In the immediate aftermath of the Cup Final we found ourselves having to play six games in thirteen days. Our schedule was relentless.

We soon propelled ourselves to the top of the Lancashire League, despite an early 4-1 defeat by South Liverpool reserves. Skip hadn't attended that particular game and, having made his feelings clear the following Monday, made sure he didn't miss another one. With Skip's presence in the dugout, we went on to win the next thirty-two matches and – despite not dropping a solitary point – we got thirty-two bollockings in return.

There were some lows to dampen the highs, though, including Andy Thackeray being released from the club. By all accounts, Billy McNeill had summoned him to the Maine Road sauna to break the bad news, our boss shattering a lad's heart into tiny pieces while he'd sat amid the swirling steam, wrapped in just a towel. Not only did this news come like a bolt out of the blue, I thought it was totally unnecessary. Andy was a great player who'd become an integral part of our unit, and I felt

McNeill's decision was a harsh one. My fellow teammates David Boyd and John Bookbinder didn't have their contracts renewed, either, and I was gutted for them, too. I couldn't begin to imagine how I'd have felt in their position.

In contrast, my career at City was on the up. Much to my surprise, in May 1986 I was selected for the first team's end-of-season tour to the USA and Canada, along with Steve Redmond and Ian Brightwell. This was a big moment for me, since I'd now crossed the threshold from youth side to senior side.

I was immediately faced with a dilemma, though, since my final A-level exams happened to coincide with the tour. Although he'd always encouraged me to pursue my education, Dad knew what I had to do and, equally as importantly, so did my mum.

'This is just too good a chance to miss, David,' she said. 'Your exams will have to wait, I'm afraid. You can always take them again.'

As it happened, I never did complete my studies. With football always remaining a priority, my motivation had waned and I'd struggled to cram in my revision and maintain good grades. The intervention of the tour was probably a blessing in disguise.

Billy McNeill had flown over to Mexico to take in some World Cup '86 action, so his easy-going assistant, Jimmy Frizzell, was tasked with chaperoning us to North America. To dub the next fortnight a 'football tour' was pushing it, to be frank; a road trip-cum-piss-up would have probably been more apt. The first-team lads had just survived relegation by the merest of margins and the manager was thousands of miles away, so we were all in full-blown holiday mode. In fact, we were so demob happy that we didn't even pack any training kit.

Our first stop-off was the Canadian city of Edmonton, where we spent a day at a water park before playing Edmonton Brickmen FC (no, I'd never heard of them either). Then we crossed over the border for a game against Seattle Storm FC, before flying down to the Californian city of San José. We arrived on the Wednesday morning but, due to a fixture postponement, discovered that our mini-tournament wasn't going to take place until the following Saturday evening.

Frizz, as laid-back as ever, gave us carte blanche to have a three-day doss-about.

'Lads, just meet me in the hotel lobby at six o'clock on Saturday,' was the long and short of it. We were issued with a couple of huge people carriers – one for the younger lads, another for the senior pros – and spent the next three days cruising up and down the Pacific coast. Our teammate Earl Barrett became our designated driver, him being the only member of our group old enough to get behind the wheel in the USA.

The senior lads visited numerous bars and restaurants along the route, while us young 'uns stopped off at a variety of roadside American diners, just like the kind we'd all seen in movies. I remember us overdosing on free soda-pop refills; we'd never come across this revolutionary drink-all-you-want concept before and would sit there for hours.

'I can't believe this,' said Reddo, mid-sugar rush. 'This is my tenth fuckin' 7 Up but I've only shelled out for one ...'

We spent most nights trying to blag our way into bars with varying degrees of success (we were considered under age in the US, of course, and had no fake IDs). If we did happen to gain entry, the senior pros would have to do shuttle runs to the bar to buy our drinks, since we couldn't risk it ourselves.

'A large beer, please, Bhuna,' I'd say, theatrically clicking my fingers as Mark Lillis got out of his chair and flicked me a V-sign.

By the time we returned to base, the senior lads weren't in the best of nick, dragging their hungover bodies around the pitch as we played Dundee (again) and San José Earthquakes. Then it was off to Los Angeles where, following the obligatory trip to Disneyland, we played the Hollywood Kickers. Our venue was a typically American multi-sport college ground, with a temporary 'bleacher' stand, a running track and a grass pitch. I remember warming up and blushing like a beetroot when I heard a few catcalls and wolf whistles coming from some college girls in the crowd.

'Hey there, City boy, why don'tcha give us a smile ...'

My embarrassment deepened, however, when, towards the end of the game, I tripped over a strip of Astroturf that was covering a long-jump sandpit, going arse over tit and landing on my head, right in front of my female admirers. What a prick.

'For fuck's sake, David ...' I heard Frizz moan in his Scottish drawl, while the girls behind me collapsed into fits of giggles.

The tour finished with matches against San Diego Sun and Los Angeles Heat – I wasn't the only player to suggest that we should have called ourselves Manchester Rain – and I'd loved every single minute of it. It was a brilliant experience for me, not only on a football level – we won all seven games – but from a social perspective, too. While our trip had taught me a few lessons about how *not* to be a footballer, it had also taught me the value of chilling out and buddying up with my teammates. Looking back, I'd been quite insular and introverted as a teenager; football had virtually dominated my life, and the Bennell situation had certainly made me less trusting and more wary of people. Our North American jaunt, however, demonstrated that, within reason, you could let your hair down with your teammates without it necessarily compromising your professionalism. It also showed me that I could actually relax on football-related trips away; this was a significant milestone for me at the time, not that the other lads would have realized.

The high jinks continued on the flight back home to Manchester. A worse-for-wear Mark Lillis had nodded off, so the lads borrowed a female passenger's make-up bag and gave him an impromptu makeover. He looked like Bet Lynch by the time they'd finished, his face daubed in blue eyeshadow and red lipstick.

And God knows how our striker Gordon Davies fared when he returned home to his wife. He was a very keen photographer, toting his precious camera to every town we visited and incessantly clicking away. If he ever left it unattended, however, one of the lads would secretly swipe it, before asking some girls in a bar to pout suggestively in front of the lens, or surreptitiously taking a snap of some random woman's backside.

'Gordon's West Coast Adventure slideshow should be interesting,' laughed one of my teammates, grabbing the poor bloke's camera and zooming in on a Los Angeles beach babe's cleavage.

* * *

With hindsight, my two-year spell as an apprentice – sweeping changing rooms, getting a bollocking, scrubbing baths, grouting tiles, getting another bollocking, cleaning boots, flattening pitches, getting yet another bollocking – provided a great grounding for my life as a professional footballer. By instilling me and the lads with drive and discipline – and by schooling us in the fundamentals of football – Skip and Glyn had taken fourteen young hopefuls and turned us into arguably the best youth team in the country.

And, while many of Skip and Glyn's charges were eventually released by Manchester City, the quality of their tutelage meant they were well equipped to establish successful associations with other clubs. John Beresford, Earl Barrett, Gerry Taggart, Darren Beckford, Mike Sheron, Neil Lennon and Ashley Ward were just some of the players who, thanks to Tony and Glyn, progressed through the City system and forged themselves a decent livelihood, albeit away from Maine Road.

My old muckers Andy Thackeray, Steve Macauley and Steve Redmond may not have become household names but they went on to enjoy fruitful professional careers at the likes of Rochdale, Huddersfield, Bury and Wrexham, which was testament to two amazing coaches.

Skip may have been the hardest of taskmasters, but he was the best football teacher I ever had. And deep down, beneath all that hot air and bluster, I knew that he was immensely proud of his class of '86. When I first broke through to the ranks of the senior squad I recall bursting with happiness when a beaming Skip shook my hand and offered his congratulations. It was at that moment that I fully understood his reasoning and rationale. Yes, his approach could be stern and uncompromising, but my coach had always been in my corner, had always willed me to succeed, and had always had my best interests at heart.

Had it not been for Skip I wouldn't have travelled on that coach up to Dundee for my first run-out with the seniors, and I wouldn't have been asked to join our star players on the USA tour. Only Skip would have realized that I was good and ready to make the step up, and only Skip would have given City's manager his royal assent.

'David's made the grade,' he'd have told Billy McNeill. 'He's all yours.'

Looking back, his influence ran much deeper, too. Along with Glyn, here was a man who I'd been able to trust implicitly and who, as such, had restored my faith in football coaching, something that had been severely tested and bruised in my childhood. For this, I remained forever in his debt.

There's no doubting that my dad was thrilled with my progression up the football ranks, although he took great pains to stay measured. In his eyes, there was still much work to be done. This latest breakthrough was just another box to be ticked, another point on the graph to be plotted.

CHAPTER 10

A Lifelong Dream

I returned to Maine Road for pre-season training in July 1986, only to discover that Billy McNeill had sanctioned a mini clear-out of playing staff. Mark Lillis had been sold to Derby County, with Trevor Christie coming the other way. Similarly, David Phillips had been offloaded to Coventry City in a deal that saw goalkeeper Perry Suckling arrive at the club. But, most disappointingly of all, our captain Paul Power had played his last ever game for Manchester City, having left our USA tour early in order to sign for Everton. Paul was a fantastic bloke – both personally and professionally – and I was upset to see him go.

McNeill, it seemed, was pinning his hopes on the squad's younger batch of players, the trio of Andy May, Clive Wilson and Paul Simpson having clearly impressed him the previous season. Nevertheless, I was still devastated that he'd released Power, Lillis and Phillips, three decent, dependable players who'd acted as brilliant mentors to us youngsters, encouraging us, scolding us and keeping us in check when required. Unlike some of their more disruptive teammates, if they ever found themselves in the reserves – often while returning from injury – they'd maintain their professionalism and always set a fine example to their younger teammates. From my perspective, the departure of these players was disastrous for the club.

I was drafted into the squad for the pre-season tour of Switzerland. We were based in the northern town of Solothurn and spent our ten-day trip driving through beautiful Alpine scenery to play matches in places like Aarau, Sion and Lausanne. Switzerland's trilingual status confused Billy McNeill, though, who couldn't quite grasp the concept that, depending on our whereabouts, the locals spoke either French, Italian or German. On one occasion, while he was giving a pre-match team-talk in Sion, there was a polite knock on the changing-room door. It was the referee, asking if he could check our studs.

'*Dos minutos!*' barked Billy, who wasn't quite ready for the interruption. He continued talking to us, while we tried to suppress our grins. There came another knock on the door, this time a bit louder.

'Fuckin' *dos minutos!*' he shouted, only for the impatient ref to rap on the door again, with even more fervour.

'Ach, for fuck's sake, *kommen sie in!*' screamed Billy, as we all fell about. It was one of many amusing moments that the gaffer provided that tour, most of them unintentional.

However, as our trip progressed, I became really unwell. I felt laboured and lethargic on the pitch – the hot summer temperatures didn't help matters – and my performances suffered as a result.

'I feel like shit,' I remember telling physio Roy Bailey, worried how McNeill would perceive my slow, sluggish displays.

It was only upon my return to the UK that I discovered the root of the problem. My chest and back had started to blister badly and I was swiftly diagnosed with a severe case of shingles that had, apparently, been triggered by a depleted immune system. My GP ordered a fortnight's worth of bed rest, which meant that I had no option but to sit out City's much-vaunted tour of Spain.

Gutted wasn't the word. As my teammates flew off to play starry sides including Barcelona, Valencia and Real Betis, I recuperated at home, lying in bed, sipping Lucozade and listening to comedy cassettes (Jasper Carrott, Billy Connolly and Rowan Atkinson were my personal favourites).

Thankfully I'd recovered in time to resume the final phase of pre-season training and to participate in the annual photoshoot day. Each July we'd get a welcome break from the rigours of training in order to have our pictures taken. Donning our new kits and sporting freshly cut hairdos, we'd kneel down in a massive line so that a procession of photographers could tiptoe along it, pausing to capture individual mugshots. This stock photo would be used throughout the season in a wide variety of newspapers, programmes and Panini albums, so the pressure not to look like a twat was immense.

'Oi, sod off,' you'd hiss to the lad next to you as he poked you in the ribs in an attempt to sabotage your mean 'n' moody pose.

Then things would get serious with the announcement of the squad photograph line-up. This was always very telling, and could get quite political. Any fringe players omitted from the list would quickly realize that their days were numbered, and the exclusion of any star names would suggest that a transfer deal was imminent.

Conversely, if a young professional got onto the picture it was a good indication that he was very much part of the manager's plans that season. On this occasion I missed the cut – unlike Reddo and Brighty – and I remember driving home that afternoon with a face like thunder, and glaring at Dad as I trudged up the driveway. Even he couldn't find the right words to placate me.

'Just bide your time, son,' he said. 'You'll get there one day. You've just got to keep grafting.'

Despite this setback I decided to knuckle down and, having fully recovered from my illness, managed to make the squad for the first game against Wimbledon. The lads enjoyed a superb 3–1 victory at Maine Road – Ian Brightwell made his debut – and this was followed up with a hard-earned no-score draw at Liverpool. I was the thirteenth man at Anfield (in the days when teams could only bring on one substitute) and, as such, felt on the cusp of a milestone league debut.

The subsequent trip to Tottenham Hotspur resulted in a 1–0 defeat and, as Billy McNeill surveyed his attacking options, I awaited my call-up. My optimism was premature. Instead of blooding his young, home-grown protégé, the manager decided to shell out £130,000 for Robert Hopkins, a right-winger from Birmingham City. Hopkins was a notoriously aggressive player who, alongside Tony Coton, Pat Van Den Hauwe, Mark Dennis, Noel Blake and Howard Gayle, had been part of the so-called 'Birmingham Six' who'd reportedly got themselves into scrapes both on and off the pitch. If this was the sort of wide-right player Billy was looking for, I had no chance. I was devastated.

Four defeats later, however, and McNeill had gone. We were travelling to Southend United's Roots Hall for a League Cup tie on Tuesday 23 September 1986, and, as per usual, he'd boarded the coach at the Manchester depot near Platt Lane. However, when it made its final pick-up at Bucklow Hill in Cheshire, McNeill promptly got up from his front seat, walked up the aisle, firmly shook our hands and said his goodbyes. He then climbed off the bus, got into a waiting car, and drove off.

Goodbye? I remember thinking. *What the fuck's going on?* It soon became clear that he'd accepted an offer to take the top job at Aston Villa, and had managed Manchester City for the last time. General Manager Jimmy Frizzell, we discovered, would be in charge for the remainder of the season. It was a strange decision by the club, given that the campaign had barely begun, and hadn't exactly started well. Frizzell would be assisted by Tony Book, however, which was fabulous news for his former apprentices.

I was named among the substitutes for the Southend tie, alongside Paul Moulden. After half an hour, Brighty received a bad knock and, once Frizz had given me the nod to strip off my tracksuit, I was crossing that white line and making my much-yearned-for debut. Watching proudly from the stands was my father, who'd very nearly not made the trip. Business for him was booming – White Reclamation had moved to larger premises in Eccles, and the firm had also diversified into waste management – so taking time off work could be tricky for Dad, even with Steve around as his right-hand man (my brother had joined the company in 1983).

'You'll never forgive yourself if you missed David's debut, Stewart,' his great mate Fred Eyre – a former City player himself – had warned him.

I don't recall too much about the game – it was a 0-0 draw – other than experiencing that *nobody-can-ever-take-this-away-from-me* feeling. I was buzzing on the coach back home, delighted that I'd achieved my lifelong dream to play for City's first team, and aware that Dad would have been cruising up the M1, experiencing exactly the same emotions.

I sampled my first proper taste of league football against Luton Town a few days later, coming on as a late sub in our 1–0 defeat at Kenilworth Road. The following Friday, Frizz called me into his office to inform me that I'd be starting the next day against Leicester City at Maine Road, as I'd impressed him with my albeit brief appearances. As my heart performed somersaults, Frizz led me into the Main Stand, where a *Manchester Evening News* photographer was waiting. I thought it would be a nice idea to have my picture taken in Block E, Row F, sitting on the seat that I'd occupied when I was a City-mad kid.

Once the snapper had captured his shot, I jogged out towards the car park and jumped into my new blue Ford Orion, desperate to get home to tell Dad and Steve the good news in person. As I turned on Piccadilly Radio, however, it seemed it had already filtered out.

'Eighteen-year-old David White is poised to make his full Maine Road debut tomorrow …' proclaimed City correspondent Brian Clarke as I drove down Kippax Street and headed towards Eccles.

* * *

Hearing the ref blow his whistle at Maine Road to signal kick-off – thus marking the fulfilment of my dream – was a moment I'll never forget. The first half saw Manchester City attacking the Platt Lane End, which meant I was playing directly in front of Dad and Steve, who were ensconced in their usual seats in the Main Stand. And, all things considered, I think I did pretty well. I felt sharp and confident, giving the runaround to my marker, Leicester City left back Mark Venus, who – if I say so myself – seemed a bit taken aback by my pace.

When we re-emerged after the interval I jogged over to assume my position in front of the Kippax Stand and was given a rousing reception by the Blues' faithful. I thought my chest was going to burst, so proud did I feel. Sadly, though, my teammates and I were unable to reward our fans with a win that day. Having been shifted inside to accommodate yours truly, Robert Hopkins had bagged our solitary goal, only for us eventually to succumb 2–1. Naturally I was disappointed with the result but, from my own perspective, my big debut couldn't have gone any better. I celebrated in Blackpool, where Dad's firm were staging their annual work do.

I maintained my place in the team for the next few league games, feeling honoured to compete against Division One big hitters like Arsenal, Newcastle United and Manchester United. I had a blinder of a game against Kenny Sansom at Highbury – prompting rave reviews in the national press – and I 'scored' at St James' Park, my shot hitting the bar and bouncing over the line, only for the ref to wave play on. My first senior Manchester derby ended all square at 1–1, with our centre half, Yorkshireman Mick McCarthy, scoring with one of the best headers I'd ever seen; it was almost Dave Watson-esque.

Overall, though, the season was a struggle for a team badly missing the experience and expertise of Power, Lillis and Phillips. With all due respect, the other senior team members couldn't begin to match their influence, both on and off the pitch. Our captain, central defender Kenny Clements, was a great guy, but he tended to be pretty quiet over ninety minutes. I don't ever recall Tony Grealish or Graham Baker having too much to say for themselves either, and I can't even remember striker Trevor Christie having been on the pitch, such was his impact.

No one could deny that tough-as-teak Mick McCarthy had an imposing presence, but his menacing demeanour could scare the living daylights out of the younger lads. We'd pray that he didn't pick us for his eight-a-side team in training because he'd wipe the floor with us if we lost. He was a born winner – his subsequent playing and managerial career was testament to that – but back in those days we needed a boost, not a bollocking.

Robert Hopkins was a strange, sullen sort – his glass was permanently half-empty, put it that way – and he was soon packed off to West Bromwich Albion in a part-exchange with Imre Varadi. Hopkins wasn't best pleased.

'I hope you all get relegated,' was his parting shot to us in the dressing room. What a charmer. City definitely got the better deal on this occasion; the new arrival from The Hawthorns was a pacey striker and a lively character who'd gladly spend time coaching the youngsters.

Along with Varadi, there was another leading light among the senior players. A talented Scottish midfielder who'd played for Tottenham, Bolton and Brighton, Neil McNab boasted a wealth of experience which he was happy to pass on to our squad's teenage contingent. He thought a lot of his junior teammates, it seemed.

'It's a pleasure to play with you guys,' I recall him telling us as we shared a few drinks one evening during a tour of Scandinavia. 'You're a credit to your club.' Coming from a top pro like Neil, that meant a lot.

Other new signings included Paul Stewart, a highly rated twenty-three-year-old who'd arrived from Blackpool for a fee of £200,000, which, at that time, was a record sale for the Seasiders. A classy forward on the pitch, and a fun-loving prankster off it, Paul was a breath of fresh air at Maine Road.

I was also thrilled to discover that Peter Barnes had rejoined the club. The thirty-year-old would be competing for my position, of course, but as far as I was concerned it was a pleasure and a privilege to rub shoulders with one of my childhood heroes.

'Watch and learn,' advised Dad. 'You won't find a better professional than Barnsey.'

Despite being bolstered by these new arrivals, City continued to struggle in the top flight, so much so that we found ourselves approaching the final game of the season requiring a victory at West Ham United (and for other results to go our way) to avoid the dreaded drop. In all honesty, it was never going to happen; we simply lacked the quality required at this level. We surrendered 2–0 at Upton Park and, as a result, were demoted to Division Two. Billy McNeill, incidentally, hadn't had the most successful season either. His failure to keep Aston Villa in the league meant that he'd presided over two of the three relegated teams that May.

I remember feeling completely numb as we made our way back to Manchester, the coach eerily silent as our predicament sunk in, and as we contemplated where we'd gone wrong. The exodus of key players hadn't helped, for sure, but neither had the over-reliance on lads fresh from the youth team – including myself, Ian Brightwell, Paul Moulden and Steve Redmond – who lacked the experience to deal with the rigours of top-tier football.

The club's preposterous staffing levels created problems, too. During that particular season, Frizz, Skip and Glyn were handed responsibility for everything: first team, reserves, youth team, 'A' team, and sometimes even the schoolboys. Frizz wasn't a tracksuited coach, either – he was a general manager in every respect – so Skip and Glyn had to work their bollocks off to compensate.

Had they been solely tasked with the first-team set-up, I'm sure the outcome would have been more positive. They were spread too thinly, however, to the detriment of players at all levels. The physio, Roy Bailey, was likewise ridiculously overworked, having to diagnose, treat and rehabilitate the seniors as well as the juniors. It was, however, symptomatic of the way all football clubs seemed to operate in those days.

It was a deeply disappointing way to end my fledgling season. While I'd been pleased with my decent start to the campaign, along with my tally of 29 appearances, the rest of it had been decidedly patchy, with an impressive performance one week being totally negated by a crap display the next. One Saturday I'd feel at the height of my powers, running rings around a full back. The next Saturday, however, I'd run off the pitch cursing my meek, ineffective performance that had seen me getting marked out of the game. This topsy-turvy inconsistency would become a hallmark of my game. Rarely your average seven-out-of-ten guy, I'd either hit the heights of a nine or plumb the depths of a five. I was fit as a fiddle, and was doing brilliantly in training, so that wasn't the problem. Something more profound was impeding my performances, something that I'd only comprehend in later life.

What the fuck's wrong with me, I'd ask myself. *Why can't I get my head straight? Why do I feel so lifeless?*

I was also anxious about my poor goal return. During my youth- and reserve-team career at City I'd scored 71 goals in 112 starts, at a rate of a strike every one and a half games. For the first team, however, I scored just once in 24 starts, against West Ham United at Maine Road. On that occasion I'd been lingering around the penalty spot from a corner when the ball had fallen kindly for me, and I'd chested it down and half-volleyed it into the bottom corner. I'd scored it in my prized number 7 shirt, too (much to my irritation, I'd been made to wear numbers 9 and 11 in some games).

It had taken me eleven games to get my name on the scoresheet – it came as much as a relief as a thrill – but my mentors warned me against being overly hard on myself.

'You played in a struggling team all season, Dave, so scoring chances were always going to be at a premium,' explained Neil McNab, noting my glum expression on the way back from Upton Park that miserable evening.

As we journeyed home, however, my mind focused on my rubbish goal rate, the poor games I'd put in, and the times when I'd been subbed. All I could do was dwell on the negative, not the positive, and the defeats, not the victories.

You could've given a much better account of yourself, you idiot, I remember thinking to myself.

Looking back, it might have helped if someone – Skip, Glyn or Frizz, maybe – had taken me aside before the start of the season to offer me a bit of context and perspective, and perhaps to set me a more realistic target.

'You're good enough to get in the team, David, and there's no doubting you'll do well,' I could have done with someone saying. 'But some players will suss you out, so there'll be some occasions when we'll rest you for games, and others when we'll put you back in. But, if at the end of the season you've achieved thirty appearances, you'll have done brilliantly.'

Sadly, though, I finished the season with my head down, my esteem low and my confidence knocked. Looking back, I shouldn't have felt like this. I should have been able to dredge up more resolve and muster more resistance. That gnawing feeling of submission had struck again.

***

Following our demotion, chairman Peter Swales sent Frizz back 'upstairs' and, much to everyone's surprise, appointed Mel Machin as our new boss. Mel had finished his playing career at Norwich City, before progressing through the coaching ranks to become the Canaries' assistant boss. His role at Maine Road was to be his first managerial appointment, a fact that many fans (myself included) found a little disconcerting. Having said that, Machin had earned himself a reputation as a progressive, innovative coach and, for that reason, I was looking forward to working with him.

He arrived at Maine Road in time for our end-of-season tour to Gabon, in West Africa. I wasn't particularly enamoured with the idea of travelling to an unfamiliar, roasting-hot country, and was delighted when – thanks to an unexpected international call-up – I received a last-minute reprieve.

That May I'd been named as a standby player for the England Under-19s tour of Brazil and Uruguay. While I was chuffed to be considered for the first time, I was disappointed that I'd not quite made the final squad (unlike Reddo, Mouldy and Brighty, who'd all been chosen, alongside the likes of Neil Ruddock, Vinny Samways and David Hirst). However, towards the end of the season one of the strikers had suffered an injury – I think it was Matthew Le Tissier – and I found myself being drafted in as his replacement.

Since there was no major football tournament taking place in 1987, the senior England management set-up – boss Bobby Robson, assistant Don Howe, physio Fred Street and doctor John Crane – had decided to join the tour and oversee this youthful 'development squad'. We all convened at Bisham Abbey for a couple of days of intensive training – Howe's sessions were notoriously regimented and disciplined – before jetting off to Rio for more of the same. One morning a familiar-looking Brazilian guy had turned up to watch us being put through our paces, standing on the sidelines and chewing the fat with Don and Bobby.

'Fuck me, Dave, that's *Zico*,' said Mouldy, my legs turning to jelly as

I jogged past one of the world's most legendary attacking midfielders.

Aside from training, we were able to enjoy some decent downtime, too. One afternoon, Doc Crane escorted us down to Copacabana beach for a leisurely swim, but he had obviously not done his homework. The sea was the roughest I'd ever swum in, and the waves were humungous, scooping us up, throwing us ten feet into the air and smashing us back down onto the sand. I remember Reddo, Brighty and I laughing hysterically and almost hyperventilating as we struggled to get upright before the next breaker sucked us in.

The Doc was panicking like crazy as we pointedly ignored his frantic yells for us to return to the shore. Bobby Robson had entrusted his colleague with the future of English football, yet the Doc found himself watching on helplessly as Michael Thomas and Paul Merson disappeared into the Atlantic for what seemed like an age, before reappearing fifty yards away, all battered and bedraggled.

'Don't breathe a word to the manager,' Doc Crane said when we reluctantly returned to the shoreline, feeling exhausted but exhilarated. 'He'll bloody kill me if he knows what you've been up to.'

The next day, I was thrilled to discover that Robson had picked me for the team to face Brazil, thus presenting me with my international debut. However, an imbalance in the squad meant that I was going to be deployed on the left wing. I'd hardly played in that role before and, although I'd never been afraid of using my other foot when necessary (and had scored plenty of goals with it), the whole concept felt alien to me.

'Take on your full back on the outside,' Don Howe had suggested before the game, but I found it hard to put the ball on my left foot when my mind was habitually telling me to manoeuvre it to my favoured right. I tried to make the most of it but, in any case, within half an hour my match was all but over. I'd knocked the ball down the outside of the Brazilian full back and, as I'd gone to cross with my left foot, he'd caught me with his right boot and smashed my ankle into the hard turf. The pain was intense. I managed to carry on until half-time, but I knew I'd done some serious damage.

My ankle had doubled to twice its normal size by the time Fred Street was able to assess me, and there was simply no way I could continue. I sat out the second half with my ankle packed in ice, watching the lads go on to lose 2–0, with Paul Merson coming on as my replacement.

I'd not broken my ankle, mercifully, but had sustained a nasty sprain that needed to be set in plaster for the rest of the trip. Mel Machin was really keen for me to come back to Maine Road for treatment, but I chose to remain with the England squad; I was having far too good a time, and didn't fancy an early return to Manchester. Our second game took place in the Uruguayan capital city of Montevideo. While I was disappointed to sit out the ninety minutes – we drew 2–2 in the Stadio Centenario, with goals from David Hirst and Gavin Peacock – I felt inordinately proud to be associated with the cream of the country's talent.

One memorable evening saw our team being invited to a reception at the British Embassy in Rio de Janeiro. Bobby Robson was a hugely patriotic man and made a massive deal of this, telling us how honoured we should feel and demanding that we all convene promptly in the hotel lobby at 6.30 p.m. We all did as requested, assembling on time and sporting our collars and ties, our smart trousers and our England 'Three Lions' blazers.

Shortly afterwards the manager appeared, dressed in his official Umbro tracksuit.

'*Boys, boys, boys ...*' he groaned, shaking his head as he surveyed his suited-and-booted young charges. 'You are *athletes*. You are professional sportsmen. You need to present yourselves as such. Go and get changed into your England tracksuits.'

Five minutes later we all reappeared, looking suitably sporty, as Bobby had requested. He still wasn't satisfied, though.

'*Boys, boys, boys,*' he said. 'We can't turn up to the British Embassy in trainers, for God's sake. Go and put on some proper shoes.'

Another five minutes later and eighteen glum footballers trooped into the lobby, sporting the bizarre combination of brown or black lace-ups and blue-and-white tracksuits. With my ankle in plaster I looked the oddest of all, though, since I could only wear one shoe.

We must have looked like a right set of knobs as we filed into the Embassy building and joined this high-class VIP reception. I'll never forget trying to have a serious conversation with a lah-di-dah ambassador while wearing a polished black brogue on one foot and a cast scrawled with tits and cocks on the other.

* * *

Fortunately, the pot on my ankle had been removed in time for my summer holiday to Ibiza with teammates Steve Redmond, Ian Brightwell, Andy Thackeray, Paul Lake and Steve Mills. This break was a bit more raucous than the previous year's, with our daytime sunbathing being followed by night-time partying. We couldn't resist buying a football, of course, and would piss around with it around the poolside, Reddo infuriating fellow tourists by suddenly getting up from his sunbed, launching a volley, and lying back down before it landed. The ball would often end up bouncing off the bonce of some fella reading a book, or landing in the middle of a lunching family, their drinks going everywhere.

'Who the bleedin' hell kicked that?' you'd hear some disgruntled dad shout while Reddo lay still, only lifting his head to give us a cheeky wink.

It was while we were in San Antonio that I really hit it off with a girl from Chester called Leanne, who'd been staying in the resort with her pals. What started off as a holiday romance quickly developed into something more serious, and we'd continue to see each other regularly when we got back to the UK.

When I returned home from Ibiza, I made it my priority to ring Jimmy Frizzell to discuss my professional contract, which was about to expire. In those days, money wasn't the be-all-and-end-all for me; I'd been earning £340 per month throughout the previous season, although first-team appearance money and win bonuses had sometimes doubled or even tripled my take-home pay. I naturally wanted to settle new terms, though, and Frizz said he'd look into it.

'David, it looks like you've still got a year remaining on your existing contract,' he said when he rang back.

'I really don't think that's the case, Gaffer,' I replied. Frizz was adamant, though, informing me that he'd confirmed it with the club hierarchy. Somewhat puzzled, I dug out the paperwork and, sure enough, on the back page was a one-year contract extension option in favour of the club. This had never been discussed or agreed at the time. I was fuming, convinced that something underhand had gone on.

'There's no way that clause was there when I okayed it,' I moaned to my dad afterwards, casting my mind back to the fact that the club had retained my newly signed contract for a couple of days before returning it in a sealed envelope that – perhaps naïvely – I hadn't thought to check.

Luckily I managed to negotiate new contract terms – I think I was paid £175 per week – this time insisting that the paperwork was countersigned there and then before I took away my copy. The whole scenario left a nasty taste in my mouth, though, as I had a sneaking suspicion that my beloved club had tried to pull a fast one.

CHAPTER 11

Sid, Jack and Fred

One hot and sunny afternoon in July 1987 I was training at the Platt Lane complex, doing the usual drills and ball-work with my City teammates. It was midway through the school holidays, so there were a few trial matches taking place on adjacent pitches, too, the sidelines dotted with parents and grandparents watching their aspiring young hopefuls.

A whistle blew to mark the end of the session, and I headed off towards the changing rooms, mopping my forehead with my damp training top.

And that's when I saw him.

Barry Bennell was sauntering around the Platt Lane Astroturf, looking exactly the same as he used to. The flash tracksuit. The curly hair. The suntanned face. The beaming smile. Walking either side of him, chatting and laughing, were two young boys wearing almost identical gear. They looked about eleven or twelve years old.

As Bennell drew nearer he suddenly caught sight of me. Our eyes locked, and I felt the contents of my stomach curdle.

'All right?' he said, with a hint of a smirk.

'All right?' I replied, stony-faced.

And then we both walked on by.

A bystander at Platt Lane wouldn't have batted an eyelid at this fleeting exchange. *There goes a former coach saying a quick hello to one of his old protégés*, he might have surmised; an everyday occurrence on a training ground. But to me, it was anything but everyday. This encounter became one of the most pivotal moments in my life, a *Sliding Doors*-type scenario that would go on to haunt me forever.

I got home that afternoon and sat slumped at the kitchen table, my head in my hands, feeling utterly shell-shocked. For over a decade I'd done my utmost to shove the spectre of Barry Bennell to the dark recesses of my mind, and had tried to box off those awful, painful memories. Yet here he was, suddenly invading my life again, catching me off-guard and resuscitating those childhood feelings of fear and dread.

I don't know how long I stayed there, mulling things over. My head pounded as I contemplated the fate of those two young hopefuls who he'd probably invited over to Platt Lane to watch the first team train. A multitude of questions began to swirl around my mind.

Would they be staying at his flat that evening? Had he hoodwinked their parents like he'd hoodwinked mine? Had he taken them 'on holiday' to Majorca, too? Had they, like me, been abused?

I sat there, trying to convince myself that everything was innocent and above board. As far as I knew, mine was an isolated case, and I'd always hoped that Bennell hadn't preyed on any other boys. But what I *did* know was that the scene that day looked horribly, unbearably, nauseatingly familiar. Barry Bennell – Svengali and Pied Piper – swanning around with two star-struck, doe-eyed young starlets, flaunting his local-hero status with promises of football fame and glory.

My anger surged as my mind's eye rewound and replayed this training-ground encounter. All the words I *could* have said, yet I had only been able to muster up two. *All right*, I'd said to the man who'd groomed me as an eleven-year-old. *All right*, to the man who'd violated me in a hotel room in Cala D'Or. *All right*, to the man who'd abused me on a makeshift bed in his house. But it wasn't fucking *all right*. By just uttering the most cursory of acknowledgements, and by choosing to walk on by, I'd taken the easiest route of all in a sea of alternatives.

I could have, by rights, marched up to the Platt Lane reception to alert them to the molester in their midst, and to tell them that he shouldn't be allowed within a mile of the place. Or perhaps I could have called those boys over, informing them that their esteemed coach was a child abuser and that they should catch the first bus home and tell their parents.

I could have, I suppose, confronted Bennell there and then.

'Who the *fuck* are you saying "*All right*" to?' I could have yelled. 'Don't ever let me see you here again, you nasty fuckin' bastard …'

But all three options would have created an absolute shit-storm, of course. Everything would have kicked off. And the reality was that – at that stage in my life – I neither had the courage nor conviction to shoulder that responsibility. No matter how just and righteous it would have been to have exposed Barry Bennell, and to have protected any other potential victims, I was unable to dredge up the emotional strength.

Besides, more than ever before, I was petrified at the prospect of my dark secret being revealed. Things might not have reached the public domain had my eleven-year-old self chosen to confide in someone – my family, maybe, or the police – but by 1987 I'd become a relatively well-known professional footballer. I was terrified that, if I blew the whistle on Bennell, the tabloids would get hold of the story and splash it across their front pages, perhaps to the detriment of my precious, hard-earned career.

I was frightened that fans, managers and teammates might react in a negative way – with disgust, even – because paedophilia still remained hugely taboo, both in football circles and within society in general. And, more than anything, I was still fiercely protective over my father. I simply couldn't bear the thought of him discovering the shocking truth.

What this Platt Lane episode showed – and what pained me to the core – was the fact that, even in my adulthood, Bennell had the capacity to exert his control and exploit my weaknesses. A whole decade had passed since the abuse, yet he still felt sure that I would keep schtum and do nothing, thus enabling him to waltz brazenly through my training ground without any shame whatsoever. And he was correct. In that split second, as Bennell breezed right past me, he'd rendered me powerless. Again.

* * *

With this traumatic incident threatening to swerve me off course, it took all my strength to keep myself together. I tried my hardest to focus on my football, and to get myself accustomed to my new manager. Mel Machin, who'd been tasked with getting us back into the big time, was a mild-mannered, softly spoken kind of guy who had a penchant for modern – if not slightly mad – coaching techniques. We witnessed this for ourselves during one of his first training sessions.

Mel, it transpired, had devised his own on-pitch communication system in order to confuse the opposition. If you wanted a colleague to dummy the ball, for example, you'd shout the code word '*SID!*' If you wanted him to flick it to the right or left you'd shout '*JACK!*', and if the player was in possession and you needed him to backheel it, you'd shout '*FRED!*' As Mel explained his logic I remember all the lads looking quizzically at each other as if to say, *What the fuck's he on about?*

Mel was insistent that we persevere with his little plan, however, and we found ourselves running around the training pitch like morons, randomly namechecking Sid, Jack and Fred (and probably 'Frank', 'Alf' and 'Bert' too, such was our confusion). I despised it, particularly when we played Norwich City, Mel's former club. Their players would be well versed in the gaffer's daft drill, of course, and would yell 'Sid', 'Jack' or 'Fred' to befuddle us and wrest possession while the crowd wondered what the hell was going on. It was progressive coaching gone mad.

By the time the new season started, Graham Baker, Nigel Johnson, Mick McCarthy, Tony Grealish, Nicky Reid, Andy May and Darren Beckford had all been moved on, with Colchester United striker Tony Adcock becoming the only significant addition to our squad (he'd compete with Imre Varadi and Paul Moulden for the second striking berth, alongside Paul Stewart). As for my former youth-team contemporaries, Paul Lake had already made inroads into the first team, and Ian Scott and Andy Hinchcliffe were on the verge of call-ups, the latter having made great headway the previous season until injury had delayed his debut.

The feeling around the club – both among coaching and playing staff – was that relegation to the second tier, no matter how painful it had been, would prove to be beneficial in the long run. I reckon City supporters probably felt the same, my dad included.

'It'll be a much safer and healthier environment for you,' he told me one evening. 'You lads were always going to struggle in Division One, because as a team you weren't good enough,' he added, explaining that a few decent victories at this level would do wonders for our confidence.

I approached the new season with extra impetus, although one player became something of a fly in the ointment. John Gidman – who'd been signed from Manchester United in October 1986 – was a great guy and a decent right back, but he and I were totally incompatible as an on-field partnership.

What I needed behind me was a reliable defender like Ian Brightwell or Mark Seagraves, a teammate who'd feed me the ball and not encroach upon my space. But Giddy, then in the twilight of his career and seemingly playing for the fun of it, just wanted to run past me all the time, usually without the ball. He wasn't the fittest squad member, either, so I spent half my life covering for him at full back while he jogged downfield, tucking his long, brown, curly mullet behind his ears as he did so.

'Why don't you say something to Mel?' asked one of my teammates, sensing my frustration.

'I dunno,' I replied, knowing full well that I didn't possess the confidence to rap on the manager's door and air my grievances. 'I might just cross my fingers that Brighty gets picked next week.'

City began the 1987–8 campaign patchily – at one point we found ourselves in 15th place – but a 4–3 defeat of Swindon Town, on Hallowe'en, prompted a respectable run of results. Things clicked for me at the County Ground that day, when I scored twice and was unlucky not to grab a hat-trick. I remedied things the following week, though, when – on Saturday 7 November 1987 – City came up against Huddersfield Town at Maine Road.

Managed by Malcolm Macdonald, and sporting a revolting black-and-yellow checked kit, the visitors started promisingly that afternoon, with Scottish striker Duncan Shearer causing us a few problems. The calming presence of Neil McNab soon steadied our nerves, however, especially when he cut in from the right to open our account with a crisp left-footed shot. Paul Stewart and Tony Adcock then scored one apiece – Adcock's first league goal for the club – and Andy Hinchcliffe and Paul Simpson began to terrorize the Huddersfield defence. With four minutes to go until half-time, Simmo more or less walked the ball to my feet, gifting me a goal from a yard out and giving us a 4–0 lead.

The second half became a rout, so much so that we were 8–0 ahead with ten minutes to go, Stewart and Adcock having each completed their hat-tricks. On 85 minutes, following a move on the right, the ball broke to me outside the six-yard box. I leathered it as hard as I could, straight into the back of the net.

'We want ten, we want ten,' chanted the Kippax faithful as play resumed.

It was Huddersfield who scored next, in fact, our former teammate Andy May converting a consolation penalty. However, deep into injury time, a rampant Simmo picked up the ball, prompting the Huddersfield defence to flee en masse as they attempted to play offside. I ran past them in the other direction, crossing the halfway line and sprinting towards my teammate's brilliantly timed pass as keeper Brian Cox came out to block. I skipped to his right, took a deft touch, and smashed the ball goal-wards to get my third and to nail a memorable scoreline.

'The Ten-One', I concede, was a freakish, stand-alone result that had been achieved against a dreadful team with an inexperienced manager. That said, bagging ten goals – including three hat-tricks – was a bit bloody special, and the dressing room afterwards was ebullient. I do remember, though, our thrifty secretary, Bernard Halford, going balder by the minute as he frantically sought another Mitre ball for the rightful Man of the Match, Paul Simpson.

'I've already given three away to the hat-trick lads,' he moaned, no doubt totting up the total cost in his head, 'and now I'm being told I've got to get one for Simmo ...'

Despite this fillip, the 1987–8 campaign never really took off for us – we finally finished ninth in the table – but I was happy enough with my season's goal count (sixteen) as well as my total appearances (fifty-plus). Things were in the ascendancy, I hoped.

* * *

In February 1988 I'd been delighted to receive a call-up to the England Under-21 squad for the European Championship quarter-final against Scotland, at Aberdeen's Pittodrie Stadium. Having lagged behind my City youth teammates when it came to international duty, I suddenly found myself ahead of them, being the first of our batch to receive an Under-21s nod. Competition was always fierce in that particular age group, though, with young wannabes like Matthew Le Tissier, Stuart Ripley and Tony Daley all vying for the same position as me.

Dad and Steve flew up to Scotland once they'd heard I'd been named in the first XI, watching from the stands as my assist provided Gary Porter with the match-winning goal. Playing alongside me that day were Newcastle United's Paul Gascoigne, whose natural talent was starting to turn a few heads, and Arsenal's David Rocastle, whose strength and flair made him the undoubted star of the show. There were some quality Scottish lads on display, too, including Stuart McCall, Robert Fleck and Kevin Gallacher.

The second leg took place a month later at the City Ground in Nottingham, a match we won 1–0 after I'd scored from Nigel Clough's cross.

'Well done, son,' said my beaming dad when we hooked up after the game. 'You looked really sharp. This level's tailor-made for you.'

In June 1988, both Steve Redmond and I were selected for the annual Under-21 Toulon Tournament in France. Reddo – who'd had a great domestic season, having become City's youngest ever captain and been voted the Blues' Player of the Year – was picked for all four games but I only figured once, against Russia.

The football was pretty intense and, with Dave Sexton cracking the whip, so was the training. We were placed under strict curfews, too, and would have to spend hours holed up in our hotel rooms. Reddo and I usually passed the time by playing cards, but, more often than not, there'd be a loud knock at the door, heralding the arrival of Paul Gascoigne. Gazza would proceed to entertain us for an hour or so, regaling us with daft stories, rooting through our belongings, changing the TV channels and generally getting up to all sorts of mischief.

Hyperactive and restless, he clearly hated spending time alone and would instead room-hop from teammate to teammate. Not that anyone minded, though. We all adored Gazza and, deep down, were flattered that the finest young player in the country was acting like our best buddy.

'Hey, Whitie, guess how much Hummel are paying me for my new boot deal,' he asked me, his eyes glinting.

'Go on, tell me, Gazza ...'

'Thirty grand, mate. Thirty grand!' he whooped, bouncing on my hotel bed as I contemplated the fact that his bonanza probably amounted to three times my City contract.

We were permitted one night out ('You'd better be back by ten,' Sexton had warned) so me and the likes of Michael Thomas, David Platt and Nigel Clough ambled off to a bar to have some beer and banter. An old-ish French guy latched onto our group, looking slightly baffled as we all took the mickey out of each other and shared a few in-jokes. Then Gazza went and overstepped the mark by insulting him in some way.

His face contorted with rage, this bloke suddenly pulled out a flick knife and held it against our Geordie teammate's throat. While the rest of us panicked – we didn't know what the fuck to do – Gazza remained calm.

'Put the knife down, pal,' he murmured, somehow managing to disarm his aggressor, who slowly retracted the blade and slunk out of the bar, badmouthing us in French as he did so. Following another round of drinks to calm our shattered nerves, we all made a pledge not to breathe a word to Dave Sexton.

'Imagine the headlines if that had gone pear-shaped?' I said, shuddering as I swigged my bottle of Kronenbourg.

This knifeman-in-France story didn't even make the final cut of Gazza's autobiography, which perhaps gives an indication of how eventful his life would become.

* * *

Back at Maine Road, in the summer of 1988, Mel Machin had drafted in some extra support on the training ground, with thirty-year-old John 'Dixie' Deehan arriving from Norwich City as a player-coach. Dixie's footballing injuries had taken their toll, however – he could hardly muster a jog – and he never made a single appearance for us. To all intents and purposes, Mel was surrendering the coaching side of his job which, other than the occasional Sid, Jack and Fred shenanigans, he'd consistently excelled in. For some reason he'd decided to devote more time to general management and administration, which I found puzzling; those areas weren't exactly his forte, and were ably dealt with by Jimmy Frizzell and Bernard Halford.

Dixie was joined by more new signings, namely Nigel Gleghorn, Brian Gayle, Wayne 'Bertie' Biggins and our keeper, Andy 'Officer' Dibble. All four were decent additions to the squad, their presence softening the blow of Paul Stewart's close-season departure to Tottenham Hotspur (City had been unable to refuse the £1.7m bid tabled by Terry Venables). Trevor Morley also came on board; a feisty and fearless striker, he'd been signed from Northampton Town in a part-exchange deal involving Tony Adcock.

The next season began disappointingly with a humiliating 4–1 home defeat to Oldham Athletic. Gradually things improved, though, with Moulden, Gleghorn, Biggins and Morley all rediscovering their scoring touch. Mouldy had never been the most graceful of footballers, but his finishing was as good as I have seen at any level. Bertie was more of a natural player, his incisive runs into the box often making it easy for me to pick him out. Tricky Trev had a bit of everything; he seemed to specialize in scoring scrappy goals, probably due to the fact that he'd fight harder than anyone else to get them.

The rest of the team was taking shape, too. With Lakey at his side, Neil McNab orchestrated the midfield, with Reddo partnering Brian Gayle in central defence, and Hinchy at left back. Fortunately for me, operating at right back (instead of John Gidman) was either Mark Seagraves or Ian Brightwell. Both polar opposites to Giddy, they supported my role, fed me the ball, and only overlapped when it was safe and risk-free.

By Christmas 1988 we were climbing towards the higher reaches of Division Two. On Boxing Day, 12,000 City fans travelled to Stoke City's Victoria Ground, the vast majority rigged up in fancy dress and carrying all manner of inflatable objects, from beach balls to blow-up dolls. This craze had started during the previous season; legend has it that some bloke had turned up to a game with an inflatable Fyffes banana, triggering chants of '*IMRE BANANA*' and prompting fellow fans to bring their own the following week. The fad caught on and reached its peak that Christmas; even a 3–1 defeat by the Potters couldn't dampen the spirit of an away end festooned with parrots and paddling pools.

New Year 1988 saw midfielder Gary Megson arriving at the club, having been lured from Sheffield Wednesday for £250,000. Shortly after Meggo's arrival – and on the eve of our game against Oldham Athletic – the manager called me into his office.

'You're on the bench tomorrow, David,' he said bluntly, as I felt the blood rush to my head. 'It's no reflection on your form, son, but I just don't think the Astroturf at Boundary Park suits your game. I'll be playing Meggo instead.'

I was lost for words. My performances had been a bit erratic that season – as tended to be the case – but I'd done well in the previous couple of games. Not only that, Mel was asking me to surrender my place to someone who didn't even play in my position.

Why isn't he dropping a midfielder? I moaned to myself as I drove to Steve and Dad's yard, becoming more agitated by the minute. *Maybe he's picked him to justify that quarter-of-a-million transfer ...*

'I'm not bleedin' playing,' I snapped as I barged into the office and slumped into a chair by Dad's desk.

'You *what*?!' he replied, aghast. 'That's bang out of order. That gaffer of yours needs to be told, David. Pick up that phone.'

Once I'd got through to the manager, I asked him why he'd felt so obliged to field his new signing, at my expense.

'Maybe Oldham's pitch doesn't suit me, Gaffer, but my form's been decent. I'm not having this, and I don't think you can justify it. With all due respect, I reckon you've got this one wrong.'

We ended our conversation agreeing to disagree, and I spent the rest of the night – and the following morning – in the biggest grump imaginable, dreading the prospect of languishing in the reserves as I fought to reclaim my place.

I arrived at the Boundary Park dressing room the following day to discover that Mel had performed a dramatic U-turn.

'You're playing, David,' he said tersely. 'I've put Brighty on the bench instead.'

Good on you, I thought. *You've seen sense. Meggo plays in Brighty's position, not mine ...*

Ian Brightwell, as it happened, didn't feature in the first team for the next fourteen games. While he was my friend and roommate – we went back years together – I felt no guilt whatsoever. Football could be callous and cut-throat, and I was unapologetically ruthless when it came to my precious shirt, my treasured position, and that hard-earned number 7 on my back. As if I was *ever* going to give them up without a fight.

Fuckin' hell, I'd better play well now, I remember thinking as I emerged from the tunnel at Oldham. We won 1–0, as it happened, with – ironically enough – a goal from Gary Megson coming courtesy of a David White assist.

* * *

I was the team's elected Professional Football Association's representative, and every year our union would send me the Player of the Year ballot forms to distribute among the lads. Andy Hinchcliffe was a renowned mischief-maker and would never take the voting system seriously, instead flouting the rules to compile his own piss-taking 'Nugget XI' of crap players. This particular year he'd cobbled together a full team – Shrewsbury Town's Doug Rougvie was invariably his captain, his Player of the Year and his Young Player of the Year – but was struggling to find a keeper.

'Hang on,' he said. 'Who was that fuckin' useless goalie who let in one of my corners this season?' To be fair, there weren't many keepers who could deal with Andy's back-post inswingers.

'Ron Green! That's the nugget,' he laughed, promptly scrawling his name at the top of the form before handing it back to me.

We all then went out for training and, as we were warming up, Mel introduced us to a goalkeeper who, due to an injury crisis, was joining us on loan for a couple of weeks. I'd actually noticed him sitting quietly in a corner of the dressing room while Hinchy and I'd been larking about with the PFA forms.

'Lads, this is Ron Green,' declared Mel, 'so let's make him feel nice and welcome, eh …'

'Oh, *shit*,' whispered Hinchy, mentally preparing his grovelling apology.

A few weeks later, on Saturday 11 March, I was suspended for the home game against Leicester City. This was a pretty unusual occurrence for me; any yellow cards I received were normally as a result of being clumsy rather than dirty.

I didn't forget that day in a hurry, however. As I sat near the dugout, close to the touchline, I found myself gaping in horror as my mate Paul Lake fought for his life on the Maine Road pitch. Early on in the game, Lakey had jumped up for an incoming corner on the edge of the box, clashing with the Foxes' Paul Ramsey as he'd done so. The impact of hitting the deck had caused him to swallow his tongue, and his whole body began to shake and twitch like he was having some kind of seizure. Physio Roy Bailey immediately raced onto the pitch to attend to Lakey, who was by now turning blue and convulsing badly.

'Bloody hell,' I remember saying to the sub sitting next to me. 'This doesn't look good at all …'

The club doctor remained seated in the Directors' Box, probably unaware of the situation's urgency. It was only when Brian Gayle ran towards the tunnel yelling '*GET THE FUCKIN' DOC!*' that Dr Luft began to fight his way to the pitch and, after what seemed like an eternity (although it was probably only a couple of minutes), he reached the scene. The Doc oversaw matters as Roy cleared Paul's airway by retrieving his lolling tongue with a pair of blunt scissors, effectively saving his life. The ground remained completely silent as my unconscious teammate was stretchered off, and the atmosphere became weirdly muted until we heard the announcement that Lakey – thank God – was okay.

'So glad you're all right, pal,' I said to my teammate when I saw him resting up in the physio room after the game, having regained consciousness following his blackout. Pale and shaken, and with two hugely relieved parents by his side, he knew that he'd had a very close call.

We approached the business end of the season with our Division One destiny lying in our own hands. Chelsea were on course to win the League, but if results went our way we'd be able to pip Crystal Palace for second place. As it stood we required just two points from two games, and by half-time in the first fixture – versus Bournemouth, at Maine Road – it looked like we'd cracked it. Two goals from Mouldy and one from Trevor had taken us into the interval with a seemingly unassailable 3–0 lead.

The mood was celebratory as we took the field to enjoy the second half and then – in true City style – it all went tits up. Ian Bishop, the Cherries' classy midfielder, proceeded to run us ragged. We conceded two goals from corners and then, in the sixth and final minute of injury time, Hinchy brought down Luther Blissett in the box, giving away a penalty which Blissett himself converted, earning his team a point and earning our team a bollocking.

Crystal Palace had succumbed to Leicester that afternoon but, a few days later, went on to defeat Stoke 1–0. To secure promotion, therefore, we required a solitary point against Bradford City at Valley Parade. If we couldn't manage that, we had to do our utmost to avoid a heavy defeat. Being just five goals better off, if we were beaten by a two-goal margin, and Palace won by four, we'd be condemned to the play-offs.

The Bradford-bound M62 was crawling with thousands of City fans that Saturday morning, and the motorway traffic was at a standstill. This time there was no need for Derek the driver to break the law, though. The team coach had been given an official police escort, which allowed us to zoom up the hard shoulder, passing cars full of supporters who beeped their horns and brandished their inflatables.

The atmosphere in the full-to-capacity stadium was incredibly tense. Both teams had chances in the early stages, but it was Bradford who took the lead on 24 minutes, with the scoreline remaining that way until the interval. We just kept plugging away in the second half – I remember hitting the post, and blasting another shot marginally wide – but as the clock ticked, the fans became more fraught, none more so than a long-haired, denim-clad lad who rushed onto the pitch.

'Palace are winning 5–0,' he yelled, raising five fingers to emphasize the fact that if we didn't score, we'd be in the play-offs. As it happened, our London rivals were only three up at the time – there was a lot of misinformation going on – but this one-man pitch invasion added to the sense of urgency.

With just four minutes to go, our goalie Paul Cooper caught a cross and immediately threw it out to Nigel Gleghorn, who quickly passed forward to Paul Moulden. Mouldy spotted my run, this time on the left, and played a great through ball. I took a touch into the box and crossed with my left foot to Trevor Morley who, as assured as ever, drove the ball past the Bradford keeper. It was a fabulous team goal, worthy of winning any promotion. The final whistle blew, Palace's result was rendered irrelevant, and we were back in the big time.

The celebrations started on the pitch, continued in the changing rooms and on the coach, and finished in Sale's Amblehurst Hotel where family and friends joined the party, including my fiancée.

Leanne and I had got engaged the previous summer, while holidaying in Gran Canaria. We'd then bought a three-bedroomed newbuild in Warrington, but had decided to keep things nice and traditional by opting not to cohabit until after the wedding. In the meantime, I remained at Dad's house in the Salford suburb of Swinton – we'd moved to a bigger property on my nineteenth birthday – and Leanne based herself in the Cheshire town of Runcorn, not far from her workplace at ICI. We'd meet up a couple of nights per week – usually grabbing an Italian meal or going to the cinema – but, without fail, I'd be home by ten o'clock to ensure a good night's sleep before training. Football, as ever, had to remain a priority.

CHAPTER 12

A False Dawn

Throughout my entire career I struggled to cope with criticism. To some players, a mocking chant from the away fans or a random catcall from the terraces would be like water off a duck's back but – me being me – I couldn't help but take things incredibly personally.

Once, during my first (admittedly erratic) season at Maine Road, I'd happened to hear the home crowd groaning when my name was announced in the pre-match line-up, over the Tannoy. It hadn't been a boo, just a murmur of disappointment that I'd been selected in the wake of a couple of poor games. On reflection, this scenario probably happened to many other professionals, but on that occasion I took it very much to heart.

From that moment on, I developed an odd little ritual that I never really shook off. Each time the team was read out, usually while I was warming up on the pitch, I shouted loudly at the top of my voice in order to drown out any sighs or grumbles that might upset me. My yells were usually muffled by the din of the Maine Road crowd, so I'm pretty sure that none of my teammates ever cottoned on to what I was doing.

I even enacted this peculiar routine when I was experiencing a good run of form. For me, it felt easier to remain soundproofed and ignorant, even if it meant blocking out any positive vibes that could have given me a welcome boost. It was all very counterproductive, of course; assuming the worst soon became my default position, and only served to exacerbate my anxiety.

It saddens me to think that I spent much of my career with my glass half-empty. Even when things were going well I'd convince myself that criticism lay around the corner, and that a pitfall loomed ahead. I found it so hard to appreciate a positive review and accept a compliment, and was forever nagged with doubt.

Don't flatter yourself, David ... I'd say to myself whenever I heard fans gleefully singing my name. *They sing everyone else's name, too, y'know ...*

If I ever failed to connect with a slightly misplaced pass, for instance, I'd wholeheartedly blame myself, cursing my own ineptitude, despite my midfield teammate also being at fault. And yet, if I happened to score a glancing header from a corner, I'd feel happier acknowledging it as a team effort rather than accepting any individual glory. As far as I was concerned, condemnation was personal, and adulation was communal. I couldn't accept the good, but I couldn't ignore the bad.

Sometimes, believe it or not, I felt a deep yearning to be average. *I'd do without all the highs if it meant not suffering all the lows,* I'd think to myself following a critical mauling from fans or reporters. I often wished I could be Mr Consistency, one of those steady-Eddie footballers who'd keep themselves on an even keel, accumulating weekly player ratings of six or seven instead of – like me – five one week, and nine the next.

Indeed, there were players around me who – while they rarely hit my professional heights – were able to fulfil their own targets on a much more regular, reliable basis. Ian Brightwell was a great example of this, I think. He performed for City for many years at a constantly good level without grabbing (or needing) the headlines. City's management and fans knew exactly what they were going to get from Brighty. You definitely couldn't say that about me.

As a sportsman, you tended to be judged on your best performances, as opposed to your average. Ridiculously, I sometimes found myself ruing the great games that I had, almost resenting the fact that expectation levels for me were set higher than for others, and worrying myself crazy that I'd struggle to meet them. It was a bizarre mindset to have, I suppose, but all too often I felt plagued by a deep feeling of unease. Only in later life would I come close to pinpointing the root cause.

I also believe that, compared with our out-of-town teammates, home-grown players were afforded much less patience and latitude from our fans. At Maine Road, familiarity often bred contempt; after my initial honeymoon period, I felt that supporters were less tolerant of a poor performance from a local-born 'graduate' like myself, as opposed to a player drafted in from elsewhere. It was almost as if our imports had an excuse not to play 'for the shirt', unlike those of us who were City born and bred.

The criticism often encroached upon off-the-pitch issues, too.

'You're always at yer dad's yard, you,' fans would sometimes yell if I was going through a bad patch. 'Try focusing on yer football, pal ...'

While I'd been appointed a director of the family business in the mid-1980s my role was far from hands-on. Occasionally I'd spend a couple of hours helping Dad and Steve with the wages, but that was the sum total of my involvement. The misconception that I was grafting at Dad's probably stemmed from the fact that, whenever a journalist or TV show requested an interview, they always wanted to meet me at the scrapyard. It gave the reporters a different angle, I suppose, and their snappers and film crews a distinctive backdrop.

'Can we get you sitting in a digger, David?' they'd say. 'Oh, and can you wear that hard hat, too?'

Naïvely, I always said yes, not realizing that I was helping to perpetuate a long-standing myth among Blues fans.

'No wonder he looks knackered ... he spends half his life at his Dad's place ...' I recall one fan saying as I trudged off the pitch following a listless performance.

Awful as it sounds, occasionally I found myself wishing that I'd been injured as a fledgling footballer, or had suffered some kind of lengthy lay-off. I think I'd have benefited from spending a bit of time in the stands during my playing career, mingling with the crowds, gaining an insight into the fans' psyche. This would have taught me, I believe, that football had the capacity to turn Mr or Mrs Average into a raging monster. It would have shown me how a vociferous, tribal passion for a team could be expressed so irrationally and illogically. It would have made me realize that these insults and outbursts were instantaneous reactions to specific incidents, and weren't always intended to be taken personally.

Other teammates, like Gary Megson, were much better at taking flak from others and taking the piss out of themselves. I rarely read any match reports or player ratings – I avoided exposing myself to any criticism – but Meggo would sit in the dressing room, scanning the tabloids, laughing like a drain at some shit that a sports journo had slung at him. Emotionally, players like Meggo and Brighty were much stronger than me; I only wish I could have mustered up a similar matter-of-fact, don't-give-a-stuff attitude.

* * *

In August 1989, following close-season trips to Australia and Scandinavia, we kicked off our Division One campaign at Anfield. City had made a couple of promising signings in the summer, with striker Clive Allen and full back Gary Fleming arriving at Maine Road, along with Ian Bishop, our tormentor-in-chief from Bournemouth.

My delight at returning to the top flight was tempered by my non-selection for our opening game against Liverpool. Mel Machin, in his wisdom, had chosen to play a midfield of new-boy Bishop, Neil McNab, Nigel Gleghorn and David Oldfield, with the latter taking my place on the right wing. I could have almost understood a tactical change to counteract the Reds' attacking prowess – maybe with a defensive player such as Brighty moving up to my position – but I was baffled by Mel's rationale on this occasion. David had been bought from Luton for £600,000 the previous year, and I could only conclude that, yet again, the manager was picking 'his' recruits at the expense of those he'd inherited.

I was seething as I sat behind the dugout at Anfield. Witnessing a centre forward wearing *my* number 7 shirt – and at one of the most iconic football grounds in the world – almost broke my heart. My misery was further compounded with a 3–1 defeat, my substitution for Oldfield coming too late for me to have an impact on the final result.

I remained on the bench for the game against Southampton at Maine Road, when the brilliant Wallace brothers – Ray, Rod and Danny – helped earn the Saints a 2–1 win. I was soon reinstated in the side, though, and proceeded to score against Spurs and Coventry. Both goals were far-post headers from Andy Hinchcliffe's curving corners, which regularly bamboozled defenders and goalies with their sheer pace and accuracy.

A pretty dismal start to the season – amounting to just four points from our opening six League games, plus a Littlewoods Cup humiliation at Brentford – meant that we went into the 111th Manchester derby as huge underdogs.

Saturday 23 September 1989 became one of 'those' days, however. Our first stroke of luck saw United arriving at Maine Road without the injured Steve Bruce and Bryan Robson – we really couldn't have hoped for a better boost – and the second involved an unexpected early-doors breather in the dressing room. The match had started very nervily for us – United were already stamping their authority – but a few minutes into the game we became aware of some crowd trouble in the North Stand. Some Reds' fans had infiltrated the home end, and referee Neil Midgley swiftly ordered the teams off the pitch while the police dealt with the situation.

Mel took advantage of this unexpected delay, making a couple of tactical changes and urging us to get the ball in the United box at every opportunity. When we re-emerged, with our heads back in gear, we were unstoppable. I crossed for David Oldfield who fired home our opening goal – Gary Pallister should have cut it out, to be fair – and it was more calamitous defending that led to our second, a rebounded effort from Trevor Morley. We went into the interval three goals to the good, Ian Bishop having added to our tally with a diving header. We could only imagine the bollocking that Alex Ferguson must have meted out to his lacklustre players in the away dressing room.

Shortly after play resumed, Mark Hughes' brilliant overhead volley pulled a goal back, but our resolve didn't waver. Paul Lake created havoc down the left flank to provide Oldfield with his second strike, and we then scored what I firmly believe to be one of the best team goals that Maine Road has ever seen. The ball broke to Ian Bishop in midfield, who swapped passes with Trevor Morley. Bish cut back on to his right foot and played a long ball over the full back's head and into my path.

Why not just take a chance, flashed a thought in my head. *We're 4–1 up, here* ... Without glancing up, I crossed the ball with the inside of my right foot on the half-volley. I was as surprised as anybody when left back Andy Hinchcliffe, positioned inside the box, met it with a bullet header, propelling it into the top corner.

It remained 5–1 at the final whistle and – much to everyone's shock and surprise – we'd thrashed our wealthier, starrier rivals. With hindsight, we couldn't have caught them at a better time. Ferguson hadn't yet found his feet at Old Trafford, and two of the Reds' lynchpin players had been out of action (we'd have never thrashed them 5–1 had Robson played, that's for sure). But we won, fair and square, and it was great to see City dominating the back-page headlines for all the right reasons.

'I'm buying every single Sunday paper this morning,' laughed my dad the following day.

Yet, while it was a fantastic occasion that will live long in the memory of players and fans, I admit to feeling slightly embarrassed about the hype and frenzy that continues to surround 'The famous 5–1'. For me, this result represented one solitary victory in an era when Manchester United's side was far superior to ours and regularly turned us over. They always seemed to have the upper hand, sadly, and never once during my senior career did I visit Old Trafford thinking that we'd be able to compete on the same level.

I feel quite ashamed by my own Manchester derby record, if I'm honest, since it comprised just one win among a litany of draws and defeats. Don't get me wrong; had 23 September 1989 been the catalyst for a reversal of fortunes and an avalanche of derby victories, I too would be reminiscing, commemorating and raising a glass each anniversary. But it didn't. It was a false dawn. There was no golden era, no dramatic revival. Ferguson's side of superstars went on to dominate English football, while City's trophy cabinet continued to gather dust.

* * *

By rights, the derby result should have injected us with added impetus and confidence that autumn, but we just couldn't seem to get going and suffered a string of limp defeats. Putting any football-related gripes into perspective, however, was a trip to Poland with the England Under-21s squad in October 1989. We'd flown over with the seniors (they were due to play a vital World Cup qualifier) and we ended up winning our game at Jastrzębie Zdrój 3–1, with myself, Lakey, Reddo and Brighty all starting. It would, however, prove to be my final Under-21s appearance.

The following day we were given the option to visit Auschwitz-Birkenau, the Nazi concentration camp where up to 1.5 million people, mostly Jews, were estimated to have been murdered. It was the most sobering experience of my life, and I witnessed some incomprehensibly shocking sights. The stark eeriness of the shower rooms and the gas chambers, for example. A hole in the ground – about the same size and shape as a telephone box – which was used for solitary confinement. Huge, room-sized cabinets each displaying left-behind cutlery, spectacles, shoes and wooden legs. The thought of these poor, innocent people being treated with such barbarity brought tears to my eyes. We were all deeply affected afterwards; not a single word was uttered during the journey back to the hotel.

The same night we watched the seniors' game in Katowice, played within an incredibly hostile atmosphere. We received enormous stick as we were escorted to our seats in the stadium and, as the game got underway, missiles were thrown between both sets of fans. The main problem seemed to be between the Polish police and the home fans, the latter ripping up the nearby seats before hurling them at the retreating officers. We had to take cover as the plastic seats scudded past us like huge square frisbees, only missing our heads by inches. The fighting got so bad, a few of us ended up sheltering on the TV gantry.

'That flight home can't come soon enough,' I remember saying to ITV commentator Martin Tyler as we watched the violence escalate.

* * *

A few days after my return to the UK, City received a 4–0 pasting from Arsenal while sporting a ridiculous, all-yellow away strip. This monstrosity suddenly appeared in the dressing room prior to kick-off, none of us having ever clapped eyes on it before.

'What the fuck's *that*?' and 'Am I in the wrong changing room, or what?' were some of the comments as we spied these hideous custard-coloured kits hanging from our pegs. Suffice to say they were never worn again.

On Saturday 11 November, a mere eight games after the so-called 'Manchester massacre', we received a 6–0 drubbing at the hands of Derby County at the Baseball Ground, our humiliation being masterminded by a tall, Scottish left-winger by the name of Ted McMinn. Despite Mel signing Colin Hendry from Blackburn Rovers – and transferring the captaincy from Brian Gayle to Steve Redmond – we couldn't halt the slide, losing at home to Nottingham Forest and Coventry City and scraping a point at Charlton Athletic. Enough was enough for a beleaguered Peter Swales who, at the end of November, promptly sacked his manager.

'I'm ringing to thank you, David, and to wish you well for the future,' said Mel when he gave me a call the following day, having made huge efforts to track me down at my in-laws' house.

'Same to you, Gaffer,' I replied. While he probably hadn't been the right fit for Manchester City, Mel had done his best for the club and, to me, that phone call was a touch of class.

* * *

By the time we travelled to Southampton on Saturday 9 December, Machin's big-name replacement was in situ. Howard Kendall was sitting in the stands during the game at The Dell, overseeing a disappointing 1–0 defeat that consigned us to the foot of the table. He knew full well that he had his work cut out, and set to task the following Monday.

You couldn't argue with our new manager's pedigree. Not only had he been a hugely respected footballer in his day, he'd done an incredible job in the hot seat at Everton between 1981 and 1987. He'd won the League championship twice – as well as the FA Cup and the European Cup Winners' Cup – and had turned low-budget signings like Neville Southall, Gary Stevens and Kevin Sheedy into top-class performers.

Some of his former Toffees colleagues promptly followed him to Maine Road, including assistant manager Mick Heaton, utility player Alan Harper and player-coach Peter Reid.

Howard's first team selection – for the away fixture against Everton, ironically – gave us a taste of his vision and ruthlessness. Controversially, he chose to drop the ever-popular Ian Bishop who, alongside Paul Lake, was probably the most technically gifted player at the club. As a manager, Howard had always preferred having two supremely disciplined players in central midfield – like Everton's Kevin Richardson and Paul Bracewell – and Bish just didn't fit the bill.

'I'm just not his type of player,' my teammate admitted at the time, aware that his days at Maine Road were probably numbered.

On the eve of the game Howard explained that he'd be putting Reidy and Meggo in midfield, and revealed that he'd be utilizing five at the back, with Alan Harper playing between Steve Redmond and Colin Hendry, and Ian Brightwell and Andy Hinchcliffe assuming deep wing-back roles. I'd be playing on the left, with Trevor Morley deployed on the opposite flank and Clive Allen operating down the middle.

The lads looked really solid at Goodison Park that day – Howard had made it our priority to stop conceding goals – and we came out with a creditable 0–0 draw. The City fans weren't convinced, however, bellowing 'We all agree, Bishop is better than Megson ...' from the away end. Winning over the supporters was not going to be easy either for the manager or for Meggo.

Howard's renowned people-management skills came to the fore in a Cheshire hotel on Christmas night 1989, on the eve of our game against Norwich City.

'You've got a midnight curfew, lads,' he declared. 'Now I don't mind you having a drink – a couple of lagers, maybe, or a glass of wine – but don't let me see you with a pint or a short.'

Unlike other notoriously dictatorial top-flight managers, who'd ban this, that and everything else, Howard allowed us some latitude and treated us like grown adults. As a result, he engendered much goodwill among the lads and, in no time, had got us all firmly on side.

His next signing came to Maine Road from West Ham, in exchange for Ian Bishop and Trevor Morley. Mark Ward, a born-and-bred Liverpudlian, was a very proficient right-winger who'd gained a reputation as a pretty aggressive player. He also happened to be a gem of a bloke, and we both got on like a house on fire.

The Everton-to-City exodus continued apace, too, with Wayne Clarke and Adrian Heath's arrival at the club roughly coinciding with the departure of David Oldfield and Neil McNab. The fans never seemed to take to Heath, though, maybe due to the fact that Howard often selected him in place of the widely admired Clive Allen. Inchy, as Heath was known, tended to be judged solely on his goal output (which wasn't great at City, admittedly) but I thought he was a very unselfish player who made the whole side tick.

At the tail end of December we beat Millwall 2–0 at Maine Road – I grabbed both goals – but, on New Year's Day, we lost 2–0 to Sheffield Wednesday. Defeats became few and far between, though, our new manager having successfully bolstered our defence and boosted our confidence. Ian Brightwell scored a left-foot screamer to earn a 1–1 draw in the Old Trafford Manchester derby on 3 February – 'I just wellied it' was his memorable post-match analysis – and we achieved the same scoreline against Wimbledon at Maine Road.

We were gutted, therefore, to suffer an unexpected 2–1 home defeat to Charlton Athletic later that month. It was a huge setback, and the lads and I felt we'd let both our manager and ourselves down.

'That drop zone is still far too close for comfort, Dad,' I said as we drove home after the game. 'The gaffer won't be happy at all.'

The following Monday morning I arrived at Maine Road full of dread. Howard had spent weeks schooling us on how to win these bread-and-butter games, and we'd blown it. I fully expected one of our routine post-match inquests, usually an 'open forum' debrief where teammates could rip you to shreds without recrimination, a video analysis session to pinpoint frailties or – if we were really unlucky – a programme of relentless running. I was confused, then, when Glyn Pardoe told us to report to the gym.

Ah, Howard's going to exhaust us all with a bleep test, I thought to myself, since it was there that the punishing, sometimes vomit-inducing straight-line running test would take place. I arrived, however, to find Howard, Skip and Reidy – and assorted teammates – playing a light-hearted game of head tennis. And that continued for an hour, with much pissing about in the process. The previous Saturday's debacle wasn't mentioned once. When that finished, Howard then directed us to the players' lounge.

'... and here comes the video replay,' I whispered to Lakey as we walked in. Again I was mistaken, as this time we were encouraged to participate in a raucous match of runaround table tennis for half an hour. Then, most bizarrely of all, the gaffer gestured to Glyn, who promptly reappeared with a crate of lagers.

'Saturday was a blow,' smiled Howard, 'but you lads have been brilliant for me over the past few weeks, and it will all come right. Help yourself to a can.'

I had a beer, got myself showered and went home feeling on top of the world, with the weekend's disappointment all but forgotten. It was a brilliant piece of man-management from Howard, and as significant a moment as we would have all season. The guy was simply amazing.

Another occasion saw us training at the appropriately named Kendall Club in Stretford, a community centre which was surrounded by some shockingly awful pitches (I haven't a clue why we trained there). Afterwards, Howard asked us to convene in the lounge, whereupon we noticed a table bearing five bottles of champagne, on ice. He proceeded to read out an officious letter from the Football League, alleging that a Manchester City player had made an obscene gesture to the crowd at an away ground.

'Come on then,' said Howard. 'Who's going to come clean?' Everyone kept schtum, until the boss told us that a similar incident had also been reported at Old Trafford, involving the very same player. The game was up – we all knew that Andy Hinchcliffe had wound up the United fans that day – and he duly raised his hand in confession.

'Lesson learnt, son,' said Howard as he cracked open all five bottles. 'Have some post-training bubbly, lads. The bill's behind the bar, Andy; settle it before the weekend, eh?'

Howard had made his point without issuing a humiliating bollocking, while at the same time lifting team morale. A more astute manager I'd never met.

Some days it seemed our luck would never turn. On Saturday 3 March, at Nottingham Forest's City Ground, an infamous goal would seal our 1–0 defeat. City keeper Andy Dibble had done well to catch a cross at the far post as Paul Lake and Gary Crosby, Forest's midfielder, had stumbled behind him to the goal line. Dibbs watched as Lakey ran back past him but, unaware that Crosby was also behind him, balanced the ball in the palm of one hand. Crosby slyly came from behind him and, quick as a flash, headed it out of Dibbs' grasp before cheekily tapping it into the net.

The City lads were outraged when the ref allowed the goal to stand.

'What have you given that for?' I yelled, the official explaining that Dibbs hadn't been in full control of the ball. The footage went on to appear on countless 'football blooper' videos.

Howard soon implemented more changes, spending £800,000 (and doing a fantastic piece of business) by bringing Arsenal's Niall Quinn to the club. The six-foot-four Irishman's first eligible game – at home to Chelsea – took place at the end of March.

Prior to the game, Howard had shocked us all by naming his new signing up front and leaving out left back Andy Hinchcliffe. The five-at-the-back formation was scrapped, with Alan Harper switching to full back.

'I also want Whitie and Wardy out wide,' he added, prompting my teammate and I to glance quizzically at each other, unsure which flank we'd each been assigned to. Howard noticed our puzzled expressions and took us to one side.

'I'm not bothered where you play, lads, just sort it out between yourselves,' was the advice. Much to my relief, Wardy agreed to occupy the left berth, which he'd go on to do for most of his fifty-plus appearances. This added a great balance to the team, as we complemented one another's games extremely well.

City v. Chelsea ended up as a 1–1 draw (I remember our visitors sporting a horrendous red-and-white horizontally striped kit). I can still visualize our equalizer; I found myself with the ball on the right, and crossed it into a dangerous area, about twelve yards out, where Niall Quinn was lurking. The Irishman – who was so lanky he barely had to jump – nonchalantly planted the ball in the corner of the net. Although it only earned us a point that night, we never looked back. The Whitie–Quinny partnership had been born.

* * *

We won five and drew one of our final six League games, comfortably securing our Division One survival and earning ourselves an end-of-season jaunt to the Canary Islands. Our week in Tenerife was a good old-fashioned piss-up, pure and simple. We faffed around by the pool all day while the gaffer and his staff took up residency in a tiny and smoky old man's bar located opposite the hotel.

The lads and I would usually venture out at 9 p.m., making a beeline to Veronica's Block, a labyrinth of dark, sweaty, seedy bars that played brilliant music. If Howard and the coaches happened to spot us passing by, however, they'd drag us in, virtually keeping us captive while the boss held court with a repertoire of songs, jokes and stories. The fact that he hardly left his seat gave us limited opportunities to escape to Veronica's before midnight.

'That man must have the strongest bladder in Tenerife,' I remember saying to Brighty. 'Does he ever go for a piss?'

After a couple of nights of this dive-bar incarceration, we hatched a plan to individually skulk out of the hotel and merge into other groups of holidaymakers, darting behind pillars and lamp posts whenever we saw Howard craning his neck. Midway through our walk, Mark Ward would often stop off at a nearby phone box to call his wife back in the UK. It transpired that, in order to keep the peace at home, he'd told her that we'd embarked upon a serious training tour in Tenerife, as opposed to a relaxing, drink-fuelled jolly. Me, Ian Brightwell and our teammate Ashley Ward would often eavesdrop.

'All right love, how's it going? Kids okay?' Mark would ask, while feeding peseta after peseta into the coin slot.

'Yeah, it's going well,' he'd add, 'but it's bloody hard work, darlin'. Howard's running the bollocks off us. In fact, I'm off to get my head down and have an early night.'

Then there'd be a pause as Mrs Ward would enquire about her husband's non-existent tour game.

'Yeah, we won, love. Four-nil. I scored a hat-trick,' Wardy would say, holding his hand over the mouthpiece so that she couldn't hear our guffaws.

We'd then continue on to Veronica's, Wardy looking immaculate in his designer jeans and tight-fitting shirt, while the rest of us probably looked like bin men in comparison. At that time, Manchester was in the midst of its Haçienda/Happy Mondays heyday, which was always my justification whenever Wardy called me a scruffy Manc bastard.

'As if you Cockneys know what high fashion is, Wardy,' I'd add, referencing his West Ham days.

'Fuck off, Whitie, I'm a Scouser and always will be.'

One morning, after a particularly heavy night on the lash, Howard challenged Wardy to a game of tennis at the hotel. We couldn't miss this match-up between a forty-six-year-old who'd had eight hours' sleep and a twenty-seven-year-old who'd had no kip whatsoever, so we all lined the court to watch Howard and Wardy slugging it out in ninety-degree heat, both sweating neat alcohol. It was a five-setter, too – I think Wardy won – and by the time they'd finished it was time to hit Howard's Bar again.

* * *

That same summer, Leanne and I tied the knot in the Cheshire village of Daresbury. Most of the family were there, including Dad and Margaret, Steve and his girlfriend Helen, and Mum and her new partner. She'd met Dave while working at a local restaurant and, regardless of their large-ish age gap – he was only seven years older than me – they soon became an item. Both Steve and I were genuinely delighted that Mum had settled down happily with such a fantastic bloke.

While I wouldn't say that my parents were on friendly terms – you'd rarely catch them exchanging small talk – they were always perfectly civil and tolerant at family gatherings. That said, there were times when I'd notice Mum despairingly shaking her head when Dad, often after a few beers, would launch into one of his right-wing rants. When sober, my father's views were quite well informed and educated but, once he'd had a drink, they could sometimes veer towards the extreme side of the political spectrum. Occasionally I'd find myself taking him to one side and having a quiet word.

'Give it a rest, eh, Dad?' I'd say, diplomatically suggesting that he consider changing the subject.

Alice (a.k.a. Nana Jack) and Auntie Betty came to our wedding, too, although the latter wasn't in the best of health and, tragically, having suffered a stroke some weeks earlier, passed away just a few days later. Among the few relatives not in attendance, sadly, were my paternal grandmother Lily – a.k.a Nanna Tom – and her companion Bert. While the latter had continued working for the family firm, at some point in the mid-1980s Dad and Lily had become permanently estranged. There'd always been a tension between both parties –

prompted largely by my great-grandad Harry Wood's bequest, which had favoured my father – but things descended into acrimony during negotiations for Dad to buy back the company shares. A settlement was finally reached but, the damage had already been done.

My father completely severed ties with Lily and, for a long time, so did my brother and I. So deep was the animosity, had we continued seeing Nanna Tom it might have damaged our relationship with Dad, which was the last thing we wanted to happen. Poor old Bert was stuck in the middle, however. While he maintained a good working relationship with Dad, and enjoyed hooking up with me and Steve at the yard, he never hid the fact that his loyalties lay firmly with his long-time friend and companion.

'If you cut her, I bleed,' he'd once said to Dad during a doomed clear-the-air family meeting.

'Well, that's how we feel about our dad, too,' I'd countered.

It was a wretched situation, without any winners.

* * *

Leanne and I had planned to spend our honeymoon in Rhodes. Howard, however, had decided to recall the lads for pre-season training a week earlier than expected, which clashed with our holiday. But, fair play to him, my manager made an exception and allowed me some extra time off, no questions asked. In order to repay his kindness and understanding, I kept myself as fit as a fiddle, running miles along Ixia beach every day and steering clear of kebabs and ouzo. As a consequence, I returned to Maine Road in better shape than some of my teammates, who'd already been training for a week.

The new arrivals that season included Watford's Tony Coton who, as well as being an incredible goalkeeper, was an absolutely brilliant bloke. Mark Brennan, a left-sided player brought in from Ipswich Town, was another decent addition to the squad. We welcomed to the fold yet another former Everton player, too – Neil Pointon – who'd come to the club in exchange for Andy Hinchcliffe.

I think Hinchy had known for a while that his career was drawing to a close at City. His departure, I reckon, had probably been accelerated after a drinking game that had got slightly out of hand. We were partway through a tour of the Isle of Man and, while staff and players were all enjoying a few beers in a local pub, Andy had been asked to think up a category for one particular game called 'Names Of …'.

'Ah, let me think,' he'd pondered, his voice laced with sarcasm. 'Names of … all the City players who've come from Everton.'

The gaffer wasn't at all impressed. He'd received enough flak from the fans and the media regarding his over-reliance on former Everton footballers, and certainly didn't need any more from his own players. The glare that he gave Andy that night spoke volumes, and it came as no huge surprise when he finally left the club.

For me, it was a huge blow when Andy departed, and Howard made a point of taking me to one side.

'I know you two were big pals,' he said, 'but Neil Pointon's a good lad and he'll do a great job for us.'

He wasn't wrong. Howard was rarely wrong.

CHAPTER 13

In a Good Place

Whenever we had a fixture south of Watford, the City squad would always stay at the same place, the Bellhouse Hotel in the Buckinghamshire town of Beaconsfield. While it was a decent enough gaff, it was located miles away from most football grounds, leading me to suspect that our penny-pinching club had negotiated some bargain-basement room rates. We'd even stop off at the Bellhouse if we were playing Luton Town, whose ground we'd bypass a whole hour before arriving at the hotel. I remember Derek the driver once turning up at Kenilworth Road on a match day with just twenty minutes to spare, and us being so pushed for time that we'd had to get changed on the coach, pulling the curtains tightly shut so that passing fans didn't get an eyeful.

I was always an early riser for away games, going down for breakfast at half-past eight and usually sitting on my tod as I had a light meal of poached eggs on toast.

If the ground was nearby I'd often tag along with the coaches and the medical team when, at ten o'clock-ish, they drove over to deliver the kits, boots and medical supplies. While they laid out the gear and checked the dressing room I'd head out to the pitch, familiarizing myself with my surroundings and performing a few stretches and stride-outs. I was a bit of a geek when it came to stadia, and particularly loved them when they were all empty and quiet.

Afterwards I'd often try to have a sneaky peek at the changing room, since the way in which the staff set out the kits and footwear could often reveal that day's team selection. If the backroom staff knew the formation, they'd place the boots under the corresponding shirt number, thus giving the game away.

'Sling your hook, Whitie,' Roy Bailey would bawl as he saw me peering through a crack in the door. 'Sod off and go and wait for us on the coach.'

Occasionally I'd creep in and nick a pair of big shorts from the pile of kit, stuffing them up my training top and saving them for that day's match. Some of the away shorts that Umbro supplied were so snug that thunder-thighed lads like me and Reddo had to cut slits up the sides with medical scissors, so I always tried to snaffle a large pair before anyone else did. For some reason, this was never a problem with the home strip.

At 11.30 a.m. the squad would usually convene for a walk around the hotel grounds. It was often at this point that Howard would have a quiet word with certain players, revealing whether they were in or out of that day's starting line-up. Getting the timing right was never easy for a manager. From a player's perspective, there was nothing worse than hearing the side being announced and discovering that you'd been dropped, without any prior notice. From a boss's point of view, though, allowing an excluded player too much advance warning often risked disruptive behaviour which, in turn, might affect his teammates' match preparation. A lot, I suppose, depended on the character of the player in question.

Pre-match meals at the Bellhouse were taken at 11.45 a.m. sharp and never failed to amuse me. The catering staff were extremely obliging, knocking up whatever we wanted to eat as long as each individual order was received a day in advance. It wasn't unusual, therefore, for fifteen totally different dishes to be simultaneously served up.

The hotel was quite a posh, traditional place. The waiting staff would waltz into the dining room at the same time, with their white napkins draped over their forearms, and with our plated-up meals steaming under those huge silver-domed lids. The maître d' would solemnly count '*One … two … three …*' while his waiters whipped off the metal lids with a flourish, shouting '*Voila!*' as they did so.

Our fellow diners would stare at this fiasco, perhaps expecting to witness the unveiling of fifteen plates of the finest chateaubriand or coq au vin for these elite professional footballers. Instead, they'd witness an array of meals that included Findus Crispy Pancakes with Spaghetti Hoops, mashed bananas on toast and Heinz Big Soup with bread and butter. Seeing their aghast expressions often made me howl with laughter.

It was following one such feast, on the afternoon of Saturday 25 August 1990, that Howard announced the team line-up for the first fixture of the season against Tottenham Hotspur. His decision to appoint Paul Lake as our new skipper was a bit of a jaw-dropper, to be honest. Although Lakey had featured in the provisional squad for Italia '90, and was developing into a world-class, Alan Hansen-esque centre half, the news of his captaincy still came as a shock to most of us. While I was genuinely thrilled for my friend – and implicitly trusted Howard's judgement – I couldn't help but feel gutted for his predecessor, Steve Redmond. Reddo had assumed skipper duties for some time, including throughout the entire pre-season, and to have suddenly found himself not only rescinding his captaincy, but also occupying the subs' bench, must have been hard to swallow.

Just prior to our departure for North London, Howard escorted the whole squad to the hotel bar. Lined up on the counter were thirteen pints of iced water, next to a pint of lager.

'Get them down your necks, lads,' grinned our boss, before downing his beer in one gulp. 'It's gonna be a warm one today!'

Spurs were far too good for us that afternoon. Gary Lineker and Paul Gascoigne were superb – they totally ran the show – and we were turned over 2–1, despite me hitting the Niall on the head – sorry – with a cracking first-half cross.

Thankfully we recovered from the disappointment, and remained unbeaten for the next eleven games. My own form took a dip, however; frustratingly, I yet again found my confidence and consistency wavering from match to match and, as a consequence, I was dropped for two Rumbelows Cup ties against Torquay. The gaffer left it until 5 p.m. to tell me I wasn't in his plans for Plainmoor, meaning that I had to quickly alert my Devon-bound father via his car phone; he promptly performed a U-turn near Birmingham and drove back home. Howard kept faith with me in the League, though, and I was back in the team for the following game versus Wimbledon. That Saturday he gave me the nod nice and early, enabling my dad to embark on an uninterrupted trip down the M1.

Our decent start to the season was blighted, however, by an injury that Paul Lake sustained in the third fixture of the season, against Aston Villa. The playing surface that day was appalling; there'd been no fewer than five concerts at Maine Road in the summer of 1990 – including Prince, David Bowie and the Rolling Stones – and groundsman Stan Gibson had resorted to dyeing huge swathes of the pitch bright green to mask all the bald patches. Not only that, days of Manchester rain had left it waterlogged.

Lakey – who like me had just been offered a new, improved contract by the club – was playing majestically against Villa that afternoon, in spite of the dreadful conditions. However, an hour into the match, he nicked the ball from Villa's Tony Cascarino, tripped over a divot, landed badly and wrenched his knee ligaments. He was carried off in agony, with Skip and Glyn bearing his stretcher. Over the next few days there was much press speculation about the severity of his injury, but he seemed upbeat enough when I chatted to him the following Friday.

'Doubt I'll be fit enough for Sheffield United tomorrow, Whitie,' he said as we both sat in the Maine Road dugout, looking across to the empty Kippax Stand, 'but I might make it in time for Norwich next week.'

Tragically, Lakey wouldn't play again for the rest of that season, or the next.

Aside from our captain's trauma, things were going swimmingly on the pitch. I played in a memorable Manchester derby at Maine Road, scoring two goals (one scrappy, one classy) and just missing out on a hat-trick. At one point we were 3–1 up and cruising, but a late fightback by the Reds saw Brian McClair twice beating Tony Coton, and we had to share the spoils. The following week I scored at Sunderland to earn us a point and, much to the delight of our long-suffering supporters, our team found itself safely entrenched in the League's top half.

And then, with our star in the ascendancy, Howard Kendall dropped the bombshell of all bombshells. He announced that he was quitting Maine Road and returning to Goodison Park, infamously describing his City stint as an 'affair' and his Everton bond as a 'marriage'. Neither the players, the supporters nor the media could quite believe the shock news. Even chairman Peter Swales had been caught totally unawares, it seemed.

Waving goodbye to this gem of a manager was really tough, and I spent that evening reflecting on how he'd worked wonders with our team. Howard had recalibrated our balance, rediscovered our belief, and reinstated our discipline and confidence. He'd given us a new lease of life, encouraging me and Wardy, for example, to seize our chances going forward and to take advantage of solid, well-drilled support from full backs Ian Brightwell and Neil Pointon. He'd injected quality and experience into our team without breaking the bank, exemplified by the astute signings of Peter Reid, Adrian Heath and Alan Harper, among others. The biggest change, however, was his commitment to simplicity. Nothing became complicated. Everything became transparent. All of us knew our jobs and responsibilities, both on and off the field.

In his short spell with the club, the gaffer had created a good side that was destined for great things. Success in football isn't always about the players themselves, but is often about the man picking those players. And Howard Kendall was, without doubt, The Man.

Some City fans were far less appreciative of him, however. Many of the Kippax faithful had never truly forgiven the boss for the departure of terrace heroes like Ian Bishop, Andy Hinchcliffe and Trevor Morley, and had resented the influx of ex-Everton players. I got the impression that Howard never really felt much love from a large section of Blues supporters, which I found a real shame. Who knows, had they learnt to value, respect and understand him more, then maybe he'd have stayed a little longer.

* * *

Rumours soon began to swirl that player-coach Peter Reid had been lined up as Kendall's successor but, judging by his cagey demeanour, Peter Swales didn't appear to be 100 per cent convinced. I, however – like the majority of my teammates – gave Reidy my full backing.

'We're in a good place, and we need continuity,' I remember telling a local reporter who collared me on the Maine Road forecourt, 'and I reckon Peter Reid can give us that.'

Reidy was duly appointed, and former Bury and Blackpool manager Sam Ellis was brought in as his assistant. The combination of enthusiastic player-manager and no-nonsense sidekick soon bore fruit, with an end-of-season surge seeing us finish a lofty fifth in the League. I scored the winning goals in our final two home games, against Derby County and Sunderland respectively. By doing so I effectively condemned both teams to relegation, muddying my name among the Rams' and the Mackems' fans.

Niall Quinn had performed heroics in the Derby game, incidentally, scoring an amazing goal in the first half and – much to the City fans' delight – saving a penalty in the second. Tony Coton had been dismissed after felling Dean Saunders in the box, prompting the big Dubliner to pull on the number 1 shirt. It came as no surprise to us when he saved Saunders' spot kick, diving full-length to his left. Niall, you see, would often challenge the lads to a post-training, best-of-three penalty contest.

'If you score two I'll give you a fiver,' he'd proclaim. 'Anything less and the money's mine ...'

Such was his save rate, he'd end up leaving Platt Lane with a fat wad of notes stuffed in his pocket.

The most memorable match of my football career was sandwiched between the Derby and Sunderland fixtures. On the evening of Tuesday 23 April 1991, not only did my team dole out a 5–1 thrashing to Aston Villa on their own turf, but I also achieved a personal feat by scoring four goals and making the other.

The home side's manager, Czech-born Dr Jozef Vengloš, had become the first overseas boss to secure a top job in Division One. He began the game with his side's biggest defensive threat, Paul McGrath, sitting in front of the back four. McGrath was without doubt one of the League's finest centre halves – he was a beast of a player, and was a supreme athlete – and had gained cult status among Villa, Manchester United and Ireland fans, particularly the latter.

Within minutes, and in spite of McGrath's imposing presence, we'd twice breached the home defence. Playing in white, Mark Brennan and Niall Quinn exchanged clever passes and, as Brenn picked up the ball in the inside-left channel, I made a run behind the centre backs. My teammate executed a brilliant pass and I finished with my left foot, low into the far corner.

Minutes later we scored a classic route-one goal with Quinny flicking on Tony Coton's long clearance and leaving me one-on-one with keeper Nigel Spink. The ball took its only bounce and couldn't have sat up for me any better. Spink was stranded as I lifted the ball over him to make it 2–0.

Those first two goals at Villa summed us up as a team; we could play both ways, either neat, intricate midfield passing to carve out a chance or, if need be, a more direct, attacking approach. At times that season we'd been criticized for being a long-ball team, but in reality I thought we were far from it. Granted, Quinny's aerial presence made him one of the game's best headers of the ball, but he was also a tremendously gifted player on the floor.

'Great feet for a big man,' I'd hear fans say, but Niall had great feet full stop, and was the best exponent of two-touch keepy-uppy in the whole squad. And, while he wasn't the quickest in deed he was intelligent in thought, regularly spotting chances and openings that others didn't.

He and I complemented each other well, too; in the early days of our partnership I created plenty of goals for him and later on, as I increasingly joined forces with him up front, he set up a fair few for me, too.

With Villa trailing, Vengloš immediately changed his formation in order to halt the slide. McGrath was ordered to police me until the interval and – despite David Platt coming close to pulling one back – the score remained 2–0 at half-time.

As the match resumed, and with an under-pressure home side chasing the game, Mark Ward put me through on the right, and I crossed the ball for Brenn to score our third. Our opponents kept plugging away, though, and earned themselves a penalty – duly converted by Platt – after Steve Redmond had handled on the goal line. Vengloš soon released McGrath from his defensive duties to try to salvage something from the game and I quickly took advantage, finding the space for Quinny to locate me with a pass to set up my favourite ever goal.

Having had a decent first touch, and with the ball at my feet, I glanced up to see Spink advancing, arms outstretched. The goal seemed like it was twenty yards wide, so confident did I feel. I visualized, believe it or not, the red-brick garage wall of my childhood and unleashed the same shot that I'd hit millions of times at home in Eccles. It was a perfect strike, the ball whacking against the stanchion before hitting the back of the net, right in front of the exultant away fans. It was my fiftieth senior goal for Manchester City and the one that gave me the most satisfaction of all.

I know for a fact that, had it not been for the thousands of hours of practice with my dad in the front garden, I wouldn't have achieved that level of power and precision. And, as I wheeled away to celebrate with my teammates, all that childhood graft and sacrifice seemed utterly worthwhile.

The Blues fans had more cause to cheer when, a few minutes later, Quinny rose again to pinpoint me with a fabulous headed pass. I cut in from the left before cannoning in a low shot at the near post, my fourth and final goal capping what, in hindsight, was to be my finest performance as a professional footballer.

Tarnishing my special night, however, was the fact that my dad hadn't been there to witness it. He'd been due to fly out from Heathrow the next morning – he was off on holiday with Margaret – and had decided against stopping off at Villa Park, possibly because my stepmother chose not to attend any games. While he'd listened with glee to the radio commentary, he'd been incredibly disappointed to miss such a landmark game.

'I'm delighted for you, David,' he said when we spoke afterwards, 'but I really wish I'd seen it for myself. I'll just have to watch the video when I get back, won't I?'

'Cheers, Dad,' I replied, 'but fast-forward through the middle seventy minutes, 'cause McGrath had me in his pocket.'

That was so typical of me. I'd scored four goals and made another, but part of me still felt like I'd failed in some way. That ingrained self-doubt continued to run deep.

* * *

In June 1991 I went on a club tour to Hong Kong, arriving back home on the morning of my brother Steve's wedding to Helen. Following a couple of weeks' rest, our 1991–2 pre-season schedule kicked in with a vengeance, although I was saddened to discover that my mate Mark Ward, along with Alan Harper, had been lured back to Everton. Among our squad's new arrivals, however, was Wimbledon's Keith Curle, signing for a fee of £2.3 million which, at that time, was a British record for a defender.

In my opinion, though, our new centre back justified all the hype and expectations. Manchester City had fielded countless quick players over the years, but shit-off-a-shovel Curley was something else, regularly trouncing me by at least five metres during our 100-metre sprints. He certainly added a new dimension to our side, encouraging us to operate higher up the pitch and squeeze the play. Opposing teams would then be tempted to launch long balls into the space behind, whereupon a turbo-charged Curley would skin them alive.

Our second game of the season, on a balmy summer's evening, witnessed the visit of Liverpool. I remember feeling a real buzz that night as I pulled on my sky blue kit and laced up my new Asics boots before running out through the tunnel and into the noisy, floodlit stadium. (My boot deal paid me £2,500 per year – a decent fee in those days – but also gave me carte blanche to raid the Asics sportswear factory in Warrington, just a stone's throw away from my home.)

Following a swift move generated by Curley and Quinny, I was able to open the scoring at Maine Road and – thanks again to big Niall – managed to double our tally in the second half. A fresh-faced young striker called Steve McManaman pulled one back for Liverpool, however, and Dean Saunders missed another penalty against us, this time sporting a different team strip. Despite being under siege by one of the best teams in the land, somehow we absorbed the pressure and managed to cling on until full time. I was overjoyed. For me, beating Liverpool at Maine Road felt like carding four-under-par at Augusta. Succumbing to three- or four-goal margins against the Reds had almost become the norm for us, so it seemed we were making progress.

A few weeks later I suffered a freak accident during a routine training drill. This exercise involved standing in a big circle with a football in the middle, while Sam Ellis shouted out various numbers in quick succession. If yours was called out, you'd race towards the ball, touch it with your fingertips and sprint back. It was a great way to maintain sharpness and dexterity.

As my number was yelled out, and as I touched the ball and turned away, I felt an incredible force clatter into the front of my body. Clive Allen had mistakenly run straight into me, the top of his head smashing right into my collarbone. Bizarrely, my first impulse was to burst out laughing – out of shock, I think – but within seconds I knew something was seriously wrong. The subsequent X-ray confirmed that I had indeed fractured my clavicle. Physio Roy Bailey told me I'd be out for at least six weeks, and I remember cursing my bad fortune as I scanned the fixture list and totted up the games I'd have to sit out.

Waiting for the break to heal naturally, with my left arm in a sling, was unbelievably frustrating. It was really painful, too; I couldn't sleep comfortably in my bed so, for three or four weeks, had to kip on the sofa. My collarbone wasn't my only concern, either, since I'd also started to suffer a slight but persistent discomfort in my right ankle.

'At some point you'll need a basic wash-out operation on that,' advised Roy as he examined my lower leg in the physio room, 'but let's get you out of this sling, first …'

I felt incredibly lethargic during my comeback match, a reserve-team game against Liverpool. I got through it intact, however, despite going arse over tit in the first minute and landing heavily on my shoulder. There were no adverse effects, thankfully, which I took as a good sign that I was on the road to recovery.

The manager started me for the Manchester derby at Maine Road, but I quickly realized that I was miles away from match fitness. Back in those days, physical conditioning and post-injury rehabilitation were still fairly primitive, so players weren't often in the best nick when they returned from a long absence. I felt nowhere near 100 per cent, I played really badly, and I ended up being substituted towards the end of a dour 0–0 draw.

After yet another shocking performance, this time against Luton Town, Reidy thought it best to drop me and give me a run-out in the reserves. I notched four goals against West Bromwich Albion (my goal-scoring rate was pretty decent in the Midlands that year) and, with that as a catalyst, my fitness and confidence levels began to improve. Reinstated in the first team, I scored in all six December games, including another brace in a 2–2 draw against Liverpool at Anfield. Yet again, both goals had been generated by the Mighty Quinn.

'That's just about the most famous one-two in the First Division,' remarked Granada TV's Clive Tyldesley in the commentary box. 'The head of Niall Quinn and the speed of David White …'

Following the second strike – a wide-angled shot that had bypassed Bruce Grobbelaar at the Kop End – I'd not been able to contain myself and, as I punched the air in delight, I yelled '*FUCK OFF!*' It was more of a joyous outpouring of emotion than an expression of abuse – it felt superb to get another brace against the Reds – but the Liverpool fans believed otherwise and, for the rest of the match, dished out some serious verbals. I arrived back home that night with '*YOU MANC BASTARD!*' still ringing in my ears.

* * *

While the likes of Niall Quinn, Ian Brightwell and I remained the experienced thoroughbreds of the City team, there were some decent young colts getting some game time, too. Bolton-born midfielder Garry Flitcroft showed great promise, as did Michael Hughes and Mike Sheron. Shez in particular was an excellent, technically adept striker who'd sometimes occupy my old right-wing role when I played up front with Quinny. He was a clever and thoughtful person, was Shez, and we got on extremely well. We lived near to each other – he was a St Helens lad, born and bred – and we'd often travel to Moss Side together.

Adding yet more wisdom and experience to our team that season was Steve McMahon, who City had signed from Liverpool on Christmas Eve, 1991. Steve had been a fantastic servant at Anfield – he'd made over 250 appearances for the Reds – and added some extra craft, grit and vision to our midfield.

Macca had no trouble settling in, although his overconfidence sometimes got the better of him. One particular afternoon we were training at Platt Lane when we noticed an old, bespectacled guy barracking us from the touchline, back in the days when the general public had open access to the complex. Wearing a tatty trench coat and a scruffy cap, this Old Man Steptoe lookalike proceeded to hurl abuse as we ran past, prompting a few of us to bat some back in his direction.

'Sod off back to your care home, you old goat,' countered one of my teammates.

This fella was unperturbed, though, and continued to harangue us as we headed off the pitch towards the changing rooms.

'White, your crossing was *shit* on Saturday,' he hissed. 'Quinn, all you can do is bloody head the ball. And as for you, McMahon, you're just so fuckin' slow …'

Macca, having risen to the bait, stopped and fixed him with a glare.

'Too fuckin' slow, am I?' he said, his voice laced with menace.

'Yeah,' replied the old bloke. 'I bet even *I* could beat you.'

That was enough for Macca.

'Right. On that pitch now, grandad,' he said. 'Let's see who's faster, eh?'

We were pissing ourselves as we watched him set up two cones about twenty-five yards apart, before lining up next to his OAP nemesis. The old guy – still sporting his cap and coat – appeared to be taking things very seriously indeed, stretching his limbs and jogging on the spot. Macca was virtually crying with laughter as he stood there, awaiting the starting signal.

'On your marks, set, GO!' we yelled, at which Macca began a leisurely canter. Much to our amazement, the old guy set off like Carl Lewis, instantly gaining three yards on his rival which, try as he might, Macca failed to make up. Crossing the finishing line first, our senior-citizen sprinter celebrated wildly, jumping up and down and punching the air as the lads and I nearly passed out in hysterics.

Then came the big reveal. The 'old guy' whipped off his coat, cap and glasses to introduce himself as Les Chapman, ex-professional footballer, notorious prankster and City's newly appointed kit man.

'You fuckin' bastard,' said Macca, playfully taking a swing at him.

Les would become an integral part of the management set-up at Manchester City. He was a hilarious bloke and a diamond of a guy, and this would be the first of many wind-ups.

CHAPTER 14

One-Cap Wonder

Leanne was expecting our first child in the spring of 1992 and, as the due date approached, I prayed that the birth wasn't going to clash with a game. I clung to the hope that we'd get the timing right, and that I'd be at my wife's bedside, not on a football pitch, when the big moment arrived.

On Saturday 4 April we played Leeds United in a game that, for once, some City fans arguably wanted us to lose. The Yorkshire side had enjoyed a fabulous season – classy players like Gary McAllister, Eric Cantona and Gary Speed had lit up their League campaign – and they were vying with Manchester United to win the First Division title. Much to the annoyance of many Blues, we thrashed them 4–0, effectively putting our red rivals in the driving seat. Howard Wilkinson's side managed to keep up the pressure, though, and were crowned title winners in May.

My wife ended up being induced at Warrington General Hospital the following Tuesday, which happened to be the same day as the Manchester derby at Old Trafford. I remember nervously clock-watching as I sat in the maternity ward, my stress levels soaring as the kick-off loomed ever closer.

C'mon White Junior, I remember thinking. *Your daddy wants to play in the Derby …*

Leanne had gone into labour at nine o'clock in the morning but, having made slow progress, found herself undergoing a traumatic emergency Caesarean section six hours later. At 3.30 p.m. our amazing son Sam was born and, after spending an hour or so gazing down in wonderment at him – and marvelling at my wife's bravery – I battled through the rush-hour traffic to join up with the squad at the Copthorne Hotel. I arrived just in time for a quick cuppa before the coach made the short trip to Old Trafford.

'Congratulations, Dad!' whooped my teammates, shaking my hand and patting my back as I made my way to my seat.

The match started at a frenetic pace, with eighteen-year-old Ryan Giggs opening the scoring with a low, left-footed strike. Shortly afterwards I made a break down the right flank, showing Steve Bruce a clean pair of heels and tempting him into a foul in the box. Keith Curle duly converted the penalty to equalize.

The TV cameras captured me giving Brucey some serious stick, shouting and swearing at him as he lay spreadeagled on the deck. I was bang out of order, and watching the footage afterwards made me cringe with embarrassment. Who on earth was I to hurl abuse at such an honest and honoured professional?

'So what exactly did you say to Bruce?' City fans still quiz me, particularly on Twitter. I never answer that question, though, because it's not a memory I look back on with any degree of pride.

In the closing minutes I had a golden chance to score the winner and seal my perfect day, but I totally fluffed my lines with a disastrous volley. A City fan gave me grief about it as I boarded the coach after the game, but I just ignored him.

No knobhead's going to tarnish one of the happiest days of my life, I thought to myself as we headed back to the Copthorne, feeling excited at the prospect of visiting my newborn the next morning.

One of the huge advantages of being a professional footballer, I discovered, was the amount of time you could devote to your offspring. Not having an average nine-to-five job, I was able to watch my little 'un grow up and reach his milestones, and – other than match days, training sessions and pre-season tours – was at home with my wife and son most of the week. I cherished each moment that I spent with baby Sam, even all those nights of early-hours interruptions and sleep deprivation.

Manchester City ended the season with a flourish. A string of four consecutive victories – including a 5–2 defeat of Oldham, with a hat-trick from yours truly – secured us a fifth League placing for the second year running.

Our domestic campaign done and dusted, I switched my attention to the 1992 European Championships in Sweden. While I relished the idea of spending my downtime watching the England seniors on TV, at the same time I realized that – sooner rather than later – I needed to try to make headway into that same side. Since my Under-21s swansong I'd been involved in three England 'B' matches, and had been given game time against France and Iceland, but clearly hadn't done enough to become a serious contender for Euro '92. I was delighted, however, to see my teammate Keith Curle receiving a late call-up to Graham Taylor's squad.

As it turned out, England performed dreadfully in the tournament, with goalless draws against Denmark and France preceding a defeat by Sweden. I watched the final while on holiday, sitting in front of a TV in a Marbella villa while bouncing baby Sam on my knee. Denmark – a late entrant to the tournament due to the troubles in Yugoslavia – rode out triumphant, confounding all critics by beating the reunified Germany 2–0.

Leanne and I managed to squeeze in another holiday before the new football season took hold. We took Sam along with us to the Swiss town of Interlaken, where the high altitude helped him sleep through the night for the very first time. What a result that was.

* * *

In preparation for the advent of the brand-new Premier League, City headed over to Italy for a gruelling five-game tour. We stayed in Northern Lombardy in the Italian lake district, an area renowned for its hugely regimented football training camps. The afternoon games were as tough as the morning drills; we lost to Brescia and Vicenza and eked out draws with Cremonese, Torino and Verona.

The day of the Verona game was a memorable one for me, and not because of my disappointingly under-par performance. That morning, Steve Redmond and Neil Pointon had announced that they were both flying back to the UK to sign for Oldham Athletic. It was a real wrench to say goodbye to Neil – he'd been a great player for us – but it was the departure of Reddo that left me absolutely devastated. I'd known him for what seemed like an eternity – he was one of my closest friends – yet suddenly, and without much warning, he'd left the tour and departed the club.

'Good luck with everything, Whitie,' he said as he clambered into his taxi. I watched the car wind its way around a Lombardy lake, feeling desperately sad as it slowly disappeared from view.

In the meantime, left-winger Rick Holden signed for the club, immediately flying out to join us in Italy. My first proper encounter with him was bizarre. Reidy and Sam had taken us all out for some beers one evening, and the night had ended with the obligatory singsong. Following some drunken caterwauling – including my time-honoured renditions of Johnny Cash's 'A Boy Named Sue' and 'Don't Take Your Guns to Town' – most of us had staggered back to the hotel.

I roomed with Brighty that night, and the next morning we were both awoken by a loud hammering on the door.

'*OPEN UP!*' shouted a northern voice that I didn't quite recognize. I did as he asked, and found Rick Holden standing there, clutching a small bag.

'Window fund. Fifty thousand lira each,' he grunted.

'Morning Rick,' I replied. 'What the *fuck* are you on about?'

Not the politest opening gambit to someone, but I was half asleep and very confused. Rick went on to explain that, after most of us had called it a night, Niall Quinn and Steve McMahon had become embroiled in a fracas which had culminated in the pair of them – plus the peace-making Rick – smashing through a shop window. In order to pacify the owner – and to keep the club out of the tabloids – the whole squad would have to share the million-lira repair bill. I gave Rick the money – the equivalent of about twenty-five quid – and he carried on with his door-to-door fundraising.

I received the one and only red card of my career during our game against Vicenza. One of their players had spat at me – dirty bastard – and I'd reacted (mildly, I'd thought) by flicking my opponent's ear while drawing his attention to the phlegm sliding down my cheek. The referee saw it differently, though, dismissing me from the field while deciding to keep the other fella on. Fortunately, the post-match intervention of a level-headed referee assessor prevented me from getting a ban.

The next day, for a bit of variety, a local military man was recruited to take us all for a run in the hills.

'Slackers will be punished,' he said. He was as arrogant as they come, and obviously hadn't factored in how fit we were. Even after an hour's worth of climbing we were more than able to sprint down the peak at pace, before embarking upon a series of ground-level interval runs and stride-outs.

'No fuckin' slackers here, Action Man,' someone said to him afterwards.

The player in the best shape of all was undoubtedly Paul Lake, who was on the verge of making his long-awaited comeback. All the signs were promising – he'd worked incredibly hard during the tour and looked strong as an ox – and we were fully expecting him to feature in our opening game of the campaign, against Queen's Park Rangers at Maine Road.

Prior to the start of this momentous season, I was among a handpicked group of City players who travelled down to London to film a BSkyB Premier League advert. Reidy, Steve McMahon, Tony Coton and I spent the day filming a changing-room scene – we were paid £1,000 for our troubles – and were joined by a troop of lively extras sporting kits and tracksuits.

The final cut – with Simple Mind's 'Alive and Kicking' as its soundtrack – was aired across the Sky Sports network, almost on a loop. As for the City-related content, it showed Reidy geeing up his players, a brief close-up of Macca's face, and a nanosecond of my and TC's backs. It was probably the easiest grand I'd ever earned.

Every striker playing in this new era of Premier League football wanted to make their mark with a 'first'. It was Sheffield United's Brian

Deane – a future teammate of mine, and a lovely guy to boot – who scored the opening goal of the campaign, against Manchester United. The following day, Nottingham Forest target man Teddy Sheringham staked his own claim to fame, bagging the first live televised goal on BSkyB by banging one in against Liverpool.

Manchester City versus QPR, on 17 August, became the channel's first ever *Monday Night Football* offering. The broadcaster made a huge deal of it and had organized all sorts of pre-match razzmatazz. It was unlike anything we'd ever seen before, with planes towing banners, music blasting from bandstands, and fireworks exploding above Maine Road. All this pizzazz, along with the fact that the Platt Lane stand had been demolished for development, made the stadium feel weirdly unfamiliar.

'I know it's difficult, lads, but try to stay focused,' said Reidy as we stretched and limbered up, the dressing room reverberating with all the noise outside.

QPR were a really classy outfit in those days – their side boasted top-notch players like Ray Wilkins, Andy Sinton and Les Ferdinand – and we knew we'd have our work cut out. Boosting our morale, however, was the fact that Lakey had indeed made the team line-up, as we'd all hoped. It was both thrilling and emotional to see this magnificent player, who I'd virtually grown up with, wearing the sky blue shirt once again.

Our formation took some time to get used to. We were still lacking a recognized left back, so Brighty filled that berth, with Andy Hill playing right back alongside Keith Curle and Michel Vonk. Rick Holden made his debut on the opposite wing to me, with Steve McMahon and Fitzroy Simpson operating between us. Niall Quinn partnered Lakey up front.

I don't recall too much about the match itself, other than on 37 minutes I achieved a 'first' of my own, notching up City's opening goal of the Premier League, one of the easiest I'd ever scored. A resurgent Lakey had been involved in the build-up, with goalie Jan Stejskal parrying a shot before I positioned myself perfectly for an easy tap-in. Andy Sinton equalized for QPR, however, and we ended up drawing the game 1–1. I'm the first to admit that, at the time, the significance of this milestone goal was totally lost on me. I'd simply never imagined how huge the Premier League would become, and how much it would transform the world of football.

'It's just the same division with a different name,' I told reporters afterwards. 'Nothing much will change as far as I'm concerned.' Hey, what did I know ...

If I'm honest, I was more gratified by the fact that Lakey had managed to stay on the pitch for three-quarters of the game, justly receiving a standing ovation when Reidy finally substituted him. Sadly, however, tragedy befell him just two days later, when he suffered yet another horrendous knee injury during our 2–0 defeat at Middlesbrough's Ayresome Park. It would be his last ever game for the club he loved so dearly.

Lakey's bittersweet memoir, *I'm Not Really Here*, chronicled his physical and emotional heartache and detailed a catalogue of mismanagement and misdiagnosis. Here was a truly outstanding footballer who'd had the world at his feet and who, had he remained fit, would have won many caps for his country. Lakey's sad but inevitable retirement from the game was English football's loss.

A month later, then, it was neither Lakey who would receive a prized England call-up, nor Mouldy, Reddo or Brighty.

It was me.

* * *

It turned out that the England boss had been keeping tabs on me since the beginning of the season.

'I think you should know that Graham Taylor's been asking after you, Whitie,' assistant boss Sam Ellis had remarked one Saturday afternoon in late August, following our 3–3 thriller against Oldham Athletic. I'd been experiencing something of a purple patch, having scored one against the Latics and, the previous Wednesday, a brace against Norwich City.

I wasn't in the business of assuming anything, though, and my dad was similarly measured when I spoke to him later that evening.

'He's probably watching lots of players, son,' he said, 'although there is that England friendly against Spain coming up soon ...'

On the first day of September, City were due to play Wimbledon at Selhurst Park. We stopped off at the Bellhouse Hotel the night before – just a mere fifty-five miles away this time – and at seven o'clock the next morning I remember being awoken by the phone ringing in my room. On the end of the line was a tabloid journalist.

'Just wondering if you've heard the news, David? Graham Taylor's selected you for the seniors for the game in Santander.'

I hadn't heard the news, actually. While it wasn't the ideal way to receive such glad tidings – City's club officials had probably planned to tell me after the Wimbledon game, and should have enjoyed the kudos of doing so – I was nonetheless delighted.

I scored the winning goal that night, grabbing two more at Hillsborough the following week as we beat Sheffield Wednesday 3–0. With seven goals in seven games, I couldn't have approached my international debut with any more confidence.

I genuinely wasn't expecting to start the England game. My odds shortened, however, when, on the day the squad convened, Leeds United's Rod Wallace was forced to pull out through injury. The right-winger had been on fire for his team and, until then, had definitely preceded me in the pecking order.

Bloody hell, I thought to myself. *I might have a chance here ...*

Following two days' training at Bisham Abbey, we flew to northern Spain to prepare for the match. To be brutally honest, the management and coaching set-up was vastly inferior to that of Bobby Robson's and Don Howe's a few years earlier. The likes of Phil Neal and Lawrie McMenemy – Graham Taylor's assistants – shouldn't have been anywhere near the England camp in my opinion; I just didn't think they cut the mustard at international level. Graham Taylor himself was perhaps a little out of his depth in his role, I feel, but I'd remain hugely grateful to him for giving me my chance, and would continue to have huge respect for him as a manager at club level.

Taylor announced the team on the eve of the game, and I was delighted to find myself in the line-up. I was also thrilled to discover that I'd be sporting my treasured number 7 as well, the safeguarding of which had become something of an obsession for me at Manchester City. I considered it a real privilege to bear the same number worn by Bryan 'Captain Marvel' Robson during an amazing career that had spanned ninety international caps.

In the Estadio El Sardinero, on Wednesday 9 September, I stood proudly for the national anthem and psyched myself up for my much-yearned-for debut. Lining up alongside me were Chris Woods in goal, Stuart Pearce at left back, Lee Dixon at right back, Mark Wright and Des Walker in central defence and a midfield of Paul Ince, David Platt and Nigel Clough. Up front, Andy Sinton mirrored me on the left wing, with our star striker, Alan Shearer, spearheading the attack. Our formation may have looked very 4–4–2 on paper but it was in fact more of a 4–3–3, with Clough dropping deep, giving me and Sinton the licence to make runs beyond Shearer.

Well that's it, I remember thinking as the whistle blew. *Whatever happens, they can't take this cap away from me ...*

Knowing that my dad and Leanne were somewhere in the crowd – and that Mum and Steve would be watching back home – only intensified the emotion of the occasion, and I stood for the national anthem with my head held high and my heart filled with pride.

The game was only eighty seconds old when Nigel Clough latched onto the ball as I made a diagonal run into an inside-left position. He located me with a perfect reverse pass and, as I looked up, I found myself beyond the Spanish back four with just keeper Andoni Zubizarreta standing between me and a dream debut goal. It wasn't to be, alas. As I adjusted my body for a right-foot shot, Zubizarreta advanced, made himself big, and stifled my goal-bound shot.

Gregorio Fonseca, my opposing number 7, was more successful on the 11-minute mark, finishing well after blocking Rafael Martín Vázquez's shot. I missed another opportunity in the second half – an easier chance than the other, in my opinion – and, after 79 minutes, was replaced by Paul Merson. England failed to equalize, and the scoreline remained 1–0 to the Spaniards.

Contrary to what most fans presume, my failure to score that early goal hardly bothered me at the time, and still doesn't now. As far as I was concerned, I'd spent my career playing against and alongside some of the best goalkeepers in the world, week after week, and had hit the back of the net pretty consistently. Granted, I'd also had plenty of efforts that had been saved, or that had missed the target, but that was football, and I was more than able to live with all the swings and roundabouts.

'You can't win the raffle if you don't buy a ticket,' Tommy Docherty used to say, and the former Manchester United manager was dead right. By merely being selected for England, I'd proved to myself that I could cope with the step up in class, and – judging by that slice of action in the second minute – that I could get myself into goalscoring positions at international level. I was more than happy with that, and had genuinely walked off that Santander pitch feeling very positive.

I was surprised and disappointed, then, when all the post-match chat seemed to focus on 'David White's missed chance'. Yeah, I'd have liked to have scored it – like any striker would have – but, to me, my squandered opportunity had been totally blown out of proportion.

'You've done well there, son, and other chances will come,' said Dad when I caught up with him after the game. Both of us were pretty hopeful that I'd receive another opportunity to show my talent and prove my worth on the England stage.

A fortnight or so later I was driving home from training, listening to the radio, when I heard the squad being announced for the forthcoming international game. Graham Taylor had only named me as one of the standby players for the World Cup qualifier against Norway at Wembley, and I felt completely and utterly devastated.

Someone's bound to get injured, I hoped, in that macabre way that players do sometimes. But it wasn't to be and, from that point on, my club form never justified another call-up, and my England career had finished before it had started. Some people said that my failure to score in that debut – and the subsequent media criticism I received – had signalled the beginning of the end. I still refute this, as I don't think my omission hinged upon one missed opportunity in Santander.

While I dearly treasured my senior England honour, I soon discovered that being a 'one-cap wonder' had a weird stigma attached to it. There existed tens of thousands of professional footballers who'd never bothered the League's top flight, never mind achieving an England call-up, but my solitary England appearance was often used by others to make me feel like some kind of failure. Strangely, such a negative judgement wasn't applied to those players who'd perhaps accumulated only half an hour's game-time play for England, but had done so across two or three fleeting substitute appearances in ties that had already been won. It pissed me off then – and pisses me off now, quite frankly – that I'd sometimes attract grief for actually achieving something.

'How many caps have you got again, Whitie?' Roy Keane once hissed as he was man-to-man marking me at Maine Road. 'Just the one, is it?'

Fuck you, I thought.

'Yeah, but it was for *England*, pal,' I replied.

I had huge respect for Roy – he did brilliantly for Nottingham Forest and went on to achieve so much with Manchester United – but I was trying to articulate the fact that there were plenty of lads playing for Scotland, Wales and the Republic of Ireland who, at that time, were nowhere near as good as me. For the record, Roy would have received countless caps for England had he been born there.

To this day, people will still try to wind me up about my short-lived international career. A few years back I remember drinking at a Puerto Banus beach bar with some pals, all of us taking the mickey out of each other, when one of the lads gestured towards me.

'And as for you, Dave, I watched you get *both* your England caps,' he said.

'Fuck off, James,' I replied. 'You know full well I only got *one*.'

'Nah, mate, I saw you get both. Your first, and your fuckin' last.'

Everyone fell about laughing, of course, including me. It's a good job he was a pal, though, because I wouldn't have taken that kind of banter from anybody else.

CHAPTER 15

Smashed Around the Edges

The passage of time had in no way dampened my dad's pushy-parent mindset. He'd never stopped living his life through my football career, even when I was an adult, and the intense pressure that he'd foist upon me often became intolerable.

Dad's mood and demeanour continued to correlate with my performances on the pitch. If I was playing well and scoring goals he'd be all sweetness and light, yet if things were going badly, he could be really hard work. One particular December, I remember having a great run of form in which I scored six goals in six games. For days afterwards, Dad's smile was as wide as the Mersey Tunnel; I was the best player around, and he was walking on air.

On the other hand, I lost track of the number of times that he totally blew his top. I remember sitting on the coach following an away game, waiting for my mobile phone to buzz. On the end of the line would be Dad, calling from his car to either praise or lambast me. Sometimes I'd pre-empt it – especially if I'd done badly – and would ring him first to get his tirade over and done with. I'd often find myself fielding a call from my apoplectic dad while my teammates sat next to me, chatting and playing cards.

'What was that sack of shit?' he'd yell. 'You looked knackered. What the hell were you bleedin' playing at?'

At times there was no real logic to Dad's thinking, either. Occasionally I'd bag a goal but not play well, and he'd be fine with me. The week later, however, I'd put in a great shift without scoring or assisting, and he'd fly off the handle. It seemed that grabbing the headlines – and the kudos that publicity brought – was more important to him than the quality of my performance. Either way, it reached the point where I could never quite trust what he was saying. This haphazard reasoning rendered his words empty and meaningless, whether he was showering me with compliments or spitting out condemnations.

Not that I fully realized it at the time, but my brother Steve often bore the brunt of Dad's bad behaviour, too. It turned out that his working week at White Reclamation would become insufferable if I'd played poorly. Dad would invariably vent his frustrations on his colleagues and employees, but most of his anger tended to be routed through Steve. Margaret and the girls would also receive similar treatment when he returned home at night, by all accounts.

I felt as torn and as compromised in my twenties as I had done in my teens. Dad had sacrificed so much for me when I'd been a wannabe footballer but, having reached that goal, I could have done with an advocate and a champion, as opposed to someone who often made me feel blameworthy. I regularly sought solace and refuge at Mum's house. While she was interested in my football, and would happily discuss on-pitch matters, City was never the primary topic of conversation. Being able to chat leisurely about her job at the Greater Manchester Council for Alcoholism, or her latest directorial role at Barton Players, came as a refreshingly welcome change.

* * *

Meanwhile, back at Maine Road, and just prior to the start of the 1992–3 season, City had signed a left back in the shape of Terry Phelan. A fellow Salfordian and a really top bloke, Terry was a Republic of Ireland international who'd figured in the Wimbledon team that had famously beat Liverpool 1–0 in the 1988 FA Cup Final. He was an excellent player, was

Phelo: whippet-fast, tough-tackling and adept in both defence and attack.

Elsewhere in the side, the devastating loss of Paul Lake had been partly alleviated by the emergence of Garry Flitcroft, who was developing into a real talent. Flitty was performing well enough to keep the energetic Fitzroy Simpson out of the team, as well as our player-manager himself. My mate Mike Sheron was doing a great job on the right, too; a very tidy player and a natural striker, he ably supported Quinny and I.

I detected some chinks in our armour, though. As a unit, I felt we were lacking in pace and tempo, and I think I'd sussed why. In Terry Phelan, we had a full-back-cum-sprinter who wanted to bomb up the pitch and, while he wasn't a renowned goalscorer, he was a great asset going forward. What he needed, however, was a player like Mark Ward in front of him. While at City, Wardy had always been skilled at moving inside and creating space for his overlapping full back. He'd loved running with the ball and making the type of reverse passes that Phelo would have thrived on.

Instead we had Rick Holden, the former Oldham Athletic winger who, stylistically, was the polar opposite to Wardy. He liked to hold his wide position, did Rick, working his full back until he could deploy one of his expert crosses. Granted, his conversion rate of crosses from possession was far superior to mine, but it often took him forever to do it, jinking from one way to the other. Often, by the time he'd whipped one in, the opposing team had regrouped and the momentum had gone.

And, while I understood the logic behind Rick's move to Maine Road – he was a decent enough player and a really unique character – I don't think the gaffer and Sam foresaw the adverse effect he'd have on our attacking style.

By now I was playing most games up front, other than a few exceptions when I'd be asked to switch to the right. Prior to our matches against Nottingham Forest, for example, Reidy and Sam would invariably inform me that I'd be up against Stuart Pearce.

'Whitie, you and Shez can swap round on Saturday,' Reidy would say as the colour slowly drained from my cheeks. 'You're better at handling Psycho.'

I don't believe any footballer on the planet would have relished going man-to-man with Pearce. A truly superb defender, he operated like a Sherman tank, had the most thunderous thighs in the Premier League and was, hands down, the best opponent I ever faced, one-on-one. You could have pitted me against him in a 100-metre sprint, on any given day, and I'd have easily streaked past him. Put Psycho on a football field, however, and he'd become a completely different animal. His supreme presence and perseverance meant that he'd win every race to the ball, often bustling his opponents into the advertising boards as he did so.

Pearcey was by no means a dirty player – he was fair, honest, and rarely fouled me – but I can't recall a physical encounter with him that didn't leave me on my arse. Amusingly, though, he'd always sportingly pick me up. During one particular City Ground match-up he gallantly offered me his hand, having just unceremoniously shunted me over the pitch perimeter.

'Cloughie's been looking at you, Whitie; d'you fancy it?' he whispered, as he hauled me back to my feet.

For fuck's sake, I thought. *He's put me on my backside, and now he's trying to tap me up …*

A few minutes later the same thing happened again, this time behind the goal.

'They pay well, you know,' he grinned, 'and there are some great places to live round here …'

The third time I found myself lying next to him on the gravel track, after all thirteen stones of him had slid into me.

'C'mon, Whitie, you'd get a bagful playing alongside Nige … what d'you reckon?'

'Bloody hell, Stu,' I replied. 'Having you kicking me around the park is bad enough twice a year. I'm not putting myself through it every day in training …'

I came up against many other excellent opponents throughout my career – Andy Hinchcliffe, Graeme Le Saux and Tony Dorigo spring to mind – but I usually held my own. I don't ever recall getting the better of Stuart Pearce, though. The man was immense.

SMASHED AROUND THE EDGES

* * *

Looking back, the turning point of my whole career occurred on the afternoon of Saturday 23 January 1993. One of City's better performances of the season had seen us beating Queen's Park Rangers 2–1 in the FA Cup fourth round at Loftus Road. Playing in purple, I'd broken the deadlock with a goal that became one of my favourites, a great strike from a wide-right position that I'd smashed into the top corner.

Later in the game, however, I got myself involved in a goalmouth scramble following a corner, the ball having broken to Michel Vonk, who finished from close range. In the mêlée, however, I challenged for the ball – with David Bardsley, I think – but, as he put his foot up to block it, I kicked through his studs, connecting with the bridge of my right foot. I felt my ankle jar and judder – the pain was horrific – but I somehow managed to carry on until the final whistle. While I knew I'd done myself some damage that day, little did I know that my career would never be the same again.

Although I wasn't forced to miss any games, I felt my ankle getting more fragile and crumbly by the day. I didn't receive a proper diagnosis at the time – no scans or X-rays were arranged – and was just told that, at some point, I'd probably have to undergo a wash-out procedure to get rid of any floating bone.

'It's like a Crunchie Bar that's still in its wrapper, but is smashed around the edges,' I used to say when people asked how it felt.

The latter stages of the 1992–3 season proved to be disappointingly inconsistent for both me and the club. Having scored seven times in seven games in the build up to the England game, I found myself failing to hit the target for nearly two months. City couldn't buy a win, either, with standout results becoming few and far between. We spanked reigning champions Leeds United 4–0 – granted, they were having a disastrous 'after the Lord Mayor's show' season – but, soon after, Spurs beat us 4–2 in the FA Cup, in a game marred by crowd trouble at Maine Road. That October we overcame Everton 3–1 at Goodison Park – I scored a cracker past Neville Southall from wide on the left – but the

Toffees exacted revenge on the last day of the campaign, thrashing us 5–2 at Maine Road and souring the end-of-season atmosphere.

Our superb goalkeeper, Tony Coton, had been unavailable for that game and young Martyn Margetson, preferred to Andy Dibble, had experienced a torrid first half. Reidy took the decision to haul off Martyn at the interval but we just couldn't recover. Had we won, we'd have finished in sixth place, which wouldn't have been too shabby considering our largely topsy-turvy season. We occupied ninth spot, though, a significant regression from our previous fifth-position finish.

Not helping our cause was the strange decision to fly the squad halfway round the world, with just three games remaining.

'The chairman wants us to take part in a tournament in Tokyo,' a slightly bemused-looking Reidy had announced after training one morning, explaining that, the following Sunday, we'd be going abroad for four days.

Our Japanese trip – which the club were presumably benefiting from financially – was the biggest slog ever. Still suffering from jet lag, we played against Urawa Red Diamonds FC on the Monday and Hitachi Omiya FC on the Wednesday, not forgetting a couple of boozy karaoke nights sandwiched in between. We returned on the Thursday feeling absolutely shattered, knowing that we had to travel to Southampton the following day. We somehow beat the Saints 1–0 – I managed to summon some energy for the goal – but the jaunt to Japan had completely done us in. We would secure just one point from our final two games.

* * *

I rarely came across our chairman, Peter Swales. He wasn't one for poking his nose into the changing room or casting his eye across the training pitch, unlike some of his more interfering counterparts. He rarely criticized us in the press, was happy to offer praise when it was due and, I believed, generally treated his players with respect. I liked the man.

I once remember Swales calling me into a private meeting after training. Part of my PFA rep role included the distribution and collection of strike ballot papers, usually relating to our union's desire to have a greater share of TV money. That particular afternoon, however, the chairman urged me to advise the players to vote against industrial action. It wasn't an attempt to coerce me, and not once did he use any leverage; he was just trying to inform and illuminate.

'All this new money is being used to improve the clubs' finances, facilities and youth systems,' he told me, explaining that there was a danger, in the short term, that all the cash would simply go into the players' coffers.

'And that wouldn't help the game as a whole, David,' he said. 'So let's try to be careful here ...'

I found his argument compelling, and agreed to pass on his concerns to my teammates. Predictably, I suppose, it fell on deaf ears. To be perfectly honest, the lads were probably voting for a weekend off so that they could spend it in the pub. Swales had convinced me not to vote for strike action, though, and as a consequence I spoiled my ballot form. No vote.

At the time I thought he would be proven right, and I believe he eventually was. It took far too long for the new television money to flow through to the bottom line in order to improve facilities, and supporters' admission prices were never adjusted accordingly because, from day one, the players held the power.

When all the additional money flooded in, many clubs sold bond schemes and shares to fans on the back of the promised new revenue streams. They then distributed this income to the players, agents and other employees which meant that – in many cases – every penny that supporters put into the clubs for share purchases was lost, as clubs had to revert to private ownership. In addition to this, ticket prices continued to rise. It was a crazy situation that, I believe, Peter Swales had predicted all along.

As our hit-and-miss 1992–3 season drew to a close, the pressure on the chairman was mounting. There was considerable and palpable unrest brewing among City supporters, many of whom were becoming increasingly unhappy with the club's lack of success, silverware and transfer activity.

'*SWALES OUT!*' soon became a common chant at Maine Road, with fans hurling insults at him as he sat impassively in the Director's Box. This had an unsettling effect upon the players on the pitch, who couldn't help but be affected by the hostile and febrile atmosphere. Personally speaking, I know that my performances often suffered as a consequence of all this unrest.

And while it wasn't unusual for clubs' head honchos to bear the brunt of supporter ire in times of difficulty, in this case I thought it was unjust. Although our team had slightly regressed, I reckoned Manchester City was still in pretty good shape with Swales as chairman and Peter Reid in charge of the players.

Swales, I think, resented that it was him, not his manager, who'd become the butt of the fans' grievances. He'd probably appointed Reidy against his better judgement – his better judgement proving wrong, as it happened – and it was no secret that the pair didn't see eye to eye. They were both incredibly strong-willed characters, with Reidy in particular refusing to be bullied by anyone. While Swales had backed him in the transfer market, shelling out huge transfer fees for Keith Curle and Terry Phelan, stories abounded that the pair had clashed over failed attempts to sign Trevor Sinclair and Kevin Gallacher.

Under fire and under pressure – and with the chairman–manager relationship at breaking point – Swales decided to install a buffer between himself and Reidy. He appointed a general manager, John Maddock, a former Mirror Group journalist who, as far as I was aware, had no discernible football knowledge or experience. Maddock denied he was merely a mouthpiece for Peter Swales, instead claiming that he was the new supremo at Maine Road, with a specific mandate from the Board.

'Who the fuck does he think he is?' I remember saying to a teammate when I spied Maddock sitting at the front of the team coach before a game, calling the shots as if he knew what he was talking about. His appointment would turn out to be a calamitous move, albeit at a time when our chairman was in a very bad place.

With Maine Road in turmoil, the squad soon disappeared to South Africa for our end-of-season tour. Upon arrival in Cape Town we headed straight to a bar on the Waterfront, where the door staff memorably asked us if we had any guns to hand in, and where we were charged a ridiculous sum for eighteen beers.

Fuck me, seven quid for a beer, I thought to myself as the barman handed me the tab, not realizing that it covered the whole bloody round.

I woke up the next day feeling really sick, but not hungover. My roommate, defender Michel Vonk, was similarly nauseous.

'You're not the only ones,' said the gaffer when we reported our ailments. 'There's a few more, too. You lot must have picked up something on the plane.'

Reidy had no choice but to insist that, illness or no illness, we all played in the two tour games that we'd committed to. This led to me and the other poorly lads being dragged out of our sickbeds on both occasions, looking as green as the Incredible Hulk as we lumbered around the pitch.

By the weekend we'd recovered enough to visit Table Mountain, craning our necks to get a glimpse of Robben Island, where Nelson Mandela had been imprisoned. Our next stop was a vineyard, where, in a massive barn, we watched the Arsenal v. Sheffield Wednesday FA Cup Final on a big screen. We were given scarves and rattles when we arrived, before being directed to stadium-style seating where we were served beer by bunny girls. Happy days indeed. Sadly, we'd moved on to Durban by the time the replay came around, so there was no return visit.

Durban was undeniably beautiful, but I was shocked to witness the racism and apartheid that still existed in the city. All the swanky bars on the beach promenade appeared to be exclusively white, and many fellow drinkers that we spoke with referred to the 'indigenous' people as if they were alien beings. The next day we took a stroll, just one block away, and it felt like we'd walked into a suburb of Mumbai. Everyone we encountered was of Indian origin, and the extent of the segregation hit home. These locals – who seemed pleasantly surprised to see a troupe of footballers in their midst – would have doubtless felt uncomfortable or unwelcome in those beachfront bars. I found it all pretty shameful.

* * *

In June 1993, having returned from South Africa, I found myself back in Cala D'Or, of all places. By then my wife was four months pregnant with our second child, and we'd fancied a quiet holiday in a family-orientated resort, staying at a decent hotel where I could keep our toddler Sam entertained while Leanne rested up on a sunbed. Majorca seemed just the ticket, even more so when we discovered that my mate Andy Thackeray and his wife Jo were going to be there at the same time.

Surprising as it may sound, I had no qualms about returning to the village that held so many painful memories for me, although I didn't go so far as to stay in the Cala D'Or Hotel itself. In fact, I'd roped off my ordeal for so long – and had yet to tell a single soul about it – that sometimes it felt as though the abuse had happened in a different, faraway lifetime.

One afternoon, however, curiosity got the better of me.

'I'm just off for a walk,' I said to Leanne, before taking a short stroll to the scene of all that past heartbreak. As I tentatively peered through the entrance, I saw that the hotel had hardly changed in nearly fifteen years. The same sun terrace – teeming with mums, dads and kids – where two eleven-year-old kids and a football coach had once showed off their soccer skills. The same turquoise-blue swimming pool in which the trio had splashed about and staged underwater races. The same clusters of loungers and parasols, where they'd sipped Coca-Cola and chatted football, football and more football.

Then, as I gazed upwards, I spotted the first-floor balcony that had been my refuge during the worst morning of my life. This time, however, my eyes weren't brimming with tears. There was no chill running down my spine, no racing heartbeat, no thumping head. Instead, I just stared impassively for a few moments, feeling oddly detached, like I was observing a photo in a holiday brochure, or a picture postcard in a newsagent's. There was no fear or dread, only a dull, flat sense of sadness.

I took one last look at the Cala D'Or Hotel and turned around, stepping out of the shade and back into the summer sun.

(Above) Me with Tony Adcock (far left) and Paul Stewart (middle) after we all scored a hat-trick in our 10–1 win against Huddersfield. Paul and I were reunited in November 2016 when the child sex abuse in football scandal hit the headlines.

(**Right**) All set for Australia, May 1987.

(**Below, left**) Me, Reddo, Ian Brightwell, Paul Simpson in Australia, 1987.

(**Below, right**) Toulon with the Under-21s. Steve Redmond and I thought Gazza was our best mate. Turns out he just couldn't sit still and was in and out of everyone's rooms. What a guy.

(Left and below) I loved Platt Lane but for a top-flight club it wasn't the most private training ground and boasted just one full-sized pitch for all full-time players!

(Above) Left to right: Howard Wilkinson, Gary McAllister and Gordon Strachan.

(Below) Just about my favourite place to be on a Saturday afternoon. One-on-one with the keeper at the North Stand End, Kippax behind me. Usually ended well!

(Right) Round about the prime of my career, 1991/92. Note the half-empty stands.

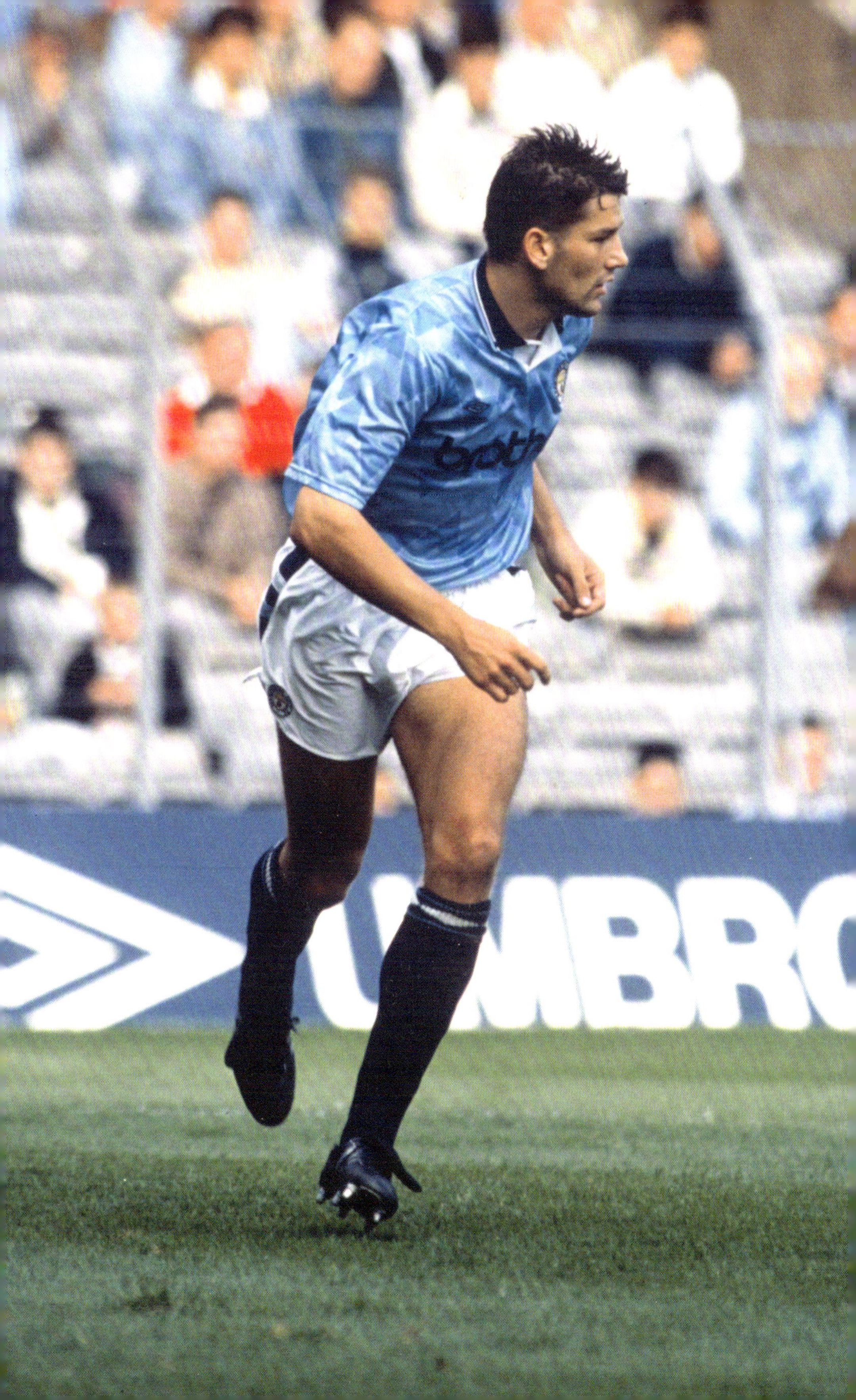

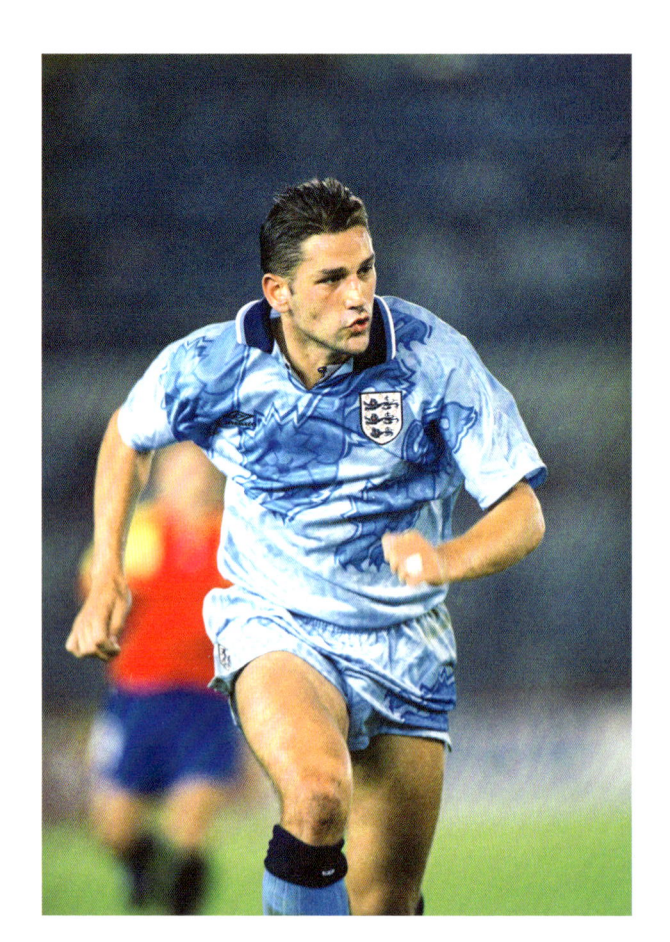

(Right) Playing for England in 1992.

(Below) With my son, Sam, in 1994.

(Left) Just about to board our chartered helicopter and leave Sun City after the best day I ever had on a football tour. Left to right: Gary McAllister, me, Gary Speed, John Pemberton. The rest of the lads went shopping!

(Right) Sam and India on a family day out in Manchester. It's wonderful how well the kids all get on.

(Left) Jordan and Georgia celebrating Jordan's eighteenth in town at another family do.

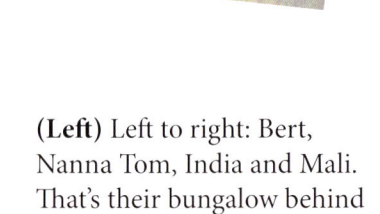

(Right) Emma and I had a 'second' wedding in Vilamoura, Portugal after Mali was born. What a weekend to share with all the kids and thirty other guests.

(Left) Left to right: Bert, Nanna Tom, India and Mali. That's their bungalow behind them.

(Below) My brother Steve and his wife, Helen, and children, Kade and Beth.

***

A few weeks later I rejoined my Manchester City teammates on the training pitches and, shortly afterwards, journeyed to Holland for our annual pre-season tour. It was a disaster from start to finish. The hotel, situated in some godforsaken Dutch backwater, was absolutely swarming with old-age pensioners. Its only attraction – a three-lane ten-pin bowling alley – was booked up solidly by the resident OAPs, and, worse still, the nearest bar was located in a sleepy village, half an hour's walk away. We had no other option but to get on with our training and play our tour matches. It was as boring as hell.

One night a group of players, including yours truly, decided we'd had enough. The gaffer had gone off to watch some game or other, and we all conspired to nip out for a beer. We were due to play a game the next day, but only against the local village team.

'What's the curfew?' we asked Reidy's assistant, Sam Ellis.

'Ten o'clock,' came his gruff reply, despite our protestations that Reidy would have given us a midnight deadline at the very least.

It was the hotel receptionist who happened to mention that there was a beer festival taking place in the locality, so that's where we headed. We went without our usual party animals, Quinny and Curley, who for some unknown reason had opted to stay indoors for a game of cards.

'Bloody lightweights,' grumbled Steve McMahon.

After a short taxi ride we arrived at something akin to a village fête, with stalls, games and pop-up bars being enjoyed by partying locals. We didn't have long – or so we thought – so we got stuck right in, with Alfons Groenendijk – our new signing from Holland – getting in the first round of drinks. We were soon full of the beer-fest spirit, trying our luck with all the sideshow games and chatting happily with various Dutch people, who seemed intrigued by our rate of beer consumption.

As half-past nine approached we reached a dilemma, however. Taxis had been booked to ferry us back, but we were all enjoying ourselves far too much, and none of us seemed in the mood for an early night. Rick Holden was having tons of fun launching beer mats around the place, and Tony 'such technique for a big man' Coton was our last survivor in the limbo-dancing contest.

I think it was Steve McMahon who finally took stock and took charge.

'Right, lads,' he said. 'If one player wants to go back – just one – we'll all leave.'

Nobody piped up, so we partied on for another two hours, returning to the hotel pissed as farts having enjoyed a noisy singalong in the minibus. Our moods changed as we entered the reception, though. Sat on the comfy sofas were Reidy and Sam, with faces like smacked arses. Not a word was spoken as we stumbled past them.

As expected, Reidy dished out a severe bollocking the next morning, and also had a huge row with McMahon that lasted the entire training session. It was hilarious – like something from Harry Enfield's 'Scousers' sketch – prompting the rest of us to prance around the pitch shouting, *'Calm down, calm down!'*

We weren't laughing after training, though, when Reidy informed us that he'd decided to fine us a week's wages. Things kicked off big-style among the lads, who were rightly aggrieved that Sam's ten o'clock curfew had, in fact, been a ridiculous suggestion in the first place, and that our midnight arrival hadn't warranted such an overblown reaction. Despite Curley being our club captain, he decided to take a back seat in this instance – fair enough, I suppose, as he'd not been involved – and I was therefore nominated to enter into negotiations with the gaffer. When the time came for us to chat, though, he'd cooled down enough to see the funny side.

'We'd have been back on time if TC hadn't been so fuckin' good at limbo dancing,' I said, which made him chuckle.

Reidy conceded that he didn't want a mutiny on his hands over something so trivial, and agreed to reduce the fine to £500 per player, to be donated to the 'team spirit' fund. I thought that was a decent deal and took it back to the lads, suggesting that they accepted it and put this sorry situation to bed. The general consensus was that it was a fair proposal, although I noticed a couple of ashen faces among the younger lads like Mike Sheron and Mike Quigley.

'What's your problem?' I asked.

'Fuck me, Whitie,' said one, 'I'm only on £300 a week.' Reidy, as even-handed as ever, would later agree that their fines could be waived.

Unfortunately, however, the beer festival episode had somehow filtered back to Peter Swales and, by the time we returned to the UK, the story had also been seized upon by the tabloids. From my perspective, it was a huge storm in a teacup; Reidy had handled our minor rebellion well and, using finely honed people skills, had succeeded in getting the lads back on side. That said, I think the gaffer realized it was going to reflect badly on him, and that the knives were already being sharpened at Maine Road.

Soon, Dad and I started to discuss my own future at the club. Sam and Reidy's days appeared to be numbered – Swales was patently no fan of theirs – and I had no confidence that any new management regime would herald an improvement. Not only that, the club's non-football structure at that time – headed up by this clown Maddock – had become absolutely farcical.

'It hurts me to say this, son, but I'm not sure City's the right place for you any more,' admitted Dad. 'You can forget any hopes of an international career if you stay at Maine Road …'

The new season began with a whimper. A 1–1 home draw with Leeds was followed by a run of three straight defeats – against Everton, Tottenham and Blackburn respectively – which didn't muster a single goal. Following the Blackburn game, Maddock had the audacity to criticize our spirit and performance, insinuating that we weren't playing for the manager. This man had clearly become the problem, not the solution.

Reidy, though, had reached the end of his tether. There was only so much he could take, and there was no way such a proud, professional person could operate under those conditions. We knew, and he knew, that it was the beginning of the end for him at Manchester City.

CHAPTER 16

The End of the Line

I was saddened, but not surprised, when Peter Reid and Sam Ellis left the club in August 1993. The ever-present Tony Book was placed in temporary charge of the players as we awaited the club's next move, hopeful that an inspirational, high-calibre manager would soon be appointed at Maine Road. With John Maddock in charge of hiring and firing, however, I deemed this highly unlikely. Maddock had neither the clout nor the credibility to recruit one of the top guys, and I doubted that any of the big-name bosses would be prepared to dance to his tune.

I wasn't wrong. As our game against Coventry City approached, news broke that the club had drafted in Oxford United boss Brian Horton as team manager.

'Brian *who*?' came the anguished cry from many bewildered Blues fans, who'd hardly heard of the guy. I was familiar with Horton as a player – he'd been a member of David Pleat's Luton Town side who had infamously relegated City in 1983 – but I was utterly gobsmacked to see him replacing Reidy. Maddock and Horton were buddies and had much in common, it seemed; both had worked within Robert Maxwell's empire, whether it was media or football, and neither had much experience of top-level club management. It seemed a nonsensical decision.

The 1-1 draw against Coventry preceded more mass 'Swales Out' protests, both inside and outside the stadium. The City fans had wanted to kick out the chairman, not the manager, yet Maddock and Horton had been foisted upon them instead. Stoking their fire was the fact that former Maine Road hero Francis Lee – who'd since become a successful and wealthy businessman – was now positioning himself as a potential investor in the club. A 'Forward with Franny' movement began to build up a head of steam, with supporters convinced that they'd found their new chairman and saviour.

The off-field unrest continued to affect me on the pitch. It felt like fans were just turning up at two o'clock on a Saturday to shout at the chairman for a few hours, with the football becoming almost incidental. It seriously messed with my head, it really did.

After a weekend of reflection I reached the sad conclusion that my future lay elsewhere. The club that I loved was being ripped apart and I was not prepared to be a casualty of all that. I'd given City fifteen years, man and boy, but I now believed that my career was at risk.

Horton's glib quotes to the press, along the lines of 'There's a lot of hard work to do,' and 'This will take a few years to sort out …' sealed it for me, I think. The man had inherited a team chock-full of highly skilled players, some with international experience (like me, Curley and Quinny) and others – like Mike Sheron, Garry Flitcroft and Richard Edghill – who were among the most exciting young players in the country. Yet Brian's comments appeared to belittle us all.

All we'd needed was for Reidy to have been backed or, failing that, a manager to come in and rally the troops and rekindle our confidence. Someone with a Howard Kendall-like intuition who could have instilled in us enough spirit to approach games without being distracted and unnerved by fan protests and behind-the-scenes unrest. Horton, in my opinion, was not that man.

My head had also been turned, I admit, by rumours that Leeds United had enquired after me. A significant transfer fee had been tabled, apparently, with Noel Whelan, Steve Hodge and David Rocastle coming to Maine Road in exchange.

That Monday morning I turned up for training with a heavy heart and my mind made up. Prior to our session, the new manager – along with his first-team coach, David Moss – gathered us together for a pep talk, telling us exactly what he expected of us. You didn't have to be an expert in body language to suss that most of us were distinctly underwhelmed.

'If anybody has a problem, my door's always open,' Horton said, slightly chippily, as if to say 'like it or lump it'. I took him up on his offer and went to see him after training. I didn't hang about.

'I think it would best for everyone if I moved on, Brian,' I said, explaining how the ructions at the club had left me feeling destabilized and demoralized.

The gaffer didn't seem interested in what I had to say, however, and just ambivalently batted away my concerns. He seemingly had no strategy or remedy, either; no plan of action to remotivate me and keep me at the club.

You're going nowhere, Whitie, just get on with it, seemed to be the general gist, and I left his office feeling incredibly deflated.

Horton's first game in charge was a 3–1 away win at Swindon Town, yet he still managed to find fault in our performance.

'You just can't afford to make any mistakes at this level,' he moaned at one of my teammates.

'How the fuckin' hell would *he* know?' hissed Rick Holden, neatly summing up our feelings.

* * *

My ankle continued to cause me no end of problems. Over the space of eighteen months the grinding pain had become progressively worse yet, other than a short lay-off following an unrelated knock, I'd hardly missed any game time due to my dodgy joint. The medical team, however, told me that I was fine to continue playing. As someone who was desperate not to miss any matches, I did just that.

In hindsight, the treatment of my injury was marred with errors and oversights. In those days, physiotherapy was basic, medical advice was sporadic, and sports science was non-existent. At Maine Road there was neither the staff nor the resources to ascertain the root cause of an ailment, or to develop an action plan, or to outline injury prevention. Back then, if you were a regular first-teamer and you said you felt fit, they simply took your word for it and named you in the line-up.

I didn't half suffer, though. Every Friday and Saturday I had to take high dosages of Voltarol in order to deaden the pain during a game and, if we were playing twice a week, I took them every day. There were plenty of occasions when I should have declared myself unfit and sat matches out, but I was desperate to avoid missing a game and losing my place.

By playing through my injury and incessantly popping pills, I was risking my long-term health, of course. Like many professional footballers I had a 'live for today' mentality and didn't waste my energy worrying about the consequences.

The detrimental effect of my ankle injury became twofold. The pain clearly impacted upon my match-day performances – I had some seriously woeful games when it was giving me gyp – but I was also unable to train properly. I'd never been a huge fan of the gym, preferring to create my own fitness routines to keep myself sharp; these would usually comprise crossing practice, shooting exercises, short sprints or interval runs. When my injury kicked in, though, I simply couldn't perform these drills without suffering intense, searing pain. I had to forsake them in order to conserve myself for a match day and – without my usual edge – my form during the Horton era dipped significantly.

A few weeks after our initial 'open door' meeting, I went to see the manager again.

'Just wondering whether you'd thought any more about my situation, Gaffer?' I asked. His subsequent shake of the head said it all.

'What am I supposed to do?' I said to Dad when I dropped into the yard for a post-training brew with him and Steve. 'He just doesn't seem bothered.'

'Just bide your time, David,' he replied. 'Sooner or later something's got to give.'

Horton's results that autumn were pretty decent, to be fair. We didn't suffer any defeats until Saturday 7 November which – unfortunately enough – just happened to be the Maine Road derby. We'd started well enough, playing in a 3-4-1-2 formation and racing to a two-goal lead courtesy of a brace of Niall Quinn headers. Worryingly, however, we were getting destroyed in midfield – Steve McMahon and Garry Flitcroft were frequently being left exposed – and our right back, Richard Edghill, without support, was being run ragged by a lively Lee Sharpe.

With that two-goal cushion we should have definitely reverted to a back four. Either Mike Sheron or I should have doubled-up with Edgy, thus sacrificing a central defender and adopting a more solid 4-4-1-1. Despite me and McMahon strongly arguing for this strategy during the interval, Brian Horton was having none of it. I was never the most vociferous in the dressing room, but I made an exception in this case; it was blindingly obvious how the game was going to pan out.

Manchester United came out all guns blazing in the second half – shock, horror – no doubt having suffered an ear-bashing from Alex Ferguson. For forty-five minutes they wiped the floor with us, scoring three goals to take the victory back with them to Old Trafford.

I stormed out of Maine Road that night, livid with the result, embarrassed by my dreadful display and frustrated at the direction the club was taking.

'I've never seen him like this before,' Dad apparently said to Steve as they'd watched me screech off the forecourt. 'I reckon it's the end of the line.'

A few days later, on Thursday 11 November, my beautiful daughter Georgia was born, adding some much-needed joy to what had been a grim few weeks.

* * *

Though it pains me to say it, the Maine Road derby was the last time I remember playing in a City shirt, and I have hardly any recollection of my last three or four months at the club. The official records may confirm that I made nine more appearances, that I was on the winning side only once, and that I failed to score any goals, but I honestly don't recall a minute of it.

It was my disastrous run of form, however, that finally spurred Brian Horton into action. Just prior to Christmas, he called me into his office.

'Howard Wilkinson's been in touch,' he said. 'He's really keen to have you at Elland Road. You can go and speak to him if you like.'

I nearly bit his hand off.

'I'd better go and have a look, then,' came my reply.

I drove over to Leeds the following morning, my first stop being a city-centre clinic for my medical. As I went through the motions, I thought it only right to raise my injury issues.

'My ankle gives me occasional problems,' I said, with some understatement, 'and it'll probably need a clean-out operation at the end of the season.'

'Oh, okay,' said the doctor. 'I'll add that to your notes.'

That was it. No questions asked, no scan, no X-ray, just a casual acceptance that I had a dodgy ankle.

With my medical done and dusted, I went over to Elland Road. I met and shook hands with Howard Wilkinson and, after some negotiations relating to the signing-on fee, I joined Leeds United that afternoon. The deal in the end became a straight trade-in for my fellow right-winger, David Rocastle. It was clearly a watered-down version of the original proposal that had apparently involved Steve Hodge and Noel Whelan, too; my stock, it seemed, had plummeted.

The following day I returned to Maine Road to gather my belongings. As it was Christmas there was hardly anybody about, and it felt incredibly eerie. I dug out my prized pair of Asics from the boot room but, sadly, failed to locate any of my precious number 7 shirts in the laundry area. Both my name *and* my squad number had featured on my back for the first time that season, and I was gutted to find that these tops had gone missing.

'I bet they're already unpicking your name, Dave,' said Steve when I caught up with him later that day. He probably wasn't too far from the truth.

Back home in Warrington, I received a well-wishing phone call from Keith Curle.

'All the best, Whitie,' he said. 'Just let me know where the tunnel to Leeds is, will you …?'

* * *

So, after 326 appearances and 96 goals, with an average tally of 45 games per season, my City career was now over. It felt incredibly weird to leave home the next morning and, instead of taking the M62 turn-off to Manchester, heading east towards Yorkshire.

Although they'd had a disastrous season the year before, I immediately sensed a huge buzz around Elland Road. Given that they'd been champions just eighteen months previously, and having observed the ridiculous situation at Maine Road, it came as no surprise that, to me, Leeds United felt a whole lot more professional.

The crowds at Leeds were almost double those I'd been used to at City, too. Only 21,000 had gone through the turnstiles at my last home league game, but 40,000 fans were packed into the stadium for my debut against QPR on Wednesday 29 December, which we drew 1–1 courtesy of a Steve Hodge goal.

The quality on show that night was incredible. In Gary McAllister it became clear that I was playing alongside a genius of a footballer and, with the superb Gordon Strachan featuring too, I almost felt like an imposter in David Batty's number 4 shirt. Gary Speed was unavailable that evening, so Hodgey completed the midfield line-up. Brian Deane was deployed up front with Rod Wallace, and Gary Kelly, Jon Newsome, Chris Fairclough and Tony Dorigo played in our back line, with Mark Beeney between the sticks.

A clause in my contract dictated that I had to move to the Leeds area, so Leanne and I found some rented accommodation in Huddersfield, close to our friends Andy and Jo Thackeray. We'd also put down a deposit to build a house on a plot of land in Holmfirth (of *Last of the Summer Wine* fame) that would give me a quick route to the brand-new training ground being built at Thorp Arch, near Boston Spa. This hi-tech facility – touted as one of the best in the Premier League – had been one of Wilkinson's main selling points.

The existing training pitches at Elland Road – located a minute's walk from the changing rooms – soon became a problem, though. I couldn't have found a worse environment for my ankle; not only was the surface rock hard and bumpy, the ground was always bloody freezing.

'It's five degrees colder than Manchester, here,' I'd moan to my new teammates as we shivered in the icy Pennine wind. 'Have you got your own microclimate in Yorkshire, or what?'

I'm no soft-arse – I never wore long-sleeved shirts or gloves for matches – but fuck me, it was like winter all year.

Given all the stories I'd heard about Howard Wilkinson being a tough taskmaster, everything seemed surprisingly casual and easy-going at Leeds. We didn't have to be on the training pitch until 11 o'clock, which was a revelation to someone accustomed to 9 a.m. starts. I'd always arrive at Elland Road at about half-nine, but some of the other lads would regularly roll up in the car park at five to eleven. These latecomers would disappear into the changing rooms before emerging onto the pitch, wiping the sleep from their eyes and pulling on their shirts as Mick Hennigan, the coach, crossly tapped his watch.

While Mick was a great guy, he wasn't the most modern-thinking coach in the world. Anyone coming to the club expecting to be dazzled by some hi-tech training methods gleaned from a recent trip to Ajax or Barcelona would have been very disappointed.

'Big lap, lads' is how he'd kick off every single training session. He used to wheeze when he spoke, too – like he was gasping his last breath – and when I first met him I seriously thought he was mid-heart attack.

While we embarked on a pointless, piss-about jog around the two pitches, our coach would start setting up his cones for the session.

'For fuck's sake, it's eleven o'clock and he's putting sodding cones out. What's he been doing all morning?' Gary Mac would say.

'What the hell's he doing now?' Gary Speed would pipe up five minutes later, as Mick lined up his eighty-seventh cone. 'Is there a fuckin' 747 due to land?'

After the obligatory warm-up we'd go into the drills which, to be fair to Mick, were top quality.

Despite my best intentions, and despite regular first-team appearances in early 1994, I never felt on top form at Leeds. My ankle continued to bother me and, deep down, I knew that my physical state would thwart my chances of playing a regular and meaningful part in this side, certainly not in the first eleven, anyway. There was little chance of me edging out the brilliant Gordon Strachan; when I'd first joined the club, Wilkinson had experimented putting the Scot out on the left to accommodate me, but even then I hadn't performed well enough to justify my place. By the spring I found myself out of favour, out of the first team, and out on the sidelines.

One of the matches I'd featured in became lodged in my mind, but for all the wrong reasons. On 23 January 1994 we played Blackburn Rovers at Ewood Park and, for the first time in my career, I nearly walked off the pitch before kick-off. Three days earlier, the death had been announced of Sir Matt Busby and, in order to commemorate one of the finest managers to have graced the game of football, it was decided that a minute's silence would be held.

I lined up on the pitch alongside Gordon Strachan, a former Manchester United player who'd doubtless known Sir Matt well. However, as the referee blew the whistle to signify the start of the tribute, the Leeds fans in the away end began to loudly boo and sing tribute songs to Don Revie. They carried on doing so for the entire 'silence'. I'd never felt so appalled, disgusted and embarrassed on a football pitch. Had Gordon decided to walk back up the tunnel, I'd have definitely followed him. However, as our side's elder statesman – and the only ex-Red among us – I felt it was probably his call to make, not mine. Gordon, his face like thunder, remained professional and decided to get on with the match in hand.

The gaffer soon hit upon a successful formula without me in the starting line-up, utilizing Chris Fairclough in midfield with Strach and

Speedo filling the wide positions. I had no complaints; my form had nosedived, my confidence had tailspinned, and my ankle was fucked. Weirdly, I became the kind of player that had always pissed me off so much at Maine Road: that super-sub who'd be brought on when things on the pitch weren't going to plan.

This situation probably affected Dad as much as me, as there became regular weekend voids when I wasn't even named in the travelling squad, let alone the starting eleven. For someone who'd spent much of his adult life driving the length and breadth of the country to watch his son play elite-level football, this must have been a bitter pill to swallow.

Out of nowhere, however, at the beginning of April, Wilkinson gave me a start against QPR. Against all odds I went on to have a blinder at Loftus Road, scoring twice in a 4–2 win which prompted the Leeds fans to loudly chant my name. I kept Strach out of the team for the next couple of games – no mean feat – but, with my ankle starting to buckle under the strain, the manager took action.

'With things the way they are, I'll have to keep you on the bench for the last few games of the season, David,' he said, explaining that he was only going to use me when he felt it absolutely necessary.

Being sidelined like this frustrated me no end, but I was pleased to have finally contributed something to the first team. The final three games of the season went pretty well, all things considered. I came off the bench to score a great 'bender' against Everton (my favourite ever goal for Leeds), notched another at home to Sheffield Wednesday and, after starting against Swindon Town, added one more to my tally. It was great to end the season on a high; not only had we finished a respectable fifth in the Premier League, but I'd also rediscovered some kind of form.

Leanne and I were also settling well into Yorkshire life, having bought a nice detached house in Scarcroft, near Wetherby (we'd abandoned the idea of the self-build in Holmfirth, since the new training complex that we'd planned to move closer to was behind schedule). Sam and Georgia were happy enough at the local nursery, and we enjoyed having family and friends over to stay most weekends. Apart from my pesky ankle, life was all right.

* * *

In May I finally had the surgery which, I hoped, would help me reclaim the form I'd enjoyed earlier in my career. I assumed everything had gone okay; the pain relief was almost immediate and there'd been no feedback from the consultant to suggest that anything was amiss.

I just about managed to get through pre-season training that year, but it was harsh. The fitness levels were very high at Leeds, where so-called veterans like McAllister and Strachan were among the most agile and athletic players I'd ever seen. At the age of thirty-seven you'd have expected Strach to have struggled to keep up with his teammates – and to have even sat out a few sessions to rest his aching limbs, perhaps – but it simply wasn't the case. He was as fit as a butcher's dog, easily lapping us during twelve-minute runs around a cricket pitch. Tony Dorigo was in fantastic shape, too, as were Gary Kelly, Noel Whelan and Gary Speed.

As time passed, Speedo became a really close friend of mine. He was a fantastic lad, he made me laugh, and we just seemed to hit it off from the get-go. We became roommates during away trips, spending hours together watching TV, playing cards and chatting about all sorts.

I roomed with him during our pre-season trip to Malaysia in June 1994, and remember staying up until the early hours to watch the Italy v. Brazil World Cup Final in the USA as Speedo snoozed in the adjacent bed. It turned out to be the worst World Cup Final in history, with Brazil only winning after Roberto Baggio skied his penalty in the shoot-out.

By the time the iconic gold trophy had finally been presented to Dunga and the boys it was time to get up for training. From then on, my sleep pattern became totally and utterly wrecked – I only had myself to blame – and for the remainder of the trip I could hardly manage any kip at night. Following breakfast, training and lunch I'd be fit for nothing, and would have to get some shut-eye in the afternoon to ease my exhaustion. I'd be wide awake in the early hours, reading book after book while Speedo slept soundly.

'Dave, you look absolutely fucked,' he'd say when he saw me the next morning, all bleary and bog-eyed.

There's no denying that Howard Wilkinson could be a pretty serious and intense character, but he revealed his lighter side in Malaysia. Once, we returned from a night out to find him holding court with the staff in the bar, with a few empty wine bottles knocking about. The gaffer promptly challenged us to a Staff v. Players knockout singing competition, which finally got whittled down to Wilkinson v. White. While I never claimed to have the best voice in the world, I had a photographic memory for lyrics. I knew every word to each song he challenged me to – from 'Sweet Caroline' to 'King of the Road' – and I trounced him. Then Howard decided to stage a Staff v. Players swimming race, so we dived into the pool – the lads in their Calvin Kleins, the coaches in their baggy Y-fronts – as the other guests looked on in bemusement. It was nice to see Howard in relaxed mode for a change.

Somehow I'd done enough to be picked for the starting XI as our 1994–5 campaign began at West Ham United. I lined up at Upton Park with Macca, Speedo and Strach, sporting my new number 14 shirt (my old number 4 shirt was rightfully on the back of a more defensive player, our recent signing Carlton Palmer). Nigel Worthington was among the other new additions to the squad, as were the South African duo of Phil Masinga and Lucas Radebe. A few months later we'd also sign Tony Yeboah from Eintracht Frankfurt for £3.4m.

My first three games went okay but, against Crystal Palace – and in the aftermath of scoring a goal – I badly hurt my left heel. I had a cortisone injection prior to the next game against Manchester United but, just fifteen minutes later, came off the pitch in agony. A resulting scan identified a stress fracture, and I had to spend the next few weeks with my foot encased in plaster. My heel felt fine when I finally made my comeback, but sadly my bastard ankle was playing up again. As winter loomed, the training pitch hardened, and the jarring pain I suffered on the rock-solid surface became unbearable.

Also causing me some grief was the gaffer's training regime which

– to put it mildly – could be tedious. He liked to plan meticulously for individual games, did Howard, and the minute one match was over, he'd immediately start preparing us for the next, starting with the Monday morning session.

'Right, Liverpool on Saturday, lads,' he'd say, before explaining that we'd be spending the next few days mocking up certain match scenarios. Not being a regular first-teamer, I'd often be tasked with pretending to be an opponent.

'You're Rob Jones for the week, David,' he'd tell me, and I'd have to modify my play accordingly, like some kind of footballing imposter. I found this charade absolutely soul destroying.

'No, Jones wouldn't do that, David ...' Howard would moan as I ran past, trailed by Rod Wallace. 'He'd cut it back to his left foot, wouldn't he? Let's do it again ...'

It was boring enough for the players who were in the first team, let alone those of us who weren't. After limping off in the morning I'd voluntarily spend the afternoon training session with Paul Hart, Eddie Gray and their youth squad. Some Tuesday and Wednesday evenings I'd also turn out for Mick Hennigan's reserve side, often operating up front on my own.

I had a spell of decent form in early 1995, however, and found myself back in the first-team starting line-up, playing eleven consecutive games including, towards the end of February, an away trip to Maine Road. I was admittedly very, very nervous about returning to my old ground. My departure from the club had coincided with one of my fallow periods, and I feared that might have left a sour taste in many supporters' mouths.

Being called 'Judas' by a lad in a City shirt as I got off the bus at Maine Road only served to heighten my concerns. My worries faded, however, when I walked out onto that familiar pitch to be met with the loudest standing ovation I'd ever received in my career.

Maybe they liked me all along, I remember thinking to myself as I acknowledged the applause and swallowed the lump in my throat, all the while recalling the paranoia that had often blighted my Maine Road career. The game finished goalless and, for once in my life, I was quite glad that I didn't get the opportunity to score. There's absolutely no way I could have celebrated.

Back at Elland Road, it was time for Gordon Strachan to bid farewell to us all, having been signed by Coventry City. Strach was an incredible professional and had been a wonderful servant to the club. Granted, he occasionally wound up some of his teammates – he expected everyone to share his exacting standards – but I think the vast majority of players and fans were incredibly sad to see him leave for pastures new.

Any hopes that Strach's departure might have signalled fresh opportunities for me were soon dashed. The manager promptly changed his team's system, with John Pemberton operating as a third central defender, Gary Kelly and Tony Dorigo pushing forward as wing backs, and Macca, Speedo and Carlton deployed in midfield. It all seemed to be working out for them, too – the new-look side put in some decent performances – so I could hardly really grumble.

In the spring of 1995 I'd reached the point where – due to my excruciating ankle pain – I simply couldn't continue playing. I told the physios, Alan Sutton and Geoff Ladley, that I needed another clean-out operation and was immediately packed off for yet more surgery. A couple of days later, when I returned to the ground to start rehab, I was greeted with a pair of gloomy expressions. Alan and Geoff had spoken with the consultant and broke the bad tidings that, in the ten months between both operations, my ankle had deteriorated badly.

'We're sorry to have to tell you this, David, but we don't think you've got a lot of football left in you,' said Alan, sadly shaking his head.

I'd always hoped to keep playing into my thirties – at this stage I was still only twenty-seven – so this news shook me to my foundations. It seemed the countdown to the end of my career had begun.

CHAPTER 17

A Bombshell

It was during my spell at Leeds that Dad shared some shocking, earth-shattering news. As with many pivotal, memorable moments in life, I can picture exactly where I was; walking past the red-brick garage next to his house in Swinton, on a warm and sunny afternoon.

'You're never going to believe this, David,' he'd said, 'but Barry Bennell's been accused of being a paedophile.'

Oh my fucking God, I thought, this bombshell news almost throwing me off balance.

I could hardly think straight as Dad explained that a complaint had been made by a young British lad who'd been on a football tour in Florida. Bennell had since been remanded in custody in the United States, pending trial. As my father went through more details, his expression incredulous, I braced myself for the inevitable question.

'You never heard about anything like this going on, did you, son?' he asked, quizzically raising his eyebrows.

'No, absolutely not,' I replied. 'Never heard a thing.'

'Are you sure about that?'

'Course I am, Dad.'

'Thought so,' he said, with a sigh of relief. 'Sounds like someone's got it in for him. As if he'd do anything like that.'

I found myself nodding my head in agreement.

'Yeah, as if …'

Shortly afterwards, though, things took a disturbing turn. Much to my dismay, I discovered that Dad had gone to the lengths of sending money to Bennell's family. He'd got married at some point, by all accounts, and – perhaps in an attempt to reinvent himself – had apparently dispensed with the 'Bené' nickname, too. Convinced that our coach was an innocent man, a group of ex-Whitehill parents had staged a whip-round, to which Dad had gladly contributed £200.

'He's locked up in a foreign country because of some daft bloody witch-hunt, and all the while his wife hasn't got two pennies to rub together,' he said. 'This is the very least I can do.'

My stomach was in knots as I drove over to Elland Road the following morning. The shocking developments in Florida had left me deeply unsettled and, not only that, the thoughts of my own father rallying round the perpetrator of my abuse – albeit unwittingly – had made me feel nauseous. Not for the first time, I'd found myself telling a lie in order to protect my father and my family. Judging by our conversation outside the garage, Dad had taken my straight-faced denials at face value; my firm rebuttals, it seemed, had been enough to confirm that Bennell had been wrongly accused, and had also dispelled any passing fears that my coach possessed a sinister side.

Sometime later, however, my father was forced to revise his opinion. News reached us from across the Atlantic that Bennell had pleaded guilty to the charges of sexual assault, and that a US judge had subsequently handed down a four-year prison sentence.

I truly don't know what Dad's exact thought processes were at the time, because he never, ever mentioned Bennell again. From then on, he was virtually airbrushed from history. Maybe my father was in denial, fearful of delving deeper and unearthing an unpalatable truth. Perhaps he felt guilt, questioning himself for entrusting Bennell with me, whether it was at home or abroad. Or maybe – and perhaps more likely, I reckon – he just moved on with a clear conscience, convinced that I'd told the truth, and confident that Bennell had never laid a finger on me. I'll never know for sure.

At some point, following Bennell's conviction in Florida, I remember having a passing conversation with Gary Speed. He'd also been one of his protégés at Whitehill FC, albeit a couple of years below me.

'You played for Whitehill, didn't you, Whitie?' he casually asked me one day at Elland Road, after a training session.

'Yep.'

'Did you play for Barry?'

'Yeah, I did.'

'Were you ever aware of all that stuff he got up to?'

'No, I wasn't, Speedo.'

'Nah, me neither. Terrible though, eh?'

'Yeah, awful.'

I got the distinct impression during this brief exchange that Gary had not suffered the same fate as me. It was my interpretation then, and it remains my interpretation now.

* * *

Leeds United's 1994–5 season ended in nail-biting fashion. To qualify for the UEFA Cup competition, as opposed to the inferior Intertoto Cup, the lads needed a result against Spurs at White Hart Lane. I hadn't made the squad but remember watching the game on TV, Brian Deane's goal earning a 1–1 draw and – thankfully – avoiding an early pre-season recall to play the Intertoto.

The squad chose Marbella again for our end-of-season team-bonding trip. We flew into Gibraltar on this occasion, my flight marred slightly by the blocked ears that I'd often suffer from on aeroplanes. I still managed a few beers on the plane, though. A couple of hours later, as we walked up to our hotel, I tried to clear my ears by pinching my nostrils and blowing. Not the best idea, in hindsight, because I immediately passed out, toppling over and smashing my face onto the pavement. As I came to, I remember seeing all the lads surrounding me, wearing concerned expressions.

'Are you pissed or what, Whitie? You only had a couple of bottles,' said Mick Hennigan.

I explained my ear issues to him, whereupon he told me that I'd have to get checked out by a doctor before I'd be allowed to go on the lash in

Puerto Banus. It felt like the most important fitness test of my life. I sat nervously in my hotel room with Speedo, my face a patchwork of cuts and bruises, as a GP gave me the once-over.

'As long as you take it easy you can go out,' he declared, and I punched the air like I'd scored a winning goal at Wembley. Within half an hour Speedo and I had joined the lads at Sinatra's Bar, where we proceeded to do anything but take it easy.

We also used our trip to Spain to host a stag night for David Wetherall, who was due to get married that summer. Plenty of drinks were downed in the pavement bars, and at one point a prankster teammate pushed Dave into the harbour. After thrashing about in the sea for a few minutes, he started to panic.

'I can't get out. The walls are too high,' he wailed, at which Speedo and Gary Kelly – who both possessed a daredevil streak – shinned down some mooring ropes, jumped into the water and hauled a bedraggled Wethers onto dry land. The poor lad was then tied to a pillar in Sinatra's, dripping with seawater as we poured San Miguel down his throat all night. Speedo and Kells, both drenched, never bothered going home to get changed, choosing just to carry on regardless, piss-wet through.

I got to know my teammate Carlton Palmer quite well during our time in Marbella. Not only was he a superb player, he was a top lad with a great self-deprecating sense of humour. I remember visiting a local restaurant with him, Speedo and our kit man, Shaun Hardy. Carlton had just returned from a pee, and in the meantime Speedo had ordered some pizzas.

'Mate, we're all having Margheritas. D'you want the same?

'Nah, fuck that fancy cocktail shit. I'll just have a vodka and orange ...' he replied, blissfully unaware of his double faux pas.

Another night, while passing around a huge bottle of peach schnapps, we noticed a flash so-and-so strutting and swaggering around Sinatra's. With his open-necked shirt and gelled-up quiff, he looked like he'd walked off the set of *Saturday Night Fever*.

'Who the fuck's this prick?' we asked, before realizing, upon closer inspection, that it was Robbie Williams. Robbie – who'd not long since quit Take That – had been partying at the other end of the bar with some Liverpool FC lads – including Neil Ruddock, Jamie Redknapp and John Barnes – and they'd told him to mince past our table, just to wind us up. He was a good laugh, to be fair, and was clearly enjoying his post-boyband freedom. Let's just say he wasn't short of female admirers that night.

Following a beery week in Marbella, and having lost a lot of fitness over the past year, I knew I wasn't in the greatest shape as our pre-season tour to South Africa loomed. Although my ankle felt much better post-surgery, I continued to be haunted by the physios' ominous tidings.

Once we arrived in Johannesburg I worked as hard as I could, though, and after four or five days of tough training sessions and testing tour games the squad was given a day off.

'Here's your spending money, lads,' declared Howard Wilkinson, presenting each of us with a brown envelope stuffed with the equivalent of £400.

'But we've got nothing to spend it on,' I remember saying to Speedo, alluding to our freebie meals and our dirt-cheap beers. While the other lads went off to the nearby shopping mall, Speedo and I joined forces with Gary McAllister and John Pemberton and headed straight to Sun City. With £1,600 in our pockets, we jumped in a cab to the airport and decided to charter a helicopter, as you do.

What we didn't realize, however, was that our five-seater chopper was going be flown by a bleedin' stunt pilot, and that we'd spend most of the flight almost shitting ourselves. He went through a full repertoire of aerobatics to keep his footballer passengers amused, from stopping the 'copter mid-air to dive-bombing down towards the Johannesburg hillsides. He even shuffled over to let us take turns in the 'shotgun' seat.

'Fuckin' hell, this is madness,' yelled Speedo as this nutter swooped over teams of farm workers, and missed electricity cables by inches while gleefully informing us that they were the cause of most helicopter crashes. Following an hour of this white-knuckle ride we landed in the Sun City golf course, enjoying panoramic views of the paradise resort.

With our crazy airman as our guide, our first stop was a flashy casino, where we frittered away some of our pocket money. Then we hit the deserted water park, hurtling down the massive slides like a quartet of overexcited kids. After wandering around the complex for a while and having a bite to eat, it was time to head back to base. Our pilot continued his air show throughout the return journey, though, and informed us that he was going to touch down at our hotel as opposed to the helipad.

Quality … I thought. Wonder what the lads will think of that …

Having finished their shopping trips, our teammates were in the hotel grounds playing games of two-touch football and head tennis. As the helicopter hovered overhead we could see them squinting up at the sky, doubtless wondering which world-famous, VIP celebrity was due to land.

They could hardly believe their eyes when me, Speedo, Macca and John clambered out, shook hands with our pilot, and gave them all a mocking royal wave.

'Bet our day was way better than yours,' we grinned as we filed past them.

* * *

It soon became abundantly clear that I wasn't going to get a look-in in Wilkinson's 1995–6 team. I didn't deserve to, in all fairness, but I realized that the time had come for me to take stock and reassess my life, both professionally and personally. While we'd really enjoyed living in West Yorkshire, Leanne and I were beginning to miss our family and friends over the Pennines and, after a long chat, we decided to put the Scarcroft house on the market and move back to rented accommodation in Manchester. The club preferred their players to live in the Leeds area but, from my new place in Worsley, I'd still able to commute to Elland Road in forty minutes.

It was nice to get the chance to see more of Mum, Dad and Steve. If there was no game at the weekend, my brother and I would sometimes venture out on the town for a few drinks and a catch-up. One such night we found ourselves getting turned away from Brasingamen's nightclub – a footballers' haunt in the Cheshire village of Alderley Edge – because, bizarrely, our smart suits had rendered us 'overdressed'.

A pissed-off (and pissed-up) Steve kicked a litter bin outside the bar and, during the taxi ride home, seemed to become increasingly agitated.

'Steve, don't get so het up about it,' I said, placing a reassuring hand on his shoulder. 'It's their loss. We can have a few drinks back at mine.'

'I'm not angry about that,' he hissed, suddenly signalling for the cab driver to stop. 'We need to get out. I want to talk to you about something.'

We then found ourselves wandering through a field in the middle of nowhere, in the black of night. I was as confused as hell, and was shocked to see Steve so upset, but everything soon became clear as he began to speak.

'It's not right what we're doing, David,' my brother blurted out. 'All this bad feeling between Dad and Nanna is starting to really upset me, and I think it's about time we started to see her again. It's gone too far. I miss her so much.'

He went on to tearfully explain that he'd heard a voice from God telling him to rebuild the relationship (unlike me, Steve has always been quite a religious and spiritual person) and that he intended to act upon this 'calling'. Indeed, this early-hours outpouring became the catalyst that prompted Steve and his family, following years of estrangement, to resume contact with Nanna Tom. I followed suit a few months later, visiting the bungalow on an albeit less regular basis with Sam and Georgia in tow.

It's true to say that my brother and I felt better with our Nanna back in our lives. My father, however, would continue to maintain his distance.

* * *

Back on the football field, I was put on the bench for the home game against Villa – I came on to score with a header – and then started at Spurs, where I did okay, albeit nothing special. I wasn't particularly surprised, therefore, when Noel Whelan got the nod ahead of

A BOMBSHELL

me for the UEFA cup tie at Monaco, in September 1995. While I was disappointed not to be in the starting line-up, I still enjoyed the experience of travelling to the principality and sampling the atmosphere of a European cup tie. Whelan fully justified his selection – he was superb – but the star of the show that night was Tony Yeboah, whose fabulous hat-trick sealed a 3–0 win.

Yeboah scored another three in our subsequent away game at Wimbledon. My own failure to be selected for that day's squad, however, made me finally decide that enough was enough. My agent at the time, Paul Stretford, convened a meeting with Howard Wilkinson, informing him that I'd assessed my situation and was looking to move on to another club. The gaffer, much to my surprise, promptly named me in the side for the return leg of the Monaco tie at Elland Road. I wasn't sure whether he was trying to placate me, but I knew damned well that, both physically and mentally, I was nowhere near ready for such a prestigious match.

As I'd predicted, I was bloody awful that night. Fortunately, our three-goal cushion proved to be too much for Monaco, although we disappointingly lost the game 1–0. Other than a brief substitute appearance against PSV Eindhoven in Holland, that was my Leeds United career effectively done and dusted.

It was while moving a vanful of belongings into my Worsley house that I received an unexpected call from Mick Hennigan.

'The gaffer wants you to go on loan to Sheffield United,' he said. It transpired that Manchester entrepreneur Mike McDonald, who two years previously had mounted an unsuccessful takeover at Manchester City, had since assumed control at Bramall Lane. Ironically, McDonald had sounded me out about the club's managerial plight a few weeks earlier, the Blades having lost nine of the first thirteen games of the campaign under Dave Bassett. He'd been a business associate of my dad's for years, and on this occasion had sought my opinion and advice. Via Dad, I'd recommended Howard Kendall and Adrian Heath as potential candidates.

After signing the loan papers at Elland Road, I hopped onto the

Blades' coach on the A1 near Wetherby, en route to a match against Sunderland. Later that evening, while at our hotel, I scanned the list of set-piece formations that had been left by the management team for the squad to digest. While I wasn't familiar with the United side at the time – and had hardly spoken to Dave Bassett about my role – I managed to decipher that 'MT' was picking up at corners, that 'RN' and 'MW' were both defending in front of the near post, and that 'NB' was at the far post for attacking corners.

'DW', however, would be taking corners on the right and would be stationed at the far post for corners from the left. According to this document, he'd also be picking up at the edge of the box for corners against. I went to bed nice and early, keen to get a good night's sleep and excited at the prospect of my first start in ages.

I was, therefore, as confused as hell when I arrived at the Roker Park dressing room, only to be informed by Bassett that I was on the bench.

I'm going to fuckin' struggle taking corners from there ... I thought and, just as I was about to angrily challenge my demotion, I clocked one of the few players that I *did* recognize strolling past and whipping the number 11 shirt off his peg. Dane Whitehouse. The left-sided midfield player. The 'DW' referred to in the set-piece sheet, of course. I afforded myself a little smile, realizing how close I'd come to making a proper twat of myself.

Incidentally, Dave Bassett claimed in his autobiography, which was serialized in the *Sheffield Star*, that I'd acted as the chairman's mole during his brief tenure at United. It was complete and utter bollocks. Never once had I spoken to Mike McDonald about the gaffer or his (admittedly poor) performance. Sometime afterwards I confronted Bassett to dispute his claims, and also spoke with the reporter who'd written them up.

'It didn't need a mole in the camp to see he was having an absolute shocker,' I said to the latter.

Bassett's inevitable sacking took place in December 1995. He'd lost 13 out of 18 games, leaving United in dire straits at the bottom end of the division. I laughed to myself when the announcement came regarding our new manager. Enter Howard Kendall – whose virtues I'd extolled to McDonald – along with his assistant, Viv Busby.

So, almost six years after he'd taken the reins at Manchester City, Howard arrived at Bramall Lane. Following his first game – against Ipswich, at Portman Road – he pulled me to one side.

'I want to make your move permanent, David,' he said. The deal was done the next day – for a fee of £500,000, if memory serves – and, once again, my ankle condition was casually overlooked.

Howard set about transforming the squad in pretty much the same way that he'd done at Maine Road. Certain long-serving players like Brian Gayle, Kevin Gage and Glyn Hodges were gradually moved on, while other United players – such as goalie Alan Kelly and his understudy, Simon Tracey – received the Kendall seal of approval. Roger Nilsen – despite being somewhat injury prone – was a very talented player, as were local lads Mitch Ward and Dane 'DW' Whitehouse. Nathan Blake was a prolific striker, finishing as that season's top scorer with a superb tally of 16.

Howard recruited a succession of really decent footballers. From Notts County came right back Chris Short, an exceptionally quick player and an immensely likeable character. Gary Ablett signed from Everton for a short spell, forming a brilliant defensive partnership with my former City teammate, Michel Vonk. Bringing some serious aggression to our central midfield was the pacey, tough-tackling Mark Patterson, and operating alongside him, with flair and finesse, were Gordon Cowans and Don Hutchison. Strikers Andy Walker and Gareth Taylor were drafted into the squad, too, as was my old pal Adrian 'Inchy' Heath, although he spent more time coaching than playing.

Howard's masterplan took a good few weeks to take effect; it was only after five consecutive draws and one defeat that things successfully started to come together. In an incredible spell of form, United amassed 39 points from 19 games at a rate of more than two points per match. An amazing feat, considering that the eventual League winners, Sunderland, had recorded an inferior rate of 83 points from 46 games. Had our campaign started the day that Howard took control, we'd have finished in second place and would have been promoted. Had it begun at the point that he made his first signings, we'd have walked it. We'd been left so deep in the mire by Bassett, however, that we eventually ended up finishing ninth.

My ankle had got through the season relatively intact, but I soon found myself on the surgeon's table for another ailment. I had a painful sports hernia – a condition also known as Gilmore's groin – which I got sorted as soon as the campaign had finished and, luckily, just prior to a Magaluf break with the players and staff.

As in Tenerife six years earlier, Howard Kendall and his entourage held court in a local bar, whiling away the time by sharing stories and downing San Miguels. There were guest appearances from Peter Reid, too – he was in the resort with his Sunderland players – as well as the then Blackpool boss, Sam Allardyce.

On the fifth night we all found ourselves in another bar, lining up the beers and watching one of those sporting blooper videos, the kind that always tend to be funnier when you're rat-arsed. I went to the loo halfway through, only to find myself cornered by three Leeds United fans. For the next fifteen minutes they proceeded to grill me about all the ins-and-outs of their club. They failed to suss that, after a while, I'd had my fill of Leeds talk and just wanted to get back to my teammates, who were continuing to have a blast watching goalies slipping on their arses. I waited for a tiny break in the conversation before politely making my excuses.

'It's been great to chat,' I smiled, 'but I'm gonna get back to my pals, if that's all right. Can I get you guys a drink?'

They went absolutely berserk at this perceived snub, hurling 'big-time Charlie' insults at me. I managed to duck away from them and back to the lads, but could feel the daggers in my back as I did so.

I thought that was the end of it, but much later that night I bumped into them again at a tiny bar, where the boys and I had been slurping cocktails through straws from a huge fish bowl. Out of the corner of my eye I noticed the Leeds lads, who'd clearly had a skinful, lurking in a corner.

'There he is, the bastard ...' one of them yelled.

Fuck me, I thought. *You had me listening to your boring shite for nearly half an hour, and now you want to kick seven bells out of me …*

In order to avoid any trouble, I turned on my heels and exited the bar, aware that my teammates would be able to calm them down or fend them off.

I confined myself to the hotel for the remaining two days of the holiday, not to avoid the Leeds meatheads but because, following five days and nights on the pop, I suddenly remembered that there were two lively and needy children waiting for me at home, and I didn't want to return feeling fit for nothing. As a result, I shunned any more alcohol and left my room just once, hooking up with my good pal Chris Short for a trip to the go-karts and a visit to a water park.

* * *

The 1996–7 season was a tough Division One League campaign, with Barnsley and Bolton Wanderers dominating from the start and the Blades spending most of the time hovering around in third place. That season's new arrivals at Bramall Lane included strikers Jan Åge Fjørtoft and Petr Kachuro, midfielders Nick Henry and John Ebbrell, and central defender Carl Tiler. David Holdsworth was also brought in from Watford and was installed as captain. Despite my glass ankle continuing to hamper my performances, I started the majority of games and was thrilled to score my 100th league goal, one of two headers scored in the 3–2 defeat against Wolves at Bramall Lane.

Despite our form fading in the latter stages, United eventually finished in fifth position, thus securing a play-off place. We were pitted against Ipswich, drawing 1–1 at home and teeing up a difficult return leg at Portman Road. I had a shocking game – I was pulled off in the second half – and Nick Henry was red-carded after some overenthusiastic play, shall we say. The lads rallied together and somehow managed to get us to Wembley, Andy Walker scoring the all-important second away goal in a 2–2 draw. A play-off final against Crystal Palace beckoned.

I contemplated the big day with mixed emotions. Judging by my awful performance at Ipswich, I reckoned I had zero chance of making my first ever senior Wembley appearance. Howard would definitely play three at the back against Palace, meaning that wing back Chris Short would be a shoo-in for a place in the starting line-up.

With eleven days to go until the final, Howard took the whole squad to the Isle of Man. Team-bonding trips certainly had their merits but, in this instance, I thought it was all a bit excessive. The trip constituted two full-on days on the beer, camping out at the appropriately named Cul-de-Sac bar (once Howard dragged you in, there was no escape). A few of us managed to make a quick getaway one night and, as we stumbled along the Douglas promenade, I remember my teammate Lee Sandford smiling and staring up at the sky.

'Look at that beautiful sunset, Whitie,' he said.

'Very beautiful,' I agreed, 'but I'm afraid it's a fuckin sunrise, Lee …'

It was all too easy to lose track of time in the Cul-de-Sac.

Back in Sheffield (and once we'd shaken off our hangovers) we resumed training. Horrifyingly, though, Chris Short – my good mate, and one of the most popular lads at the club – broke his leg during a morning session. He was utterly devastated, as were all his teammates. I took no pleasure out of the fact that, as a direct consequence, I'd now be taking his place at Wembley.

We stayed at the good ol' Bellhouse Hotel before the play-off final and, as we made our preparations, I was absolutely buzzing. Like most footballers, I'd always dreamt of running out at Wembley, and that momentous day had finally arrived. Making it extra special was the fact that most of the family – including Mum, Leanne and the kids – had made the trip down to London to share in my big occasion, Sam and Georgia sporting special 'DADDY' T-shirts.

Sheffield United walked onto the pitch that afternoon wearing a brand-new, all-white away kit – not unlike the Leeds United home strip at the time – and, although I say it myself, we looked the dog's bollocks. We felt great, too; having beaten Palace 3–0 a few weeks earlier, our confidence was sky-high.

The match itself was an incredibly tight affair, with little opportunity for me to push forward. Petr Kachuro went off with an injury in the 26th minute and then, crucially, we also lost Don Hutchison with a broken collarbone just prior to half-time.

As the clock ticked by, and with no goals scored, extra time seemed likely. However, with just a minute remaining, the ball was headed clear from a Palace corner. Eagles' midfielder David Hopkin controlled it, calm as you like, and hit a brilliant curling shot into the top corner to win the game and secure promotion. It was virtually the last kick of the match.

When the final whistle blew, I just collapsed to the ground and sobbed. My Wembley dream had ended, and my one last chance to get back into the Premier League had been snatched away. Sheffield United versus Crystal Palace, on Saturday 26 May 1997, would be the last time I ever played a full ninety minutes of professional football.

CHAPTER 18

Doing This For Dad

Sheffield United's failure to secure promotion wasn't just a personal tragedy; it had massive financial implications for my family, too. My father's business had invested a considerable amount of money when, in 1995, the club had been floated on the stock market, the shares almost doubling in value. Two years later, however, the Wembley defeat had slashed their value, eventually rendering them almost worthless.

Dad's interests in the club weren't just money-related, though. Not long after my arrival at Bramall Lane, Chairman Mike McDonald had invited him onto the board of directors, handing him the remit of overseeing Russell Slade's youth-team set-up. Mike had realized that Dad, having immersed himself in my career for two decades, was a 'proper football man' who had a great deal to offer the club. It was a role that he came to love dearly.

I underwent yet another ankle operation in the summer, around the same time that Howard Kendall announced his departure from Bramall Lane to return – once again – to his beloved Everton. It was a shocking blow, considering that Howard had done an incredible job in his brief time at the club.

Nigel Spackman was asked to step up – he'd previously worked as Howard's player-assistant manager – and soon brought in former Manchester City legend Willie Donachie as his coach. Training was great that summer. Willie was still fighting fit – he loved taking us on long runs – and, having worked really hard, I felt in decent shape. Joining the lads on the training pitches were a couple of exciting signings too, namely Brian Deane – a lad I knew well from Leeds – and my old Aston Villa nemesis, Paul McGrath. Star players Dean Saunders and Ian Rush also arrived at Bramall Lane, as did Portuguese striker Marcelo and Greek full back Vas Borbokis.

On the eve of our tour to Norway I badly strained a calf muscle. I was gutted, but was still keen to make the trip. I remember the lads giving me grief when I arrived at the airport armed with two huge sports bags.

'Bloody hell, Whitie, how much gear are you bringing? We're not off to Marbella …'

What my teammates didn't know was that I'd visited this part of Norway before, and knew there was fuck all to do. Mindful of this, my spare bag contained a huge roulette game, which soon took up permanent residence in the hotel lobby. We literally spent every spare minute gathered around the wheel, taking it in turns to give it a good spin.

'What a lifesaver this is,' said Dane Whitehouse as the ball bobbled from red to black. 'You've played a blinder, Dave …'

We staved off the boredom with an afternoon's trip to Oslo, too, a few of us getting a cab and spending a couple of hours sitting on a moored boat and enjoying some beers. I loved the Norwegian capital; it was probably one of the most beautiful cities I ever visited as a player.

* * *

The Sheffield United lads started the 1997-8 season unbelievably well, losing just one game out of the first nineteen. Spackman had adopted a wing-back system, with Borbokis operating on the right. The Greek lad was an outstanding player, and I remember observing him from the stands, realizing that, even if I returned to full fitness, I'd struggle to oust him. Striker Brian Deane was in brilliant form, as was Dane Whitehouse at left wing back. Paul McGrath was everything that you'd expect, too: the guy was sheer class.

Once I'd been passed fit and ready to play, my appearances were mainly brief and were generally ineffective. I figured in a League Cup tie against Wrexham, but the usual aches and pains led to an abysmal performance and, as the game went on, I had a sinking feeling that I'd reached the end of the line. Five years earlier I'd played for my country, yet now I couldn't even pass muster against a Division Two side. I trudged off the pitch with my head hung low, feeling mentally and physically shattered.

The next morning, I awoke to a loud knock on my front door. Standing there was my dad, his face contorted with rage.

'You're ruining my life,' he yelled, clearly referring to my calamitous cup tie. No sympathetic noises, no soothing words, no fatherly hug. His golden boy was losing his lustre and it seemed he couldn't cope.

The fact that he'd made a special trip to my house in order to vent his spleen broke my heart, though. I felt completely and utterly devastated. I just stood impassively in the doorway, with no answers, and with nothing to say.

I can't be doing with this any more, I remember thinking to myself. *I've had enough.*

Nigel Spackman ended up offering more help and sympathy than my dad, sending me to a specialist in London for a last-ditch consultation regarding my ankle. People were forever telling me that I was limping – I hadn't noticed it myself – but the doctor's video analysis revealed that, while my left foot ran straight, my right leg flicked markedly to the side. My left calf, he noted, was also considerably larger than my right. It was the first time I'd ever benefited from 'modern' sport science and, while I was grateful to Nigel for doing something positive for me, I felt it was a case of too little, too late.

The prognosis from the specialist was depressing.

'You've only got a very slim chance of playing again, David,' he said, 'and even that would be dependent on major surgery and lengthy rehabilitation.'

* * *

A few days later, despite feeling as creaky as an OAP, I travelled with the squad to our match against Huddersfield Town. At one point, Nigel took me aside for a quiet word.

'I've been thinking a lot about this, David, and I reckon it might be a good idea for you to find another club,' he said.

It was the last thing I needed to hear.

'No disrespect,' he continued, 'but you and I both know you won't be getting much game time here. It'd be for your own good.'

'I'm going nowhere, gaffer,' I replied tetchily, explaining that I'd decided to see another specialist about the possibility of ankle surgery, this time in Manchester, and that I intended to stay at Bramall Lane and see out the remaining two years of my contract. Nigel couldn't really argue with that.

The appointment with the consultant yielded a make-or-break dilemma. The procedure, he told me, would involve cutting into my ankle bone in order to generate some artificial cartilage that would act as a buffer. There would be no guarantees, though. If the operation was a success, the pain might subside slightly, and there'd be a fair chance that I could resume my career. If it failed, the discomfort would continue and I'd be finished as a footballer. I knew the odds were stacked against me, but couldn't bear the pain any longer.

'You need to decide whether you want to go ahead, David,' said the surgeon.

I took the plunge. Just before my thirtieth birthday, I checked into the BUPA hospital in Whalley Range, a mile or so away from Maine Road. The operation went to plan, apparently, and I was sent home on crutches the following day. Within hours of discharge, however, I collapsed in agony, flailing around on my lounge floor while attempting to make frantic SOS phone calls to family members. I'd never experienced such excruciating pain in my life. Eventually, my sister-in-law, Helen, came to my rescue and whisked me back to hospital, where I was kept in for another week.

Once I'd recuperated, I resumed my daily Stockport-to-Sheffield rail trips, often sharing a carriage with my Blades' teammates, John Ebbrell and Nick Henry. Chugging through the Peak District on a train was always far less hassle than getting stuck in traffic jams over the Snake Pass, and it gave us a good opportunity to have a chat. John and I shared a similar predicament – both of us were trying to come back from chronic injuries – and we'd often train together at Shirecliffe, going for long, laborious jogs, far away from the first team.

During the last few months of the season I tried my best to remain upbeat and positive, convincing myself that I could somehow prolong my football career. I remember telling John that, if I carried on working hard, I'd soon be ready for a run-out with United's reserve team. I also mulled over the idea of playing lower-league football, where I could have still earned some decent money.

'The Conference would probably have me, John,' I'd say to him, 'and I might just be able to get away with my creaky ankle, too …'

I was kidding myself, of course. I was light years away from any semblance of match fitness. The injury and the surgery had robbed me of my balance, for starters – I often felt like I was wobbling around on stilts – and my trademark pace and acceleration had diminished. I found myself shirking away from training-pitch scenarios that I knew would cause me discomfort, and I'd do my utmost to avoid that tackle, to dodge that sprint, to shirk that free kick. Most tellingly of all, just the mere anticipation of pain made me fearful of kicking through a football. Deep down, I knew I couldn't get away with such a negative mindset in the game of football, at any level.

So, in the summer of 1998, I sadly and reluctantly accepted that my life as a professional was over. I was a spent force, and there was no point in damaging myself even further. It was time to quit, once and for all. Oddly, once the decision had been made, the financial wranglings that took place between myself, the club and the PFA superseded any deep feelings of sadness and regret.

* * *

It was in 1998, while still training with Sheffield United, that I'd received an unexpected telephone call.

'Hi there, is that David White?' enquired the voice at the end of the line.

'Yes it is … who's speaking?'

'Sorry to bother you, but I'm calling from Cheshire Police. We're investigating a former football coach of yours, Barry Bennell, and we're just wondering if we can ask you a few questions …' he added.

I almost dropped the phone in shock.

'We'd like to come and interview you at home, David, if that's okay with you?' continued the officer.

What the fuck do I do now? I thought. *I can't exactly say no to the police, can I?*

'Yes, of course,' I said, trying to conceal the fear in my voice.

I agreed to meet the police at my house in Worsley the following evening, and in the meantime descended into full-blown panic mode. I'd spent two decades trying to block out the abuse that I'd suffered, banishing those gruesome memories to the back of my mind. I'd lived with this dark secret since I was eleven years old, keeping schtum to protect myself, my family and my career. Now, however, this criminal investigation threatened to blow everything wide open.

Around that time, I'd been aware that, having served his sentence in Florida, Bennell had at some point returned home to Britain, only to be arrested in connection with a number of historical offences. Not only that, in 1997 Channel 4 had broadcast a *Dispatches* documentary titled *Soccer's Foul Play* that had exposed the scale of his abuse within north-west football circles.

The programme, which I watched somewhat warily, chimed with me in many ways and exhumed lots of painful memories. It described how this Pied Piper-type 'star-maker' had obtained the trust of lads and parents, promising them a route to their football dreamland. With their mums and dads on side, he'd invited these unsuspecting kids to various trips and tournaments, where he'd sexually abused them.

The documentary also featured interviews with various football-club officials, who'd suggested that Barry Bennell had become revered and admired for scouting a steady stream of talented young players, the implication being that his rumoured dark side had almost been glossed over.

The *Dispatches* team had managed to trace some of Bennell's victims, too, who'd painted a familiar picture of their coach's Derbyshire home, describing a youngster's paradise boasting video games, takeaway food, freebie football gear and pet animals. Harrowing testimonies and statements described instances of horrendous, intimidating assaults far beyond that which I'd suffered. To say that I was flabbergasted by the widespread nature of his abuse was an understatement.

Soccer's Foul Play then proceeded to namecheck various professional footballers whom Bennell had coached as youngsters. My heart nearly leapt out of my mouth when I saw my name and picture being flashed up – along with Rob Jones, Gary Speed and Andy Hinchcliffe – although there was no suggestion by the programme makers that we'd been among his victims.

Even though I'd been spotlighted in this manner, I'd never once contemplated that the police would try to make contact with me. I hadn't told a soul about the events of eighteen years earlier and, perhaps naïvely, had always assumed that my vow of silence and my veil of secrecy would protect me forever.

As I journeyed back from Sheffield that afternoon, though, I made the gut-churning decision to tell my wife about Bennell. With the police now involved, I knew I'd no longer be able to conceal things from her.

Describing what had happened to me in a Cala D'Or apartment, in a Butlin's chalet, and in a Derbyshire living room became one of the most difficult and emotional conversations that I'd ever had in my life. Leanne and I both broke down in tears as I revealed all the secrets, the lies and the heartache. With my say-so, she then rang my brother Steve who, within five minutes, had arrived on our doorstep with his wife, Helen. He was distraught to discover the truth of my ordeal and, again, the emotions overflowed. At one point I found myself in the strange situation of having to console my loved ones, instead of the other way round.

'It's fine, honestly,' I remember saying to my brother as he sat in my lounge, in a state of utter shock. 'Everything will be okay …'

We stayed up until the early hours, my feelings of relief so palpable as I was able to open my heart and talk things through. Following a long discussion, Steve and I decided that my parents – particularly my dad – shouldn't be told about Bennell, and all four of us made a pact to keep things between ourselves for the time being.

Nonetheless, I still felt that I needed some urgent advice as regards my stance with the police. I rang a friend of mine, a shrewd, clever guy with tons of life experience, who I knew would be able to guide me through the fog. He drove over straight away, and we sat down and talked things through. It wasn't long before my pal tackled the crux of the matter, addressing the huge moral dilemma that I now faced.

'Your priority is to protect Stewart, isn't it, David?'

I sighed, and thought for a moment.

'Yes, it is,' I replied. 'There's no way Dad can find out about Bennell. It would break his heart. It would destroy him.'

'Then if that's the case, maybe it's best if you keep the truth to yourself,' he suggested.

I'd found myself in a really awful predicament – I was planning to withhold information from the police, for fuck's sake – but that night I remained convinced that I'd made the correct call. First and foremost, I was doing this for my dad.

Less than twenty-four hours later I found myself nervously perching on a sofa in our conservatory, sitting opposite two suited-and-booted detectives. They posed a variety of searching questions, with my answers wavering between truths and untruths.

'So, David, did you ever visit Bennell's house in Chapel-en-le-Frith?'

'Yes, I did.'

'Did you ever go away on football trips with him?'

'Yes.'

'Did you attend any tournaments at Butlin's in Pwllheli?'

'Yes, a few times.'

'Did he ever take you abroad?'

'Yes, he did.'

'Where did you go?'

'I went to Majorca for a week.'

This particular disclosure prompted them to exchange sidelong glances.

'Okay, David. I'm afraid we've got to ask you this, but were there ever any occasions when you were sexually abused by this man?'

I paused for a moment.

'No, never.'

One of the coppers then looked at me and smirked.

'You mustn't have been his type, then, eh?' he said.

Hey, that's really fucking professional of you, I thought to myself, doing my damnedest to mask my anger.

'I suppose not,' I replied, deadpan.

'Did you ever hear about Barry Bennell abusing any other boys, David?'

'No, I didn't.'

'Okay, just a few more questions, if you don't mind...'

They then asked me if I was able to pass on any contact details of past teammates and parents who'd had connections with Bennell. I feigned ignorance about that, too. The last thing I wanted to do was to implicate any other lads who, like me, might have chosen to conceal their abuse for myriad reasons. And, judging by the lack of tact and sensitivity that I'd just witnessed, I'm not sure these policemen would have prompted any victims to unburden themselves in any case.

The detectives then thanked me for my time, shook my hand, and walked out of my front door. I never saw or heard from them again.

In June 1998, at Chester Crown Court, Barry Bennell was sentenced to nine years' imprisonment for historic sexual offences against a number of under-age boys, dating back to the late 1970s. The abuse had been prolific, his sickening crimes ranging from molestation to rape.

And, while my heart went out to those young men who – unlike me – had possessed the strength, courage and wherewithal to give evidence, I believed that I'd made the right decision for the sake of the White family unit. In my mind, and at that point in my life, I truly felt I had no alternative.

* * *

The late 1990s saw me gradually acclimatizing to life outside of football, edging into the active directorship that my father had vacated within the family businesses. Not having accrued much commercial experience, there was a lot of learning on the job and thinking on my feet to do, but somehow I managed to find my way. I can't say I grasped this new role with much enthusiasm, though; with the best will in the world, working in recycling and waste management was never going to compare with the heady heights of top-flight football.

Dad, however, continued to enjoy life within the game. His position as Director of Youth Development at Bramall Lane had seemingly filled the vacuum created by my retirement, and he devoted a lot of time and effort to the role, forging a fruitful working relationship with the club's Youth Development Manager, Russell Slade.

My father was well respected by United's new chairman, Kevin McCabe, and as such would often be asked to help with staff recruitment. There was a pretty high turnover of managers at the Lane in those days, and Dad told a story of once interviewing a candidate – a former Manchester United player – who'd rolled up with an agent in tow.

'I got up and walked out after two minutes,' I remember him saying. 'I told him I was trying to find a bloody manager, not someone who needed a manager themselves.' That was him all over.

We began to see less and less of Dad on a day-to-day basis as he channelled his energies into Sheffield United and embarked upon various golf trips and exotic holidays. As bad luck would have it, though, once he'd taken a back seat from business matters and had started to contemplate retirement, he began to experience health problems. He fell victim to serious chronic fatigue, and was eventually diagnosed with Myalgic encephalomyelitis, commonly known as ME. Sadly, there came a point when he had to all but give up his role at Bramall Lane, just as he was getting a real feel for it.

* * *

As I gradually adjusted to my new career in business, I also embarked upon a stint on local radio, co-commentating on Manchester City games alongside the BBC's Andy Buckley. While I generally enjoyed being involved on a match day, City just didn't feel like the same club I'd left five years previously. Much had changed, including its ownership.

Francis Lee had eventually taken control of the club in January 1994. While I liked him as a person, and respected him as a footballer, I was never convinced that he wanted to become Manchester City's chairman. From my perspective, it looked as though he'd almost felt obliged to take on the role, having been virtually carried to Maine Road on a tidal wave of 'Forward with Franny' goodwill. I might have been very wrong, but that was my overriding impression.

Peter Swales had reluctantly resigned as chairman a few months' earlier – he'd buckled under the constant abuse and intense pressure – and it came as no big surprise when the incompetent John Maddock followed him out of the door, too.

Nobody doubted that the modern game of football was fast overtaking Swales – I think even he realized his relative financial clout was dwindling, as were potential investors to the club – but, even so, the circumstances that prompted his exit were appalling. Say what you like about Peter – and I know plenty of fans and players who'll think I'm more than charitable towards him – but, in my view, he was a devoted Manchester City fan who cared deeply for the Blues. He made mistakes, of course – notably, in my opinion, promoting assistant managers in John Benson and Jimmy Frizzell, who both took us down a division – but his chairmanship wasn't half as bad as people made out. I reckon his unpopularity probably stemmed from the fact that his arrival at Maine Road followed a remarkable golden era, and the longer it took to restore those glory days, the more impatient the fans became.

Swales' judgement and decision making, I believe, had been clouded by the criticism that had come his way. To deflect some of the incessant flak, he'd handed over control to Maddock, who had proceeded to ride roughshod over the club, its staff, its players and its fans. Had Peter Reid been kept in situ – and I firmly blame Maddock for Reidy's departure – I've no doubt that City would have gone on to achieve great things much earlier than they eventually did.

Swales wasn't daft – he knew that his days were numbered at Maine Road, particularly with the emergence of fans' favourite Francis Lee. However, given some time and respect by the City fans and the new regime, I think he'd have managed his own exit properly and correctly – as opposed to being hounded out with such haste and hatred – and would have passed on the mantle with his head held high. At the very least, I believe he should have been invited to remain at the club in some capacity, perhaps as an Honorary President like Aston Villa's Doug Ellis.

I was greatly saddened by the fact that, towards the end of Swales' tenure, Manchester City seemed to bring so many problems to his door. He left Maine Road a broken man, by all accounts, amid allegations that his family had received vile threats from disgruntled supporters, something that I found both outrageous and abhorrent. He was treated appallingly by a section of militant City fans, I believe; it certainly soured my view of the club, and probably expedited my eventual departure.

Brian Horton tried his best in the aftermath of the takeover, encouraging a brand of attacking and creative football courtesy of flair signings like Uwe Rösler, Paul Walsh, Peter Beagrie and Nicky Summerbee. While his side won him plenty of plaudits from the terraces and in the press box, from where I'd do my match commentary (in the mid-1990s, the BBC occasionally asked me over to Maine Road whenever my playing schedule at Leeds or Sheffield allowed it). Not enough points were amassed, however. In his two seasons at Maine Road, Horton's City finished 16th and 17th in the league, avoiding relegation by just four and five points respectively. His win percentage of 30.21 per cent was significantly less than Reidy's 43.38 per cent (yes, I did the maths).

In the summer of 1995 the club parted company with Horton, and Lee promptly appointed his good friend, former Everton, Arsenal and England star Alan Ball, as his replacement. During his stint as Southampton manager, Ball had got the best out of the mercurial Matthew Le Tissier and the hope was that he'd be able to replicate this with City's £2 million summer signing, Georgi Kinkladze, who'd been recruited from Dynamo Tbilisi.

There was no doubting that the Georgian was a superbly gifted footballer; in fact, I'd go so far as to say he was a genius. However, the policy of building a team around a lad who scored at a rate of fewer than one goal in ten games, and who hardly ever defended, was deeply flawed. In fact, deploying such a maverick player in central midfield – and asking Garry Flitcroft and Michael Brown to drop deep to cover for him – was plain ridiculous. At times City even played three central midfield players to protect a fourth, and I'd often find myself airing my grievances across the BBC's airwaves.

'It's a crazy situation,' I'd moan from the press box. 'Kinkladze should be told to operate from a wide position with a proper full back behind him, or should be played as a number ten.' Decent midfielders like Flitty and Brownie, I explained, were being sacrificed to protect him.

Rumours soon began to fly that Alan Ball was presiding over a very unhappy camp. Not only were the players irked by the over-reliance on Kinkladze, they'd also had enough of Ball forever reminding them of his own (admittedly illustrious) football career.

'If he mentions his World Cup medal one more time I'm going to request a transfer,' one fed-up player revealed to me after a home game.

Top players like Paul Walsh, Terry Phelan and Garry Flitcroft were soon shipped out of the club, only to be replaced by arguably inferior players in the shape of Mikheil Kavelashvili, Michael Frontzeck and Scott Hiley. Ball's assertion that new signing Martin Phillips would become the UK's 'first £10 million player' was always going to backfire on the manager, too.

All hopes continued to be pinned upon Kinkladze, but it was this ruinous plan that largely contributed to City's eventual but predictable downfall. Following a calamitous game against Liverpool in May 1996, their relegation to Division One was confirmed. It wasn't lost on many that Peter Swales – who'd not long died of a heart attack aged just sixty-three – was given an immaculately observed minute's silence prior to that day's kick-off.

Alan Ball resigned his position just three days into the new season. What then followed was a farcical merry-go-round of managers, with Asa Hartford, Steve Coppell, Phil Neal and Frank Clark all taking ill-fated turns in the hot seat. While City managed a 14th-place finish in May 1997, things were looking ominous. Even the appointment of the highly competent Joe Royle came too late to arrest the slide, and a year later his team was relegated to the third tier of English football.

The Francis Lee period had been largely disastrous. From the sacking of Reid to the appointment of Royle – with a conveyor belt of unsuitable managers in between – Manchester City had seemed to go backwards with Franny, not forwards. It would take two decades to restore the club to the status that it had enjoyed under the tenure of Peter Swales and Peter Reid.

Plenty of mistakes were made off the pitch, too, the biggest being the development of the towering new Kippax Stand. This money-sapping white elephant of a project was a total eyesore, with no constructional link or architectural similarity to the rest of the ground.

'This isn't the Maine Road I know and love,' I remember saying to Dad when I visited my old club as a Leeds player. While I'd really enjoyed coming 'home', the ground and the atmosphere hadn't quite felt the same without the famous old terraces.

CHAPTER 19

A Flight to Mumbai

In April 2000, at the age of eighty-seven, my nan Alice – Nana Jack – passed away. I'd been on holiday when I'd received the sad news, and flew back in time for the Friday funeral. The next night I went over to Mum's for a few drinks – well, more than a few – and, with our emotions teetering, we ended up talking about family matters until the small hours. We shared happy memories of Alice – she'd been a wonderful mother and grandmother – as well as of her sister, Aunty Betty, who'd died a decade earlier.

The conversation also turned to Dad, as it often did when the wine flowed, with Mum revealing the extent of his obsession with me and my career.

'Stewart's energies were focused on you and the football, David,' she said, regretfully. 'You were always the conversation topic; always. Steve and I hardly got a look-in.'

I'd never properly considered the adverse effect that this must have had on other family members. It was only now, aged thirty-two and brimful with sauvignon, that it began to dawn on me.

'Don't blame yourself, love,' she continued, no doubt heeding my glum expression. 'It wasn't your fault; it's just the way he was.'

Hearing Mum's words really saddened me. And whether it was a result of the alcohol loosening my tongue – or a childish cry for parental sympathy, perhaps – that night I ended up telling her all about Barry Bennell.

'Oh you poor thing,' she said gently, once I'd unburdened myself. Then, as everything slowly began to sink in, her expression turned to anger. 'The bastard,' she hissed. 'The *bastard* ...'

Mum went on to tell me that, like all the other parents, she'd put her trust and faith in Bennell, and hadn't for one minute suspected that he'd had any ulterior motives. My father had assured her that the various trips, tournaments and stay-overs were all excellent opportunities for my football development, and she'd had no reason to doubt that.

'Dad can't find out about any of this, though, Mum,' I pleaded.

'I won't say a thing, David, I promise,' she replied.

Mum stayed true to her word, as I knew she would.

* * *

Around the same time, I joined forces with an old pal of mine, Les Edwards, to set up The David White Soccer Roadshow. Les had spent most of his life working in regional football, either as a coach or a scout, at one point enjoying a stint at Sheffield United alongside my dad.

Together, he and I devised some high-quality football sessions for children of all ages, which we ran during term times and school holidays. Les agreed to coordinate things behind the scenes, and I'd turn up on the day to teach the kids various skills and drills (well, those that wouldn't aggravate my ankle, anyway).

We took the roadshow into various schools in the Greater Manchester area where, after spending an hour or so on the pitch, we'd chat informally to the boys and girls and host a question-and-answer session. It went down a storm and, within weeks, attendances had grown dramatically. However, the more the roadshow expanded, the less time I could devote to it. Due to increased work commitments at the recycling yard I couldn't attend every single session, and Les had to delegate some of the workload to other football coaches that we'd previously trained up.

Inevitably, these coaches – as well as teachers and parents – became frustrated that David White wasn't turning up to his eponymous soccer schools. Soon enough, our disgruntled employees started to take the piss. Les and I would turn up unannounced at a school where we'd already received payment for twenty-five kids' places, only to find forty wannabe soccer stars running around. A couple of our coaches, their pockets no doubt crammed with extra fivers, were clearly taking us for a ride. Most of our staff were totally above board but, unfortunately in this case, the greedy minority ruined things for the honest majority.

The final straw came when I learnt that one coach was planning to relocate one of our weekly skills sessions and rebrand it as his own. Les and I didn't have the time for all this – we were far too busy with other stuff – so we reluctantly decided to wind down the Soccer Roadshow. Sadly, time and time again I'd come across similar deceit and dishonesty in the world of business. Les, however, was one of the most loyal colleagues I ever had, and still remains a great friend.

I continued my broadcasting work with BBC Radio Manchester, most memorably for the Manchester City versus Gillingham Second Division play-off final at Wembley on 30 May 1999. Although I never believed that Joe Royle's boys would fester in the league's lower echelons for too long – they were huge favourites that afternoon – I certainly didn't foresee the emotional roller coaster that occurred that Sunday. With just minutes to go, and with City trailing 2-0, many Blues fans had poured out of the Wembley exits, having resigned themselves to defeat. All hell let loose, however, when Kevin Horlock clawed a goal back on the 90-minute mark, and then Paul Dickov scored a dramatic injury-time equalizer.

When the Scotsman made it 2-2, my colleague Andy Buckley – Radio Manchester's Head of Sport and a huge Blues fan – promptly ripped off his headphones and legged it halfway down the stand to embrace his family. It was left to me to try to describe the goal, waffling down the microphone against a backdrop of deafening noise. City famously went on to win the penalty shoot-out, and the First Division beckoned.

It was a fantastic day all round, made sweeter by the fact that every City fan I met that day seemed to treat me like a hero.

'Whitie, you legend, WE'RE GOING UP!' they hollered, before grabbing me for a kiss, or a photo, or both. Whichever way you look at it (and despite more relegation–promotion see-sawing under Royle and his successor, Kevin Keegan), the play-off final marked a huge change in Manchester City's fortunes.

As the 2002–3 season came to a close, I was fortunate enough to attend another momentous day in the club's history. Manchester City v. Southampton was to be the final ever fixture at Maine Road, prior to the imminent relocation to the new City of Manchester stadium at Eastlands. I was invited to attend as a VIP guest, and would be paraded before the fans alongside City stalwarts like Tony Book, Mike Summerbee and Dennis Tueart.

I had a bizarre little encounter with former Blues boss John Bond at the Platt Lane Complex, as we waited to be transported to the ground.

'You're the boy White, aren't you?' he said (I was thirty-five at the time).

'Yep, that's me,' I replied.

'It never really happened for you here, did it?' he added, shaking his head.

After fixing him with a *what-a-fuckin'-weird-thing-to-say* stare I half-contemplated having a pop back – something along the lines of 'more than it fuckin' did for you, John' might have done it – but managed to rein myself in. There was no way some strange remark from an odd bloke was going to mar this special day.

It was a lovely occasion, only slightly tarnished by an anti-climactic 1–0 defeat. As I gazed across the famous pitch for the very last time, taking in the centre circle, the penalty spots and the goalposts, it struck me that a decade had passed since I'd last worn a sky blue shirt at Maine Road.

I'm going to miss this old place, I thought to myself. It truly felt like the end of an era.

The move across the city to an impressive new stadium, originally built for the 2002 Commonwealth Games, was an amazing development for the club. I soon began working there as a match-day host, rubbing shoulders with assorted ex-players including Peter Barnes, Gary Owen and Tommy Booth. My role generally comprised putting in guest appearances in the hospitality suites, where we'd chat with corporate supporters and sign autographs. I'd often be asked to visit an executive box to mark someone's special occasion, in spite of the fact that many of them didn't have a clue who I was.

'And who's this handsome chap, Derek?' some old dear would ask as I wished her and her husband a happy diamond wedding anniversary. Once, a sullen-looking birthday boy disparagingly looked me up and down before demanding to know exactly when Shaun Wright-Phillips – or another first-teamer – would be visiting his dad's box.

'Sorry, mate, I'm afraid you're landed with me,' I said through gritted teeth.

'Oh, right,' he replied glumly, before passing me his empty glass. Cheeky little toerag.

After a couple of years, with the business swallowing up even more of my time, I decided to quit my hospitality role at the stadium. I scaled down my radio work, too. In both cases, I found that a day's work was leaving me out of pocket; after forking out for extra family tickets and allowing myself my usual pre-match flutter, I was often walking away £100 worse off.

It was a decision I'd deeply regret. Without necessarily realizing it at the time, by severing ties with my Soccer Roadshow, with the BBC and with Manchester City, I'd created a barrier between myself and live football. I'd still watch matches on TV and would do the occasional radio interview, but it's safe to say that my interest in the game began to wane, and for a while I virtually abandoned the sport that I'd loved since childhood.

The family firm had to take priority, though, so I continued to run White Recycling with Steve, putting all my physical, emotional and financial resources into an industry that, as each year had passed, I had grown to despise more and more. It was a pivotal time in my life: a period in which nothing happened, but then *everything* happened.

A FLIGHT TO MUMBAI

* * *

The horrific accident that Dad had suffered thirty-five years previously, when a steel girder had crushed his left leg, had continued to blight him in later life. His ankle remained purple and swollen and caused him constant pain. I remember the whole family once visiting Center Parcs, a few years after my retirement. Dad and I, despite having enjoyed a few beers the night before, had both awoken at eight o'clock-ish (we were both early risers). We'd slowly eased ourselves out of our respective bedrooms, he with his arthritic left ankle, and me with my arthritic right.

I can visualize myself hobbling into the kitchen, walking with my right foot pointing outwards, almost at a ninety-degree angle, to counteract the acute pain. In my right hand was a glass of water, and in my left hand – which was propped against the wall for balance – were two painkillers.

Simultaneously, my dad lurched into the kitchen with his sore left ankle facing outwards, a glass of water in his left hand and two tablets in the right hand that he was using to steady himself. I remember squinting at this other bent-over figure – having gained some weight after giving up football, I now shared his bulky frame – and thinking, *Who the fuck put that mirror over there?*

At that moment we both clocked each other and – despite the pitiful figures that we must have cast – we both burst out laughing. A daft but spontaneous moment that I still treasure to this day.

The subject of Dad's dodgy ankle had been brought up after a routine prostate cancer check in 2001. Following the examination, the specialist had asked if there were any other health problems that needed to be flagged up.

'I sometimes notice a bit of blood when I go to the loo,' he admitted, almost in passing, 'but that's because of the pills I take for my ankle, isn't it?'

Dad had been told that his daily cocktail of painkillers and anti-inflammatories would inevitably cause side effects. Problems with bowel movements, he'd assumed, were part and parcel of this.

'Apart from that, I'm feeling okay,' he went on to assure the specialist, also explaining that the ME he'd suffered from for several years was generally under control, too.

'The medication may not be the sole cause, though, Mr White,' warned the doctor, who, as a precaution, booked him in for some more tests.

A few weeks later, Dad revealed the shock news that he was seriously ill. Although I know I was at work, I can't remember if he told me in person or on the phone (I think I had some kind of memory block) but I recall him being very matter-of-fact. Dad didn't do melodrama.

'I've been diagnosed with bowel cancer, David,' he said bluntly, 'but I'm going to do all I can to fight it.'

This revelation knocked me for six, of course, and the rest of the White family were devastated. There were no tearful hugs or emotional meltdowns between Dad and me, though; while we loved each other dearly, we just didn't have that kind of tactile, demonstrative relationship.

Dad subsequently underwent surgery on the tumour at Wythenshawe Hospital, and was fitted with a colostomy bag. Like many cancer patients, his life was never the same again. He was a battler, though – he never shirked a challenge – and confronted the disease head on. He doggedly refused to let his illness mar his enjoyment of life, and continued his glamorous holidays with Margaret. Whenever anyone asked us how Dad was feeling, it became commonplace for Steve and I to answer, 'Yeah, he's doing fine and on a cruise', or, 'No, he's not so good, he's on chemo.' It was invariably one or the other: cruise or chemo.

It was around the same time in my life that underlying issues in my marriage finally came to a head. In fact, had it not been for Sam and Georgia – then aged seventeen and fifteen – maybe Leanne and I would have called it quits a few years earlier. We finally separated in July 2009, on the first day of a twelve-night Mediterranean cruise. We'd been together long enough to not let this decision upset the kids and ruin a family holiday.

It broke my heart to see the children having to cope with the anguish of their parents splitting up, but they were ever so grown up about it and behaved like stars throughout. Leanne remained in the family home – I agreed to move out – and, as it turned out, we both found new partners fairly quickly. I'd met Emma in one of Manchester City's corporate lounges, while she'd been doing some promotional work. We'd soon got chatting – I was struck by how smart, pretty and funny she was – and I knew almost instantly that I wanted to spend the rest of my life with her.

Within weeks, Emma and her ten-year-old daughter, Jordan, had moved into the two-bedroom flat I was renting in Worsley. To say I had a houseful was an understatement – some weekends there'd be two adults, three kids and four dogs – and it became inevitable that I'd have to move once more. Emma and I relocated to a new rented house in March 2010, the same month that she announced that I was going to be a dad again.

Despite being in the early stages of a relationship, we were thrilled with the news. Only a few weeks previously, Emma had suffered an ectopic pregnancy which, traumatic though it was, had made us realize how much we wanted to have children together. However, before we'd even had the chance to consult with a doctor, I received a dramatic, life-changing phone call from India.

It was a message concerning my dad.

* * *

Every couple of years, Dad and Margaret would embark on an extended, three-month holiday and, in January 2010, their plan was to spend a few weeks in South Africa before boarding their favourite ship, *Crystal Serenity*, in Cape Town. However, alarm bells started to ring when, a fortnight into the holiday, Dad was admitted to hospital near Sun City, suffering with a painful open wound. He ignored our pleas to come home – 'I'll be okay,' he assured us – and, after receiving medical attention, he travelled over to Cape Town as scheduled.

Steve and I didn't hear much from Dad and Margaret for the next couple of weeks. We assumed that their varied itinerary – which included dockings in Zanzibar, Mombasa, the Seychelles, Maldives and Mumbai – was proving to be as exciting as it sounded. That wasn't the case, sadly. It turned out that Dad's health had remained a concern, and that he'd been in and out of the *Crystal Serenity*'s medical centre. When they reached Mumbai, on Tuesday 2 March, the ship's medics insisted he got himself checked out at the local hospital, doubtless seeking reassurances that he was fit to travel. The cruise ship's agent also suggested that, as a precaution, he and Margaret take their packed suitcases with them.

Dad sounded fairly positive when he phoned us from his bed, in Mumbai's private Saifee Hospital.

'At the very worst I'll be here for a couple of days,' he said, explaining that, once he was sorted, he was going to fly over to Oman and rejoin the ship.

We weren't entirely convinced by his optimism, though, and agreed that our stepbrother Phil – Margaret's eldest child – should go to Mumbai, not only to support his mum but to report back to us, too. I'd have gone myself, had there not been a million reasons why I needed to be at home at that point in time. Emma was pregnant, anxious for everything to go smoothly. Georgia was in her final year at high school, approaching her all-important GCSEs. And the company financiers, the Bank of Ireland, were rapidly retreating from mainland UK and had become ominously uncontactable. Steve and I were effectively shackled to the office, trying to sort things out.

We had to visit the Indian Embassy in Birmingham to sort out Phil's emergency visa – a hugely drawn-out process – but he finally landed in Mumbai on Wednesday 10 March. It was then that I received the critical phone call, Phil having spoken with Dad's consultant.

'I'm really sorry, Dave,' he said down a muffled telephone line, 'but I've got some bad news for you. They reckon Stewart's cancer is spreading very aggressively. It's not looking good at all.'

That conversation changed everything. My dad's health was rapidly deteriorating, and bringing him home as soon as possible became an urgent priority. UK medics advised us that the treatment he'd receive in Mumbai would be far inferior to that in Manchester and, even if successful, would entail a long lay-off and a travel ban. Following a long heart-to-heart with Steve, we decided that I should travel to India straight away to organize his homecoming while Steve kept things afloat back home.

It'll only take a few days, we thought.

* * *

After another few hours of chaos at the embassy in Birmingham, I caught the Heathrow–Mumbai flight sporting a warm-weather combo of T-shirt, shorts and Birkenstocks. My tiny on-flight bag contained the bare necessities for a whistle-stop trip: a pair of swimming shorts, two short-sleeved shirts, underwear, toiletries, laptop, mobile phone, passport and credit card. In a weird way, I was quite looking forward to the challenge ahead. Hop on a plane. Fly to Mumbai. Get to the hospital. Bring Dad home. Get him better. Easy enough, I thought, as I touched down at the city's Chhatrapati Shivaji Airport.

An agent from *Crystal Serenity* had sent a cab to collect me, one of hundreds of tiny black-and-yellow Fiats that swarmed around the airport. As I exited the terminal I was engulfed by a wave of searing, burning heat; it was like nothing I'd ever experienced before. The journey to the hotel was a proper eye-opener, too. It took me through acres of shanty towns, comprising hundreds of rickety wooden huts precariously perched upon steep hillsides and cliff-sides. It transported me over the huge, six-kilometre Bandra–Worli sea link, from where I could see the smoggy haze lingering over India's largest city.

Despite being located in Mumbai's vibrant, arty Colaba area, Margaret and Phil's hotel was pretty grim. It was also a stone's throw from the famous Taj Mahal Palace Hotel and Leopold Cafe, both of which had been targeted in the terrorist bombing attacks just eighteen months earlier.

'I'm not being funny, but I don't fancy staying here,' I told my stepmother and stepbrother, and within hours I'd organized our relocation to the Marine Plaza, a much nicer hotel situated nearer to Dad.

My first trip to the hospital was pretty eventful. The cost of the ten-minute taxi ride, in one of the tiny Fiats, was the equivalent of 30p. However, after experiencing one of these terrifying white-knuckle rides for myself, I reckoned I was being massively overcharged. It was a nightmare from beginning to end, whether it was the car's total lack of suspension and any working doors, or the absence of any air conditioning and legroom.

I'd soon learn that you were pretty much guaranteed to have some sort of accident in a Mumbai cab, however short your journey. Forget your Highway Code; drivers could speed up at will and, with the absence of road markings, the number of lanes was dictated purely by how many vehicles could squeeze into a road, door to door, bumper to bumper. Car horns blared constantly – even if you were legitimately stopping at a red light – and pedestrians were treated with utter contempt. Drivers would rarely stop for anything crossing their path, whether it was bikes, rickshaws, prams or people. The only exception was cows.

On pretty much every journey we hit something – a kerb, a wall, a roadside stall – and one day we eventually (and inevitably) hit a human being. I remember seeing this young lad jogging in front of us – our cabbie had no intention of slowing down to avoid him – and hearing a thud of flesh against metal, followed by a screeching of tyres.

Jesus Christ, I hope he's not dead, I remember thinking as the driver zoomed ahead, cursing the stupidity of the pedestrian he'd just hit. Fortunately, the boy managed to scramble to his feet.

The online photos of Saifee Hospital had depicted it as luxurious and palatial, like some five-star Dubai hotel. However, in reality – and without the airbrush – it was less salubrious. Once inside, though, I was thrilled to see my dad. He looked much better than I'd expected, and his face lit up when I entered the room.

'I'm not so bad, David, not so bad …' he said when I asked him how he was feeling, his voice sounding much stronger than it had done in our previous phone conversation. Apart from the odd bout of confusion

– he occasionally rambled a little, talking nonsensically – he seemed pretty comfortable.

'We'll have him home in a couple of days, I reckon,' I typed in an email to Emma, Steve and Mum, attaching photos of Dad lying in his hospital bed, looking relatively upbeat.

* * *

Sadly, my optimism was misplaced. Not long after my arrival, Dad's condition took a downturn, with recurrent bowel perforations causing him terrible problems. Sometimes I'd arrive for an afternoon visit – Dad having seemed okay that same morning – only to discover that he'd suffered another episode and had been rushed into the operating theatre.

My hopeful 'couple of days' soon became a week, which then stretched to a fortnight, which subsequently turned into a month. Over the next thirty days I'd make almost one hundred visits to Saifee Hospital, usually amounting to three or four trips per day.

Dad had to undergo four serious operations, each one representing a huge step backwards. His stomach was also fitted with five or six tubes which, out of sheer discomfort and frustration, he'd often try to wrench out. Alarmingly, sometimes I'd turn up to find that his hands had been manacled to the bed with bandages, like he was some kind of prisoner. I was horrified, and tore a strip off the hospital management. Not only did this pitiful sight break my heart, it also motivated me to employ two additional male nurses to monitor Dad round-the-clock. The other staff didn't object to their presence – they lightened their workload, I suppose – and paying for this extra care became one of the best decisions I ever made.

'While Dad's awake, I want you to hold his hands,' I said, telling them that under no circumstances were they to allow anybody to restrain him.

During one particular visit, another nurse summoned me to the hospital's blood bank. She gave me no indication as to why, and I remember worrying like crazy.

They're about to tell me his blood's contaminated, I surmised. *Or maybe there's some awful genetic problem and they want to admit me as well ...*

As I sat in the waiting room my mind was working overtime, and I found myself entering serious panic mode. Soon all became clear, though. It was *my* blood they were after. In India, when a patient received a blood transfusion, it was common practice – expected, even – for a relative to replace it. However, bearing in mind there'd been a superbug outbreak at the hospital – Dad had contracted it at one point – I made my excuses and scarpered. I felt a bit bad about it, but the last thing I needed was to fall ill myself.

My journeys to and from the hospital became less fraught as time went by, as I hired myself a reliable private taxi driver who collected me three times a day in his people carrier. Although he drove in a similarly haphazard fashion to Mumbai's other cabbies, I just felt slightly safer in a bigger car whenever we suffered the inescapable collisions.

Each day we'd drive past the same sights, such as the Charni Road railway station. Entire families would live and work outside this transport hub, squeezed into small blocks of pavement no more than ten feet across, with scant shelter from the sun or rain. Though I'd never before witnessed such abject poverty, it was also strangely inspiring. Despite their desperate predicament, these street-dwellers just seemed to be getting on with things. I'd see a grandmother lovingly tending to a baby while, just a few yards away, its mum and dad created beautiful jewellery that they'd sell to tourists. Next to them, another child would sleep soundly (due to the lack of space, the blankets would be used in rotation). There was a real sense of order – everything seemed so clean and tidy – which amazed me every time we passed by.

Things would become a little more menacing outside the hospital, though. Being a private facility, as opposed to state-run, the Saifee would attract hordes of homeless people seeking money from its comparatively wealthy visitors. Sadly, most of these beggars were young kids, despatched by parents who'd lurk around the corner. It was an awful situation. Whenever you handed over a few pennies these poor children would often be attacked by other kids, who'd try to prise the money out of their hands. I remember feeling distraught when I saw two girls, who couldn't have been older than six years old, fighting viciously over a few coins as their families watched on.

* * *

In Mumbai, like most parts of the world, you couldn't get away from football. The number of live televised games on the various sports channels was incredible, including most Premier League fixtures. Bearing in mind the time difference of plus five-and-a-half hours, I could find myself watching Champions League games until 4 a.m.

'United or City?' I recall a cab driver once asking me, upon learning that I hailed from Manchester. Gone were the days, thankfully, when foreigners just trotted out the standard 'Ah … Manchester United!' response. City's 2008 takeover by the wealthy Abu Dhabi Group, spearheaded by Sheikh Mansour, had certainly done wonders for the club's global profile.

'I actually used to play for City a few years back,' I explained to the driver, which prompted a lively chat about football and sport in general.

'Ah,' he smiled. 'Tonight there is a big match at the stadium, starting at eight o'clock. You should go.'

'I think I might,' I replied, grateful for the tip. 'I could do with a change of scenery.'

There were two sporting arenas in central Mumbai. One of them – the unfortunately named Wankhede Stadium – was being redeveloped so I made my way to the other venue, the Brabourne Stadium. I bought a ticket from a tout for the equivalent of about thirty quid (*That's a bit steep*, I remember thinking to myself) but, having spent a gloomy day at hospital, I paid up. I was in the mood for some live football to take my mind off things, and reckoned it would be a nice diversion.

It was only when I got settled into my seat that it dawned on me that there were no goalposts and no pitch markings. There were, however, two sets of wickets, two huge sight-screens and a perimeter rope.

I glanced down at my ticket. *Mumbai Indians v. Chennai Super Kings* it read. *Indian Premier League Cricket.*

Bollocks. Perhaps I'd misunderstood or misheard the taxi driver – my head would often be swimming after a hospital visit – but there was no way I could face watching cricket for three hours, particularly since I'd set my mind on some football. I left the stadium before leather hit willow, and watched some soccer on my hotel telly instead.

Most nights I'd order my evening meal via room service. I'm a really faddy eater – especially when I'm overseas – and I'd routinely ask the kitchen to bake me a simple lasagne. The hotel worker who always brought my meals over was a great guy; polite, professional and genuinely concerned about my dad. One evening he knocked on my door and, with a kindly expression, handed me some prayer beads.

'To help your father get well, sir,' he smiled.

They never once left my grasp while I remained in Mumbai.

CHAPTER 20

Dusting Myself Down

By early April 2010, Dad's situation had become desperate. The more he deteriorated, the more determined I became to get him back home before he died, or before it became medically impossible for him to travel. The family knew, deep down, that his passing was inevitable, but we wanted him to be in Manchester, not Mumbai, when that time finally arrived.

Making things more pressing was the fact that Margaret and I had also made a 'do not resuscitate' pact with the consultants. In the event of Dad taking a turn for the worse, we'd agreed that he shouldn't be kept alive artificially. Reiterating that conversation with Steve over the phone was as difficult as you can imagine.

'I feel so helpless, Dave,' I remember him saying, 'but I'm so glad you're there with him. Just hope you get him back home soon.'

At one stage I tried to persuade Margaret to fly back to the UK which, in hindsight, was both illogical and insensitive. My stepmother wasn't coping very well – seeing my dad in such a bad way had naturally taken its toll – and, if I'm brutally honest, I wasn't in the best frame of mind to give her much emotional support, particularly since Phil had returned home shortly after my arrival. The medical team, however, urged her to stay on, which she did. Margaret and I managed to get along okay in Mumbai, all things considered, occasionally whiling away the time by the hotel pool or playing games of Scrabble.

I do recall feeling very, very down on Good Friday, though. Everyone in the UK was enjoying an Easter break with the family, yet here I was, keeping a vigil at my poorly father's bedside while pining for my pregnant partner and my children.

A couple of days after making yet another hotel move – this time I'd upped sticks to the Taj Mahal Palace – Dad's consultant told me he was thinking about finally sanctioning his discharge. It was a decision, I believe, that was prompted by financial rather than medical developments. While my father's condition hadn't improved – he remained gravely ill – it seemed that a long-awaited insurance payment for previous treatment had finally been authorized. The hospital had been reluctant for Dad to leave until the bill was paid, so I'd spent days on the phone to the insurers in order to speed up the process and secure the £25,000 payout.

I immediately booked three British Airways flights for Thursday 7 April 2010, which also happened to be Sam's eighteenth birthday. For obvious reasons I was desperate to get back home in time, even if it just meant catching a couple of hours with my son on his big day. I did everything by the book, securing the vital 'permission to travel', pre-informing the airline of Dad's health issues and obtaining the necessary medical reports.

On the eve of our planned departure I'd visited a local sports shop to buy Dad a T-shirt, a tracksuit and some trainers. The next morning, when Margaret and I arrived at the hospital, my heart leapt when I saw Dad sitting up in a wheelchair, dressed in his pristine new gear and sporting a huge grin. Despite the ravages of the cancer – he was so weak, and still very confused – I'm convinced he knew that he was going home to his beloved Manchester.

Sadly, things didn't go to plan. With our flight being scheduled for 12.30 p.m., we'd organized an ambulance to collect us from Saifee three hours earlier to give us enough time to negotiate the Mumbai traffic. For whatever reason, though, we still found ourselves on the ward at 11 a.m. The medical team had spent two hours faffing about – if it wasn't unsigned paperwork, it was misplaced medication – and I was becoming frantic.

'Can we please get things sorted?' I yelled. 'If we don't leave soon we're going to miss this bloody flight.'

I got the impression that the staff were stalling for time; I could only guess that the insurance money hadn't yet been wired over, and they'd been ordered not to release Dad until the transaction had taken place.

Eventually we were discharged but, as our taxi trailed Dad's ambulance, I had a sinking feeling that trouble lay ahead. The temperature had hit a roasting 100 degrees and, since we were now behind schedule, both vehicles were travelling at breakneck speed over potholed roads. We finally reached the airport, only to find we'd missed the general check-in. *Shit, shit, shit.* The heat was blistering and my dad was flagging; in fact, he looked so pale and frail I honestly thought he was going to collapse and die there and then.

Then the panic set in. 'We must get this flight,' I begged a member of staff as I tightly clutched my prayer beads. 'You've got to help us … please.'

Within minutes the British Airways' pilot himself turned up on the scene, clearly having been alerted to Dad's condition. He took one look at him, and shook his head.

'I'm sorry, but there's no way your father's in a fit state to fly.'

No matter how much Margaret and I pleaded with him, he simply refused to budge. We were devastated. I remember ringing Emma and the kids from the airport, in floods of tears. Not only was my rapidly declining Dad marooned in Mumbai, I was also going to miss my precious son's milestone birthday.

I honestly didn't know what to do for the best but, since Dad was fading fast, I knew I had to act quickly. I was loath to return to the hospital in the ambulance, because I didn't want him to die there (and that's if he even survived another bumpy journey). I decided upon a last-ditch attempt to fly us home. I checked us into an airport hotel, drafting in the brilliant nurses I'd previously employed to care for Dad, while I sorted things out with a local travel agent.

After three days of exploring every option, I finally had a breakthrough: Air India somehow agreed to sell us first-class flight tickets to Heathrow on Saturday 10 April. I'm not sure whether they regretted this when we arrived at the airport, though. The ground staff and cabin crew were visibly shocked by Dad's fragile state, and the porters literally had to roll him out of the wheelchair and into his seat.

The nine-hour flight was an ordeal for Margaret and I. Fortunately Dad slept for most of the time, but we were struggling to keep his tubes intact and his dressings affixed. It can't have been very pleasant for our fellow travellers to witness, although not one person complained.

As we finally touched down in London, I discovered that I'd lost my precious prayer beads. I'm not at all religious, but they'd given me great comfort for a fortnight and I'd not been anywhere without them. *This has got to be a bad omen*, I remember thinking.

A private ambulance met Dad off the plane, which transported him straight to a local hospital to have his wounds tidied up. I remember one particularly unsympathetic consultant glaring at me, more or less questioning my rationale for bringing Dad back to the UK. *What's the point flying all this way? He's going to die anyway* ... pretty much summed up his attitude. Although, in my heart of hearts, I knew Dad wasn't going to pull through, I was staggered by this doctor's total lack of compassion.

Once Dad had been patched up, we headed north towards Wythenshawe Hospital. Emma had met me at Heathrow, so I travelled with her while Margaret accompanied Dad in the ambulance. After thirty days in Mumbai, it was fabulous to see my other half again, and to catch up with all her baby news.

'If it's a girl, maybe we should call her India', I remember saying as we zoomed up the M6.

While in transit, I texted a photo of Dad to Steve and the kids. I labelled it 'LEGEND', illustrating how he'd heroically clung on for the previous three days.

Over the next week, my father was reunited with all his favourite people, even managing to rouse a smiley 'hello' for Sam and Georgia, which was an emotional moment for us all. There were to be no more false dawns, however, and he died peacefully in hospital on Saturday 17 April 2010. Poignantly, as he slowly slipped away, the Manchester derby was being played out on his bedside TV, almost as if this lifelong Blue had planned it that way.

Along with the gut-wrenching grief came an almost guilty sense of relief that his suffering had finally ended. I also took a great deal of comfort from the fact that Dad had gone to his grave never knowing the awful truth about Barry Bennell. I'd done my utmost to shield and protect him for nearly three decades, and felt beyond pleased that I'd succeeded.

Dad's funeral, and the subsequent wake, was jam-packed with family, friends and colleagues. His close friend Fred Eyre spoke in the church – as did Steve and my niece Beth – and local entertainer Vince Miller sang a tear-jerking rendition of 'Abide with Me'. And that was it. My dad was gone forever.

There was much talk and reflection among my family in the aftermath. Most of us – including me, Steve and Mum – agreed that, while it had been a pleasure and a privilege to have Dad in our lives, it had also been bloody hard work (no doubt Margaret and her children would have concurred, too). My dad was, without doubt, the single biggest positive influence on my life and career. At times, however, he was the biggest negative, too. Despite his faults and failings, though, I'd never stopped loving him, and I knew that I'd miss him hugely.

On a sad note, Dad and his mother, Lily, never resolved their differences and remained estranged throughout his illness. It wasn't that my nan didn't care – 'David, you did so well getting your dad back from India,' she said on the day he died, and she chose to attend his funeral – but circumstances never prompted a reconciliation. I found it all utterly heartbreaking.

Not long after Dad's passing, the family were invited to a Sheffield United game, where a minute's applause was held in his honour as his picture was flashed up on the big screen at Bramall Lane. I remember bumping into my ex-Leeds teammate, Gary Speed, just before kick-off.

Though we didn't have much time to chat, I took the opportunity to tell him that Emma was expecting a baby.

'Ah, that's great news,' said Gary, flashing one of those sparkling smiles of his. 'Really hope everything goes well for you all.'

A few months later, our beautiful daughter arrived in the world and, as planned, we named her India.

I'd soon meet Gary again, albeit unexpectedly. I was holidaying in the Algarve in the summer of 2011, looking after our newborn while Emma and the rest of the White clan were go-karting. I was sitting by the track, minding my own business, when I heard a familiar voice.

'Oi, Whitie, what are *you* doing here?'

Much to my surprise it was Speedo, whose kids were lining up in the same race as my lot. It was great to see him again – he seemed in really good spirits – and we had a catch-up chat, Gary telling me about his new role as Wales manager and how he was planning to fly to Brazil for the World Cup draw. The karting race over, we shook hands, wished each other well, and said our goodbyes.

Just three months later, I was driving through Manchester, listening to talkSPORT, when the broadcast was interrupted by a sombre voice announcing Speedo's sudden passing. I was totally and utterly stunned. I nearly lost control of the car as I shouted 'NO!' at the top of my voice.

Over the next few days, more details began to filter out about Gary's tragic death, including the fact that he'd been found hanged in the garage of his Cheshire home. Like many others who knew him, I could hardly comprehend what had happened. All I knew was that he was a superb footballer, a brilliant manager and a diamond bloke. He'd been a great friend and roommate to me at Leeds United – I'd had some fantastic times in his company – and his passing felt like a hammer blow.

As the weeks passed, some sections of the media began to explore connections between Gary and Barry Bennell. A *Sunday Times* journalist, perhaps having seen our names in the *Dispatches* documentary, contacted me to request an interview for a piece they were writing. I declined. I thought that the resulting article, while thought-provoking, was a tenuous attempt to link Gary's death to his childhood associations with Bennell. No concrete evidence was ever put forward, either at his inquest or within the newspaper report itself, to suggest that Gary had been a victim. In my opinion – and that of the police at the time – I don't believe my friend's death was in any way related to Bennell.

* * *

In March 2012 Emma gave birth to our second daughter, the gorgeous Mali. We'd also managed to fit in a wedding beforehand, finally tying the knot near Stratford-upon-Avon, surrounded by our closest family and friends. However, life would soon take a downward turn. Having lost a parent, gone through a divorce and moved house on several occasions – all within a year or so – I found myself facing yet more stress. The collapse of my business, and the loss of my livelihood, was looming around the corner.

I'd given seventeen years of my life to the family firm, yet I can safely say that I'd hated every single minute of it. When I retired from football I hadn't hesitated in joining up with Dad and Steve, never for one moment realizing how traumatic it would become. Between 2000 and 2015, I don't think there was one night that I didn't go to bed dreading the next working day, or worrying myself sick about employees, equipment or finances.

Our problems stemmed from the fact that the waste industry brought together two elements that, logically speaking, should have always been kept apart: large, automated, potentially dangerous machinery and fallible, vulnerable, occasionally careless human beings. It didn't matter what systems were put in place, what training was carried out or what warnings were given; it was an almost uncontrollable combination.

In 2003, tragedy struck. An employee of ours, Rick Buckley, died on site as a result of a dreadful accident. I was in the car with the kids when I received a call from Steve, who was at the yard.

'We can't find Rick.'

A few minutes later he rang again to relate the awful news that his workmates had found him, buried under waste.

It was a horrific time for everybody, and Steve and I did all we could to support his grieving family and his distressed colleagues. The Health and Safety Executive attended the site of the accident and, although they found no reason to close the yard down or change any working practices, we were told to expect some kind of prosecution. The inquest, which took place eighteen months later, recorded a verdict of accidental death.

When we finally attended court, a further three-and-a-half years down the line, we were initially charged with five offences, three of which were withdrawn. In July 2008, however, the company was found guilty on two counts, namely 'failure to adequately separate vehicles and employees' and 'failure to adequately separate vehicles and third parties', which were basically the same offence. We were served an improvement notice that, in effect, required us to build a walkway at the side of the road (this, in all honesty, wouldn't have actually prevented the accident from happening, and I was aware of no other similar yard in the area with this measure in place). The financial loss incurred as a result of the incident – mainly due to lack of productivity in the aftermath – was crippling. We lost hundreds of thousands of pounds, although this obviously paled into insignificance when compared to the loss of human life.

The bad news didn't end there, though. As the result of another accident, this time out on the road, one of our skip loaders collided with a cyclist on a roundabout. The driver concerned was adamant that he'd indicated to exit as the lad on the bike had undertaken him. Steve and I had the unenviable task of telling the driver the awful news that the cyclist had subsequently died.

After these incidents things were never the same again, and I found myself living on a constant knife-edge. I'd wake up bolt upright at 5 a.m., fretting about my employees as they arrived on site. Each time the phone rang my heart would be in my mouth, fearful that yet another accident had happened. The pressure was unrelenting. It was awful.

Because I detested my working life so much I was constantly trying to change the business, to make it different and saleable so I could get away from it all. Over the next decade, however, we just seemed to suffer a series of false dawns.

The final straw for our business came in October 2014. I was sitting in the office when a member of staff alerted me to some smoke emanating from one of the waste piles. At first we didn't think it was a major issue, but it ended up burning for a fortnight. We had no other option but to close down the yard for safety reasons until it was quelled.

'This is the last thing we need,' I said to Steve, aware that our cash flow had never been tighter.

I remember going to watch that year's Super League Grand final between Wigan and St Helens at Old Trafford, not long after the fire had broken out. I can't describe the emotional torment that my brother and I were suffering that evening. We tried to enjoy the rugby while drowning ourselves in beer, as you do, but with our stomachs knotted and our minds racing, nothing could rid us of that tight, tensed-up feeling of dread. We were two men on the edge.

Following the match, we hailed a cab back home. We passed by our eerily empty yard, trying (but failing) to ignore the smell of the burning waste filtering through the car window, and the plumes of smoke snaking up into the night sky.

During the next couple of months it became impossible to control revenue or costs. We were unable to send wagons out, we'd been unable to tip waste as a result, and we'd had managers and workers bailing out left, right and centre. To all intents and purposes the business was on its knees but we still fought on to try to turn things around. As we returned after the Christmas break, however, everything became too much for poor Steve who, clearly in the midst of a physical and emotional breakdown, collapsed in the office one morning. He was hospitalized shortly afterwards.

Despite our best efforts, and following a horrendous run of bad luck, Steve and I were unable to save White Recycling from going into liquidation in early 2015.

I happened to be at Peel Green cemetery when I took the pivotal phone call from the Environment Agency. I often went over to the graveyard, not just to visit Dad's resting place but to seek some much-needed peace, quiet and solitude. It became my haven, my retreat.

'I'm afraid it's not good news, David. We're going to have to shut the yard down until the waste is back down to permitted levels,' said the voice at the end of the line.

While not a regular occurrence, this had happened before – and we'd always got through it – but in my heart of hearts I knew there was no way out this time. We were done.

I walked back to my car, took a deep, deep breath, and drove off. While I felt completely distraught, there was also an underlying sense of release.

These next few months are going to be shit, I remember thinking to myself, *but they can't be as shit as what we've just been through …*

I spent the following week meeting with various officials, visiting a recuperating Steve, and making covert night trips to the yard office. I knew that very soon we'd be barred from the premises, but I needed to recover various personal belongings and sentimental items – signed shirts, framed programmes, old football contracts – before the administrators or landlords got their hands on them. By the looks of things, the site had already been plundered by various creditors of ours who, having heard the news that we were in trouble, had fleeced us of vehicles and machinery in lieu of what the company owed them.

While Steve and I faced personal financial ruin – we'd transferred funds from our reclamation firm to refinance our recycling firm – there was no escaping the fact that the company also owed a lot of money to other parties, and that we'd suddenly acquired a lot of enemies in the process. Inevitably, I became subject to some threatening and intimidating behaviour, and let's just say there were times when I felt that my personal safety was compromised. Though nobody ever turned up at my doorstep or laid a single finger on me, I'd occasionally receive timely 'visits' at a temporary office where I'd based myself.

As I tried to cope with the ramifications of the business collapse, my life hit an all-time low. There were times when I felt incredibly down and despondent – I remember lying in bed contemplating methods of suicide – but being surrounded by an amazing family and support network helped to keep these dark thoughts in check. I never for one second thought about acting upon things, but I can imagine how those feelings could have easily escalated. I consider myself very lucky that they never did.

* * *

Following the company liquidation, Steve and I were all set to agree Individual Voluntary Agreements with our creditors, notwithstanding the fact that, by doing so, we'd be putting ourselves under lots of pressure to meet the monthly payments. Despite the bank supporting us, the other two major creditors weren't having any of it, though, preferring instead to declare us bankrupt. I think they were convinced that the White family were secretly living an opulent, luxury lifestyle, and that they'd be able to seize all the holiday homes, flash cars and South African diamonds that we'd squirrelled away. They couldn't have been more wide of the mark. By 2015 I had no assets. I didn't have a bean. It didn't stop them from trying it on, though.

'We've heard that your brother's on a yacht in Florida at the moment,' was one of the more spurious claims.

'No he's not, actually. I think you'll find him sitting next to me, watching football with a beer,' I replied, as Steve and I shook our heads at the sheer ridiculousness of it all.

On Tuesday 6 October 2015, Steve and I were both declared personally bankrupt at Manchester County Court and ordered to rescind our directorships. I then underwent a three-hour interview in which my personal finances were pored over in forensic detail. I had £600 remaining in one bank account, which I needed to pay some costs, and £2.74 in another. Peculiarly, they allowed me to keep the £600, but swiped the £2.74!

All my outgoings were assessed – from grocery shopping to gas bills, from cars to jewellery – which, for the next twelve months, would be covered under the terms of the bankruptcy agreement. My financial plight was inevitably raked up by the *Manchester Evening News* – the media revel in a good down-on-his-luck story – but I just tried to ignore it, in a 'tomorrow's chip paper' kind of way.

Then I tried to get on with my life as best I could. Without intending to trivialize things, bankruptcy wasn't as dramatic as it sounds. Nothing earth-shattering happened in those twelve months, other than people occasionally poking their nose into my financial affairs.

Having your every move being tracked can be hard, though. In late 2015 my son set up a travel business, Living It Travel. It was an avenue I was entitled to pursue with him as long as I didn't earn over a certain amount, and I avoided taking up a directorship. Part of the business set-up process involved flying down to Marbella for a five-night seminar. As soon as I returned, however, I received the inevitable phone call accusing me of gallivanting abroad.

'We hear you've been on holiday, Mr White. Could we ask how you found the funds for that?'

'First, it wasn't a jolly, it was a conference,' I explained, my hackles rising. 'And second, my son paid for it.' I understood that the trustee was only doing her job but from time to time she seemed to be following up on false and malicious information.

On Wednesday 5 October 2016, I emailed the Insolvency Service to confirm that I'd been discharged from bankruptcy. A terse 'Yes, that's correct' response confirmed that was indeed the case.

These circumstances have taught me a lot, though. In my late twenties and early thirties I enjoyed what I'd consider to be a privileged, though not lavish, lifestyle. We lived in big houses, had nice cars, went on great holidays and ate out whenever we so desired. During my first year at Leeds United, my wages, bonuses, appearance money and signing-on fees probably totalled £300,000 gross, an amount that I'd probably earn in less than a month if I were still playing now! If I wanted to spend £400 on a meal-for-two at San Carlo, I did. If I wanted to fly the whole family out to Florida, I did. There were never any ifs, buts or 'shall I's?' since money enabled us to do whatever we wanted.

Don't get me wrong, I'd love to be in that position again. But recent experiences have opened my eyes to the value of things and, having been forced to cut my cloth accordingly, I've become far more sensible with money. I'll shop at Aldi instead of Waitrose. I'll have a pint in a pub, but will swerve a meal in the adjoining restaurant. I'll lease-hire a Ford because I can't afford a top-of-the-range Lexus. I'll wander around the Trafford Centre without picking up every gadget that takes my fancy. I've learnt that you can still enjoy life within your means, and without spending the earth. A good job, really, given that I've had no cash to splash over the last few years.

But, while I've coped fairly well with this new-found frugality, it's broken my heart to see Emma and the kids being deprived of certain things, through no fault of their own. We didn't have a family holiday this year, for example, and the Christmas-present budget is nowhere near what they all deserve for the support they have given me. But when I feel myself faltering, I try to put things into perspective. Some people would probably kill for the life I've led so far. Being a professional footballer was a wonderful privilege – for the majority of the time – and I now find myself surrounded by a wonderfully supportive family who've been at my side through the hardest times as well as the happiest.

The last few years have been tough, however, and the end of the tunnel isn't yet in sight. I can't deny that I've struggled both personally and professionally, but I've now reached a stage where I'm taking stock, dusting myself down and starting all over again.

'Unclear … but exciting,' is my reply when people ask how my future's looking.

I'm forging a career in travel and hospitality – two things I've always had a great passion for – and I have some sport-related ventures in the pipeline. Emma works as a personal trainer – she's brilliant – and occasionally competes in 'Bikini Fit' competitions up and down the country, which is a form of women's body conditioning. I'll often tag along as her chief supporter and bag-carrier.

Mum's great. She's had a rough time of it over the past few years – predominantly worrying about Steve and me – but, like us, is now doing all she can to look on the bright side. I catch up with her as often as I can, stopping by for a chat and a brew in between her various art classes and theatre productions.

Steve – my big bro, my best mate – continues to spearhead our scrap-metal business, White Reclamation, which we managed to keep ticking over following the collapse of White Recycling. We're both well aware that, had the firm not diversified into waste management all those years ago, the White brothers would probably have become very wealthy scrap-metal merchants. But c'est la vie. It'll probably take years before we finally see some profit, but hopefully that day will come.

Once my work life is back on track, I'll aim to get myself in shape. Like many ex-pros I've put on some timber since my playing days, and I'm more than aware that it's something I need to address. My pain-ridden, arthritis-ravaged ankle is partly to blame – until I have surgery, most sporting activity is out of the question – but there have been other contributory factors, too. When you're in the middle of a business collapse and a bankruptcy order, it's all too easy to switch your priorities away from yourself and onto more pressing matters. When my life was unravelling at the seams, the last thing I felt like doing was going for a swim or joining a gym.

'You've got to start devoting more time to yourself, David,' Emma will often tell me. She's right, of course, and I will.

As for football, I'm glad to say that I've fallen back in love with the game. I can often be found at the Etihad Stadium on a Saturday afternoon, taking in a City match with Sam, India and Mali in tow. Sometimes, though, when I'm watching Raheem Sterling and Kevin De Bruyne zipping around that pristine Etihad Stadium pitch, I can't help but reflect upon my own career in sky blue.

While I tend to look back with a tinge of regret – I don't think I ever truly fulfilled my potential – it's always outweighed by a huge dose of satisfaction. During my thirteen years as a professional I was lucky enough to play with and against some fabulous footballers, under the guidance of great coaches and managers. I performed in the finest grounds in the land – in front of the loudest, most loyal supporters – and I was lucky enough to figure in a string of memorable matches.

Not everything went to plan, of course. Yes, I'd have liked to have reached my 100-goal milestone at Manchester City (I was only four goals shy) and yes, I'd have loved to have savoured a Sheffield United victory in that 1997 play-off final. In an ideal world it would have been fantastic to have earned fifty-plus international caps and, in hindsight, I'd have much preferred not to have quit the game at the relatively young age of thirty.

But, all things considered, I'm incredibly proud of my achievements. I made 403 senior league and cup appearances. I scored a grand total of 125 goals. I received a coveted England cap. I played at Wembley stadium. I signed for three top clubs, including that very special one in Moss Side that captured the hearts of me, my brother and my dad.

And nothing, and no one, can ever take that away from me.

Epilogue

On a warm summer's day in 2015, in the midst of all my financial troubles, I sat down with a laptop and decided to write my memoirs. As the family business collapsed around me, and my livelihood lay in ruins, I reckoned that putting my thoughts into words might be a cathartic exercise and a timely distraction. I had no inkling that it would, in fact, prove to be such a life-changing, soul-searching journey.

The more I wrote, the more I remembered. The more I remembered, the more I reflected. And as I did so, something suddenly dawned on me. It was one of those revelatory light-bulb moments. My story wasn't just about one man who had shaped and influenced my life and career. It was about two. One, of course, was my father. The other was my abuser.

As words became sentences, and paragraphs became chapters, everything began to make sense. I could finally justify and rationalize the insecurity and self-doubt that had dogged me for years. From the secrets and skeletons-in-the-cupboard at home, to the confidence and consistency issues on the pitch, one individual linked them all.

For almost four decades, I'd gone through life believing that Barry Bennell's actions hadn't profoundly affected me.

Writing this book has made me realize that they did.

* * *

EPILOGUE

If I'm honest, the physical nature of Bennell's abuse rarely haunted me. I think he inflicted far worse on other young boys, and I consider myself one of the luckier victims who escaped his clutches before the cruelty escalated to levels that I now know others had to endure.

For me, the deepest trauma he inflicted was psychological, and stemmed from my fateful trip to Cala D'Or. Prior to that so-called holiday, I'd considered myself a pretty strong-willed, single-minded and carefree kid who possessed an almost obsessive desire to win and succeed. But those awful events of May 1979 – the humiliation in a hotel room, the intimidation in a bowling alley – changed everything. I returned to Manchester a completely different boy, with my confidence shattered, my trust betrayed and my innocence stolen. The continuation of the abuse back home in England only prolonged my suffering.

This mental fragility lingered throughout my childhood and adulthood and, on many occasions, was unwittingly transferred onto the football pitch. My game hinged so much upon self-belief and, with hindsight, I'm convinced that much of my notoriously patchy, see-saw form was linked to latent feelings of fear and surrender. Whenever I faced pressure or adversity – the prospect of defeat, perhaps, or some jeering from the crowd – I'd often feel myself caving in. Try as I might, I'd be unable to revive that spirit, that vitality, that never-say-die attitude that – prior to Bennell's intervention – had defined me.

This on-field disintegration would baffle and infuriate my managers and my father, as well as legions of supporters, no doubt.

'Why didn't you play like last week?' Dad would yell after a game. 'Why didn't you go for that header? Why didn't you look bothered? Why did you give up?'

'I don't know, Dad. I just don't know ...' I'd reply, sharing his bewilderment.

My football coaches seemed similarly perplexed, too.

'Your shoulders were sagging, your head was down,' they'd observe in the wake of a lackadaisical performance. 'Your fitness isn't the problem, David, so what is?'

I truly believe that, had Bennell not blighted my life, my career would have borne more fruit. On my day I was a more than capable player, and was as good as any of my top-flight contemporaries. When I was in peak form – flying down the wing, firing over crosses and scoring at will – I was pretty much unstoppable, my four-goal bonanza at Villa Park in 1991 being a prime example.

Conversely, there'd be days when the weight of the world seemed to rest heavy on my shoulders, and when that lingering sense of insecurity would rise to the surface. Feeling mentally flimsy – and still not realizing quite why – my impassive displays would invariably trigger those catcalls from the terraces and those bollockings from my dad.

What I desperately needed at that time was professional help to address my confidence and consistency issues. In the 1980s and '90s, however, football clubs had neither the staff nor the know-how to identify and support a player suffering with emotional issues. In those days there was nowhere to turn to for psychological advice and guidance; no counsellors, no therapists, no welfare officers.

Theoretically, had the right help been available, I'm convinced that I'd have eventually opened up about my childhood experiences. All it would have taken, I think, would have been a probing conversation or a pointed question to gently coax out my story.

'What's bothering you, David?' a sympathetic sports psychologist might have asked. 'You're brilliant on the pitch one week, but dreadful the next. Is there something on your mind? Are you worried about something? Do you need to talk?'

With specialist intervention, I'd probably have revealed all about Bennell, and I'd like to think that I'd have been believed, supported and protected. I might have been offered therapy to understand how my problems and anxieties could be rationalized and traced back to my past. I might have been given coping strategies to allow me to move forward and keep myself on an even keel, for the sake of my career.

With the best support and strategies in place – and with my head firmly back in gear – I'm sure I'd have put in better displays, played with more swagger and scored more goals. And, by performing to my

EPILOGUE

best ability, on a more consistent basis, I reckon I'd have amassed many more international caps.

Furthermore, had I sought and received professional help in my younger years, I believe I'd have been equipped and empowered to discuss those delicate abuse-related issues with my family, and would have been able to finally let go of the secrets and lies that had encumbered me for years.

Learning the truth about Bennell would have floored my dad, I'm certain of that. But, following some sensitive counselling – and some time and space to deal with his feelings of shock and guilt – I think he'd have eventually come to terms with this bombshell. Knowing Dad, he'd have then done everything in his power to help me; there'd have been no barriers in terms of personal or financial sacrifices, and he'd have tracked down the best psychologists in the land to help me work through what happened. While he had his faults and failings, deep down all he ever wanted was the best for me.

Hypothetically, had I been able to open up to my father at that time, I think we might have enjoyed a closer and calmer relationship. I believe he would have acted far more compassionately towards me, perhaps not pushing me and pressuring me to the extent that he did.

Sadly, though, all these best-case scenarios never materialized. In the 1980s and '90s the football world – and society in general – was not yet sophisticated or mature enough to adequately tackle the issue of child sexual abuse and, as a result, I had to bottle things up and cope alone. I ended up suffering professionally and personally, my emotional frailties not only jeopardizing my performance on the field, but also affecting the relationship with my dad. Until the day he died, there always remained a barrier, a distance and a disconnect between us both, and I lay the blame for this squarely at the feet of one person. Barry Bennell effectively sabotaged that precious father–son bond, undermining what should have been a magical journey together for a football-crazy dad and lad.

* * *

In November 2016, Bennell was once more catapulted to the forefront of my mind when ex-footballer Andy Woodward gave an interview to the *Guardian*'s Daniel Taylor. In it, the former Crewe Alexandra, Bury and Sheffield United player bravely revealed the sickening abuse that he'd suffered at the hands of Bennell throughout the 1980s, and disclosed how he'd struggled to live with his dark secret for three decades.

A few days later, Andy outlined his harrowing ordeal on the BBC's *Victoria Derbyshire* show. I watched the programme in my mum's lounge, overcome with emotion as he recalled his hideous experiences with searing candour and honesty. Not only was I deeply moved by his strength and courage, I was also shocked at how so much of his story chimed and resonated with mine. Though his trauma seemed to have been more severe and prolonged, I could only empathize with the emotional and psychological torment that he'd suffered through the years.

Andy's revelations lit a powder keg within the world of football. The next few days witnessed a steady stream of ex-pros waiving their anonymity and coming forward to report their own ordeals, including Crewe's Steve Walters, who revealed that he too had been preyed upon by Bennell, and my former Manchester City teammate, Paul Stewart, who described being abused by Frank Roper, another youth-team coach based in the north-west.

Various footballing bodies – including the FA and the PFA – expressed their shock and support, and dedicated helplines were set up to cater for other troubled ex-players. Bennell's image was plastered all over the media, accompanied with reports that he'd not long been released from a two-year prison sentence for abusing a young boy at a Macclesfield football camp in 1980.

There came a point when I felt it was time for me to step forward, too. On the afternoon of Wednesday 23 November I composed a written statement confirming that I'd also been victimized by Barry Bennell as a child. Everything went berserk. For the next week my phone buzzed incessantly with calls from reporters, and my picture and story appeared on TV news bulletins and tabloid front pages. My social-media feeds

EPILOGUE

went completely haywire, and the messages of goodwill just flooded in, ranging from compassionate tweets from complete strangers to supportive calls from friends and family.

One message in particular caught my attention. Mark, the Whitehill FC teammate who'd accompanied me and Bennell to Majorca, had decided to get in touch via Twitter; he'd seen my press statement, and was keen to offer his support. There then followed an exchange of direct messages that began fairly light-heartedly – 'How are the family?' ... 'What are you up to?' – but became progressively more serious at the first mention of Bennell.

'What you should know, mate, and I'm sorry if this shocks you,' I wrote, 'is that my abuse started when we went to Majorca.'

His message flashed up a minute or so later.

'It's not a shock to me, David. He tried to do the same to me.'

Mark's words made me flinch. It wasn't just sympathy that he was offering, it was empathy. Bennell had got to us both.

* * *

My advice to anyone who has experienced abuse of any kind, in any walk of life, is simple: please talk. Talk, talk, talk … and then talk some more. Whether it's confiding in a loved one – a partner, a parent, a sibling – or speaking to an organization – the NSPCC, the PFA, the police – I urge you not to suffer alone. Reaching out to someone – especially for the first time – may be upsetting, but it will ultimately make things better. That I can almost guarantee.

It was only after I'd opened up to my immediate family – other than my dad, of course – that I began to pluck up the courage to talk to close friends about my experiences. During my late thirties I decided to take some long-standing pals into my confidence, a trusted network of individuals who'd convinced me they could keep a secret and shield my father.

People reacted in different ways – shock, anger, sadness, unease – but every single person, without fail, offered their love, comfort and support. This helped me no end, and also made me wish that I'd confided in them years earlier. Not only could I have started my recovery process sooner in life, I could have done so safe in the knowledge that my father would have remained none the wiser, such was my friends' discretion.

For a variety of reasons, divulging my innermost thoughts became a very liberating and enlightening experience. Disclosing my abuse enabled me to unshackle myself from the secrets, the shame and the stigma. My willingness to speak up demonstrated that the old abuser-versus-victim, control-versus-vulnerability dynamic that existed between Bennell and me had all but disappeared. Moreover, having the confidence to lay my feelings bare proved that I still possessed an inner strength and fortitude that I thought I'd lost forever.

Sharing my story also helped people to understand me as a person, and doubtless shifted a few opinions and preconceptions. Friends who'd once questioned my occasional introversion and oversensitivity could now pinpoint a probable root cause. Those who'd once observed my wariness and caution in certain situations could see how it stemmed from age-old trust issues.

For instance, when Sam was a kid, I'd kept him away from his Cub Scout group because, in passing, he'd told me that he'd not enjoyed himself.

'Oh, just get on with it,' other parents might have said, steering their sulky kids into the church hall on a Tuesday night. But not me. To my suspicious mind this was a possible cry for help that couldn't be ignored, so Sam stayed at home with me, under my care.

My son also joined forces with a local football team for a while but – contrary to all expectations – I didn't encourage him as I should have done. My caginess was born out of fear, of course; I vividly remember sizing up the coaches on the sidelines and thinking – quite wrongly, I'm sure – *What are your motives, mate? Why exactly d'you like working with kids, then, eh?*

Often my cynicism knew no bounds. I once sent Mum and Leanne to Wales to 'babysit' Georgia while she was on a school trip. All it took was one tearful, homesick telephone conversation to get my alarm bells

EPILOGUE

ringing and I insisted that, instead of sleeping in a dormitory, she spend each night in a nearby B&B with her mum and grandma.

In all instances there was no indication whatsoever that anything untoward was going on but, with the spectre of Bennell skulking at the back of my mind, I was never, ever prepared to take that risk with my own children.

Fortunately, I'm not as sceptical these days. I'm confident that we now live in a more alert and enlightened society that's far less likely to give sex offenders the scope to torment children on a prolific scale, whether it's within the world of football or beyond. I'm ever hopeful that modern-day safeguarding policies and protection procedures, so lacking in previous decades, are infinitely more stringent, watertight and fit for purpose. I'm also heartened by the number of clubs, charities and associations that are now committed to offering support and sanctuary to those who have been abused, or those who are at risk of abuse.

For the sake of future generations, however, we must never be complacent about this issue. We should continue to raise awareness and remain vigilant in order to ensure that all paths are closed to paedophiles, thus preventing any more youngsters from suffering in silence. We need to foster a climate of care and compassion in which child-abuse survivors are able to come forward, to open up and to start their recovery. Only by finding their own voices, and by telling their own stories, may that healing process begin.

If you have been affected by any of the issues in this book, please do not suffer in silence. Speak to a friend or family member or, alternatively, contact one of the following organizations:

The NSPCC's helpline (in conjunction with the FA)
is 0800 023 2642

ChildLine, for children and young people,
can be contacted on 0800 1111

The National Association for People Abused in Childhood can be
reached on 0808 801 0331

Samaritans can be contacted on 116 123

Acknowledgements

Writing this book has been a long and testing process, and there are so many people who have helped me along the way. I couldn't have reached this point without my co-author, Joanne Lake, who accepted the challenge to knock my own 100,000 words into shape. Diligent and efficient, while at the same time sensitive and understanding, Jo was quite simply a delight to work with. I know she was deeply affected by some of the discussions we had, but her professionalism never once wavered.

A friend of mine referred me to my literary agent, Rory Scarfe from Furniss Lawton, which proved to be a very wise move indeed. Rory has been there for me when I've needed him, offering excellent advice and support throughout this project. I was thrilled when Rory linked us up with our publishers, Michael O'Mara Books, and would like to thank Clare Tillyer, Clara Nelson, Fiona Slater, Jane Pickett and the rest of the team for all their help and guidance during some pretty taxing times.

I'm also grateful to Gary James – an expert on all things Manchester City – for casting his forensic eye over all the facts and figures, as well as the dedicated people at the City Til I Die and Bluemoon websites whose statistical resources have been invaluable to me over the past twelve months.

I don't think words can quite do justice to the love and support I've received from my family during the writing of this book – and over the past few years – but I'll try. My mum, Elaine, has been a calming influence and has provided sanctuary from the sometimes troubling world that I still manage to find myself in. She is more of a mum than a mum and more of a friend than a friend, and I love her and her partner Dave dearly.

My children mean the absolute world to me and enrich my life every day. Sam, Georgia and Jordan are adults now, but we can't seem to shake them off (and if they tried to go anywhere we'd drag them back anyway). There's nothing more satisfying than your grown-up children constantly ringing you up and asking what you are doing over the weekend; they should be ideal babysitters, really, but they're always tagging along with us!

My youngest two, India and Mali, are helping to keep me young. They're both beautiful girls and, although there are sixteen months between them, they're often mistaken for twins. Their characters are poles apart, though; India is timid and mild-mannered whereas Mali is the Tasmanian Devil. Even I'm scared of her!

I love my gorgeous wife Emma so much. In the seven years we've been together she's been through a great deal personally – including a life-threatening ectopic pregnancy – and she suffered alongside me as we lost the business and entered personal bankruptcy, something that deeply affected the whole family. During this time, however, she has also given birth to two amazing children, has tied the knot with me (what was she thinking?!), and has never stopped working. My admiration for my wife's loyalty and tenacity knows no bounds, and I hope that the better future that she so richly deserves lies ahead.

I feel blessed to be fully reconciled with Nanna Tom and Bert, which means that my little girls can now cause havoc in their bungalow just like my brother Steve and I did over forty years ago. I continue to miss my Nana Jack and Auntie Betty, though, who brought so much love and laughter into our lives.

Steve and I have been through so much together, and he has supported me unstintingly, whether it's been within the world of football or the world of business. We've hardly exchanged a cross word during childhood and adulthood and, when our partnership is functioning at its best, our skill sets complement each other perfectly. He's the rational

ACKNOWLEDGEMENTS

thinker, the voice of reason, and has often dragged my head out of the sand when problems have loomed. Circumstances have taken their toll, however, and I was seriously worried about my brother's health when the business collapsed. Since then, I'm glad to say, I've detected a steadily increasing determination that I know will bring happiness and prosperity to him, his lovely wife Helen and their children, Kade and Bethany. I could not have hoped for a better brother, and if there's one hero in this book, it's him.

Picture credits

Page 1: Elaine McCann personal collection (top, middle and bottom)
Page 2: Elaine McCann personal collection (top, middle and bottom)
Page 3: David White personal collection (top and bottom)
Page 4: David White personal collection (top and bottom)
Page 5: ANL / REX / Shutterstock (top); David White personal collection (bottom)
Page 6: Hutchison / ANL / REX / Shutterstock (top); David White personal collection and Manchester Evening News (bottom)
Page 7: Paul Lewis / ANL / REX / Shutterstock (top and middle); PA Images (bottom)
Page 8: David White personal collection (top); Colorsport / REX / Shutterstock (bottom)
Page 9: David White personal collection and Mirror Group Newspapers
Page 10: David White personal collection (top, middle and bottom)
Page 11: David White personal collection (top and bottom)
Page 12: Daily Mail / REX / Shutterstock (top); David White personal collection and Manchester Evening News (bottom)
Page 13: David White personal collection
Page 14: Getty Images (top); David White personal collection (bottom)
Page 15: David White personal collection (top); Sam White personal collection (middle and bottom)
Page 16: David White personal collection (top and middle); Steve White personal collection (bottom)

Index

A

'A' team, Manchester City FC's 79–81
Adcock, Tony 130, 132, 135
Ablett, Gary 219
Alder Park School 29
Alice (DW's maternal grandmother) 21, 22–3, 156, 238
Allison, Malcolm 39–40, 88
Ardiles, Osvaldo 68–9
Arsenal FC 60, 149
  FA Youth Cup 103, 105–6
Asics sportswear contract 168
Aston Villa FC 162, 165–7
athletics, British 19
Auschwitz-Birkenau visit 148

B

Bailey, John 96
Bailey, Roy 84, 114, 134, 160, 168
Baker, Graham 118
Ball, Alan 236, 237
Barnes, Peter 41, 43–4, 53, 119
Barrett, Earl 109
Barton, Manchester 14
Bassett, Dave 217, 218–19
BBC Radio Manchester punditry 234, 236, 240, 242

Beckford, Darren 78, 94
Bell, Colin 40–1
Bell House Hotel, Beaconsfield 159, 160–1, 222
Bennell, Barry 'Bené'
  abuse of DW 53, 57–60, 62–6, 268–75
  arrest and imprisonment in Britain 229, 232–3
  arrested and imprisoned in Florida 210, 211
  Cheshire Police enquiries 12, 229–32
  coach and talent-spotter 34, 46–9, 52, 53, 61
  Majorca 53, 54–60
  returns to Maine Road 127–9
Betty, Aunty (Alice's sister) 21–3, 156
Biggins, Wayne 'Bertie' 135
Bishop, Ian 145, 146, 150
Blake, Nathan 219
Blue Star FC 71
Bond, John 68, 241
Book, Tony 'Skip' 38, 39–40, 52, 74, 79, 82, 84, 86, 88–92, 93, 95, 102, 107, 111–12, 120, 196
Booth, Tommy 41

Borbokis, Vas 225
Boyd, David 106
Bradford City FC 139–40
Brasingamen's nightclub, Alderley Edge 215–16
Brazilian/Uruguayan tour, England under-19s 122–5
Brennan, Mark 158
Bridgewater Canal 15
Brightwell, Ian 82, 103, 108, 115, 122, 123, 125, 136, 137, 143, 151, 170
British Embassy, Brazil 124–5
Bruce, Steve 146, 173
BSkyB Premier League advert 176
Buchan, Martin 40
Buckley, Andy 234, 240
Buckley, Rick 259–60
Busby, Sir Matt 204
Butler, Bryon 39
Butlin's Pwllheli 64–5

C

Cala D'Or, Majorca 54–60, 192
Canada 108
Cape Town, South Africa 190–1
caravan holidays 24–5
Carr, Franz 94–5
Chapman, Les 171
Chapple, John 35
Charlton Athletic FC 98–9
Chelsea FC 104–5
Cheshire Police enquiries 12, 229–32
Christie, Trevor 118
City of Manchester Stadium 241–2
Clements, Kenny 118
Collins, James 29
Corrigan, Joe 40, 41
Coton, Tony 115, 158, 164, 188, 194
Courtney, George 97–8
Crane, John 122, 123

Crompton, Steve 76, 93, 102
Crooks, Garth 69
Crosby, Gary 153
Crystal Palace FC 139–40, 222–3
Cunningham, Tony 98
Curle, Keith 167, 174, 194, 202

D

David White Soccer Roadshow 239–40
Davies, Gordon 110
Davies, Ted 52
Deane, Brian 176–7, 225
Deehan, John 'Dixie' 135
Dibble, Andy 135, 153, 188
Dispatches 229, 258
Donachie, Willie 40, 224–5
Doyle, Mike 43, 44
Dutch tour 193–5
Dyson, Jack 13

E

Ebbrell, John 228–9
Eccles Church of England school team 72–4
Eccles Town FC's Under-11s 29–32, 45
Edwards, Les 239–40
Ellis, Sam 164, 168, 175, 178, 193, 194, 196
England Football Squad 11, 148–9, 174, 178–82
  under-19s 122–5
  under-21s 133–4, 148
Eryl Hall caravan park 24–5
European Championships 174
England under-21s 133

F

FA Cup Finals 13, 19–20, 60, 68–9, 191

INDEX

FA Cup rounds 187–8
FA Youth Cup 94, 97, 102, 103, 105–7
Ferguson, Alex 147
Flitcroft, Garry 170, 185, 236
Frizzell, Jimmy 108–9, 116, 117, 120, 122, 125–6
Full Members' Cup 104–5

G

Gabon, West Africa 122
Gascoigne, Paul 133, 134–5, 161
Gayle, Brian 135, 136, 139, 219
Gibson, Stan 83, 162
Gidman, John 131, 136
Gillingham FC 240–1
Gleghorn, Nigel 135, 145
Godfrey Ermen Memorial Primary School 21, 29
Gordon, James Alexander 39
Gorton, Andrew 29
Gowling, Alan 44
Grealish, Tony 118
Green, Ron 138
Griffiths, Freddie 38, 77

H

H. Wood (Patricoft) Ltd. 16–17, 18
Halford, Bernard 132
Harper, Alan 150, 163, 167
Heath, Adrian 151, 163, 217, 219
helicopter trip, South Africa 214–15
Hennigan, Mick 203–4, 212–13, 217
Hinchcliffe, Andy 78, 101, 130, 132, 138–9, 147, 153, 158
Holden, Rick 175, 185, 193, 198
Holdsworth, David 221
holidays, childhood 24–5, 70–1
Holland 193–5
Hopkins, Robert 115–16, 118–19
Horton, Brian 196–7, 198–9, 235

Howe, Don 122–3, 179
Huddersfield Town FC 131–2
Hughes, Michael 170
Hutchison, Tommy 68–9

I

Ibiza 125
Irwin, Miss 29
Isle of Man 222
Isle of Wight junior tournament 47–9
Italy 174–6

J

Johnstone, Bobby 13
Jones, Peter 39

K

Keane, Roy 182
Kendall, Howard 150–5, 156, 158, 161, 162, 163–4, 217, 219–20, 222, 224
Kennedy, Alan 95
Kidd, Bert 17, 18–19, 74, 156–7
Kinkladze, Georgi 236

L

Lake, Paul 101, 106, 125, 130, 136, 138–9, 147, 161, 162, 176, 177, 178
Lancashire League 94, 96, 107
Lancashire Youth Cup 80, 98, 102
League Cup Finals 42–3, 221–3
Lee, Francis 197, 234, 235–6, 237
Leeds United FC 11, 172, 187, 197
  DW at 201–5, 207–9, 212–19
  Malaysian tour 206
  Marbella trip 212–14
  South African tour 213–14
  UEFA Cup 216–17
  youth trials 78

Lewis, Mike 37, 42–3, 44
Lillis, Mark 101–2, 110, 113, 118
Littlewoods Cup 146
Liverpool FC 168, 169–70, 236–7

M

Macauley, Steve 111
Macdonald, Malcolm 131–2, 217, 218, 224
Machin, Mel 122, 124, 130, 135, 136, 137, 138, 145, 149
Macrae, Keith 41
Maddock, John 190, 195, 196–7, 235
Magaluf 220–1
Maine Road
   DW's league debut 117–18
   final match at stadium 241
   first time playing in the 'A' team 79–80
   training at 52–3
   watching matches at 37–9, 40, 237
Majorca 53, 54–60, 100–1, 192
Malaysia 206–7
Malta 70–1
Manchester City FC 11, 29–30, 36–44, 68–9, 75, 234–7, 241–2
   'A' Team 78, 79–80
   Bobby Glennie testimonial game 103–4
   Cape Town tour 190–1
   Central League reserves 95–6
   Dutch tour 193–5
   DW's apprenticeship 81–7, 89–98, 101–2, 111–12
   DW's 1st league season 116–22
   DW's 2nd league season 130–1, 133
   DW's 3rd league season 135–40
   DW's 4th league season 145–54
   DW's 5th league season 158
   DW's 6th league season 167–74
   DW's 7th league season 176–8, 184–8
   DW's 8th league season 195–201
   DW's final match at Maine Road 240–1
   FA Youth Cup 94, 97–8, 102, 105–7
   first *Monday Night Football* match airing 177–8
   Full Members' Cup 104–5
   Italian tour 174–6
   Manchester Derby matches 118, 146–7, 162–3, 169, 172, 173, 200
   Salford Boys 76–7
   Swiss tour 113–14
   Tokyo tournament 188
   USA and Canada tour 108–10
   Youth Team training 84–7, 89–90, 91–2
Manchester Evening News 42, 117, 264
Manchester United FC 40–1, 60
   FA Youth Cup 106
   Lancashire Youth Cup 80, 98
   Manchester Derby matches 118, 146–7, 162–3, 169, 172, 173, 200
Mansour, Sheikh 251
Marbella 212–14
Margetson, Martyn 188
Mark (Whitehill FC player) 54–7, 58–9, 61, 273
Marsh, Rodney 40
McAllister, Gary 202, 206, 214
McCabe, Kevin 233
McCann, Elaine (DW's mother) 13–14, 15, 22–3, 25–6, 27, 29, 51, 184, 238, 266
McCann (MP), Jack 14, 16
McCarthy, Mick 118–19

INDEX

McFarlane, Ian 38
McGrath, Paul 165, 166, 225
McMahon, Steve 170-1, 175, 176, 193, 194
McMenemy, Lawrie 179
McNab, Neil 119, 121, 132, 136, 145
McNeill, Billy 78-9, 84, 96-7, 98, 101, 104, 107-8, 112, 113, 114, 115-16
Megson, Gary 136, 145, 150, 151
Merson, Paul 123
Mills, Steve 125
Monaco 216-17
Monday Night Football 177
Morley, Trevor 135, 140
Moulden, Paul 76, 77, 78, 82, 103, 105, 106, 122, 123, 135
Mumbai 246-56

N

Neal, Phil 179
Neill, Terry 60
Newcastle United FC 42, 43-4
FA Youth Cup 97-8
Norway 225
Nottingham Forest FC
FA Youth Cup 94-5
youth trials 78

O

Oldfield, David 145

P

paedophilia, 1970s lack of awareness 66-7
Pardoe, Glyn 82, 88, 89, 90, 91-2, 111, 112, 120, 152
Patricroft recreation ground 21, 28
Patterson, Mark 219
Pearce, Stuart 185-6
penalties, DW and 102-3

Peter Barnes Football Trainer 32-3
Phelan, Terry 184-5, 236
Phillips, David 98-9, 113, 118
photographs, team 114-15
Pointon, Neil 158, 175
Poland 148-9
politics 15-16
Potter, George 42
Power, Paul 107, 113, 118
Premier League opening season 176-8
Professional Footballers' Association 137-8, 188-9

Q

Queens Park Rangers FC 177-8, 187, 205
Quinn, Niall 153-4, 164, 165-6, 168, 169, 175

R

red card, DW's 176
Redmond, Steve 76, 77, 78, 82, 86, 94, 103, 105, 106-7, 108, 111, 115, 122, 123, 125, 133-4, 136, 175
Reeves, Kevin 69
Reid, Peter 150, 164, 169, 176, 177, 185, 188, 190, 193, 194-5, 196, 220, 235
Robinson, Miss 29
Robson, Bobby 122, 123, 124, 179
Robson, Bryan 146, 147, 180
Rocastle, David 133, 201
Roper, Frank 272
Royle, Joe 240
Rumbelows Cup 162

S

Salford Boys 76-7
Sandford, Lee 222

Sansom, Kenny 118
Santander, Spain 179, 180–1
Scott, Ian 82, 100, 103, 106, 130
scouts, football 30, 53, 76
Sexton, Dave 60, 133–4
Sheffield Wednesday FC 95
Sheffield United FC 11, 41, 177–8, 217–20, 224, 225–8, 233
   Isle of Man trip 222
   League Cup 221–3
   Magaluf trip 220–1
   Norway tour 225
Sheringham, Teddy 177
Sheron, Mike 170, 185
Shirecliffe training ground 11
Short, Chris 219, 222
Simon (childhood friend) 29–30, 33–4, 48
Simpson, Paul 99, 132
Sinatra's nightclub, Marbella 213–14
Smith, Gordon 98
Soccer's Foul Play 229–30
South Africa 190–1, 214–15
Southampton FC 150–1
Southend United FC 116–17
Spackman, Nigel 224–5, 226, 227
Spain 178–81
Spalding, Chris 72–3
Speed, Gary 206, 211–12, 213, 214, 258–9
Sports Report 39
St Asaph, North Wales 24–5
Stewart, Paul 119, 132, 135, 272
Strachan, Gordon 204, 206, 208–9
Street, Fred 122, 124
Stretford, Paul 217
Sunday Times 258–9
Sunderland, Alan 60
Sunderland FC reserves 95
Sutton, Derek 103–4, 159
Swales, Ken 72, 73–4

Swales, Peter 38, 39, 88–9, 101, 122, 149, 163, 164, 188–90, 195, 196–7, 234–5, 237
Switzerland 113–14

T

Talk of the North nightclub 18
Taylor, Bill 52
Taylor, Graham 178–9, 181
Tenerife 154–5
Thackeray, Andy 76, 78, 82, 94, 106, 107–8, 111, 125, 192, 202
Thomas, Michael 105–6, 123
Tokyo tournament (1993) 188
Tottenham Hotspur FC 68–9, 161
Toulon Tournament, under-21's 133–5
Trautmann, Bert 13
Tueart, Dennis 42, 44
Tyldesley, Clive 169

U

UEFA Cup 216–17
United States of America 108–10
Uruguayan/Brazilian tour, England under-19s 124–5

V

Vengloš, Dr Jozef 165, 166
Veronica's, Tenerife 154–5
Villa, Ricky 69–70
Vonk, Michel 191, 219

W

Walters, Steve 272
Ward, Mark 151, 154, 155, 156, 167, 185
Watson, Dave 40, 44, 53
wedding and honeymoon 156, 157
Wembley Stadium 13, 43, 104–5, 221–3, 240

INDEX

West Ham United 119
Wetherall, David 213
White, David
  ankle injury 11, 187, 198–9, 201, 203, 204, 206, 207, 209, 224, 226–7, 243
  bankruptcy 263–5
  Barry Bennell's abuse of 57–60, 62–6, 268–75
  BBC Radio Manchester punditry 234, 236, 240, 242
  birth and earliest memories 13–14
  birth of children and fatherhood 172–3, 200, 244–5, 259, 274–5
  Cheshire police enquiries 12, 229–33
  childhood holidays 24–5, 70–1
  City of Manchester stadium host 242
  confides in family about abuse 230–1, 239
  dealing with criticism 142–5
  divorce 243–5
  Dutch tour 193–5
  Eccles Town FC Under-11s 29–32, 45
  England senior squad 178–82
  England under-19s 122–5
  England under-21s 133–5, 148
  FA Cup Final (1981) 68–70
  FA Youth Cup win 105–7
  family business 16–17, 18, 116, 144, 157, 184, 233, 242, 259–63, 266
  father's illness and death 233, 244, 245–51, 252–6
  father's influence 31–3, 45, 49–52, 54, 60, 62, 74, 75, 80, 96, 111, 183–4, 226
  first training session at Maine Road 52–3
  formal qualifications 81, 93, 108
  Gary Speed's death 258
  girls/girlfriends 75–6, 87, 125
  impact of seeing Bennell in 1987 127–9
  Isle of Wight junior tournament 47–9
  Italian tour (1992) 174–6
  League Cup Final at Wembley 223
  League Cup match Wembley (1976) 42–4
  leaving Manchester City FC 201–2
  Leeds United 201–5, 207–9, 212–19
  Magaluf 220–1
  Maine Road league debut 117–18
  Majorca 53, 54–60, 100–1, 192
  Manchester City FC (1st season) 113–22, 142
  Manchester City FC (2nd season) 130–1
  Manchester City FC (3rd season) 135–40
  Manchester City FC (4th season) 145–54
  Manchester City FC (5th season) 158
  Manchester City FC (6th season) 167–74
  Manchester City FC (7th season) 176–8, 184–8
  Manchester City FC (8th season) 195–201
  Manchester City FC end-of-season tour (1986) 108–9
  Manchester City FC first senior squad game 103–4
  Manchester City FC YTS apprenticeship 81–7, 89–98, 101–2, 111–12
  Manchester City FC's 'A' Team 79–81

287

Manchester City satellite teams 71–2 (*see also* Whitehill FC)
Manchester City Switzerland tour 113–14
Marbella 212–14
most memorable match 165–7
Mumbai 246–56
parents' divorce 25–7
Patricroft recreation ground 21, 28
physical health 11, 77–8, 114, 168, 207, 220 (*see also* ankle injury)
Salford Boys 76–7
school and Cubs football 28–9, 72–4
Sheffield United FC 11, 217–28
signs first professional contract 102
Soccer Roadshow 239–40
South African tours 190–1, 214–15
Tenerife 154–5
wedding and honeymoon 156, 157
Whitehill FC 29–30, 31, 34–5, 45–8, 52–3
White, Emma (DW's wife) 245, 246, 256, 258, 259, 265, 266
White, Leanne (DW's wife) 125, 140–1, 156–7, 172–3, 192, 230–1, 244–5
White, Lily (DW's paternal grandmother) 16–17, 18, 21, 156–7, 216
White, Margaret (DW's stepmother) 26–7, 184, 244, 245–6, 253–4, 256
White, Steven (DW's brother) 14, 15, 18–19, 20, 21–2, 24–6, 33, 37–8, 42–3, 68, 69–70, 102, 156, 167, 184, 215–16, 230–1, 253, 259–60, 261–2, 266
White, Stewart (DW's father) 13, 14, 15–18, 20, 25–6, 35, 36–9, 42, 68, 69, 157, 224, 231, 232, 233–4, 239, 243–4, 245–58
  son's football career 31–3, 45, 49–52, 54, 60, 62, 74, 75, 80, 96, 111, 183–4, 226
  the truth about Barry Bennell 210
White, Tom (DW's paternal grandfather) 17
Whitehill FC 29–30, 31, 34–5, 45–8, 52–3, 212
Wilkinson, Howard 201, 203, 204, 205, 206–8, 214, 217
Williams, Robbie 213–14
Wood, Harry (DW's paternal great-grandfather) 14, 16–17
Woodward, Andy 272

Y

Yeboah, Tony 217
Young, Neil 36
Youth Training Scheme apprenticeship 81–7, 101–2, 111–13

Z

Zico (Arthur Antunes Coimbra) 123